FAMILY RECONSTRUCTION: THE LIVING THEATER MODEL

Sharon Wegscheider-Cruse
Kathy Higby
Ted Klontz
Ann Rainey

Printed in the United States of America.

Library of Congress Card Number 94-069597

ISBN 0-8314-0083-8

Cover design by Will Derksen
Interior design by Robin Penninger
Typesetting by Robin Penninger
Printing by Haddon Craftsmen

TABLE OF CONTENTS

PART ONE

THE HISTORY
OF RECONSTRUCTION
AND PREPARATION FOR
THE PROCESS

The real voyage of discovery consists not in seeking new landscapes, but in having new eyes.

—Marcel Proust

FOREWORD

"The world can doubtless never be known by theory:
practice is absolutely necessary; but surely it is of great use
to a young man, before he sets out for the country, full of
mazes, windings, and turnings, to have at least a general
map of it, made by some experienced traveller."
— Lord Chesterfield

I first met Sharon Wegscheider-Cruse as a member of the audience while she demonstrated the family roles in the chemically dependent family. The pain I experienced was so unbearable that I wanted to cry out to her to stop. She had the inimitable ability to draw in observers from the audience, to passively and actively invite them to participate in the experience of the drama as it unfolded through the volunteer role-players. Each such experience was very personal, re-lived instantly, and utterly real. It was painfully obvious to me, newly in recovery from addiction, that I must know more of her work. I had no idea then that I would also *feel* it.

In ensuing years I was fortunate to participate in numerous family reconstruction workshops, and eventually to undergo my own personal family reconstruction. My life since has been totally changed. Subsequently my wife and I continued to work with Sharon and her husband Joe in family reconstruction workshops, in the Living Centered Program, in sessions for professionals, and in couples' groups. The latter was my favorite as we were so frequently rewarded by revisiting with couples as their relationships were revitalized and enhanced far beyond their original expectations. Still, the core element was the family reconstruction process.

When Sharon first began talking of decreasing her role in all of these programs, many of us who knew her were afraid that all of her experience would be lost if others were not prepared to follow her. A.A. Milne's beloved Winnie the Pooh said, "Always watch where you are going, otherwise, you may step on a piece of the forest that was left out by mistake." This is what I feared most when Sharon spoke of cutting back her role at Onsite Training and Consulting—that a piece of the forest would be left out by mistake. Fortunately, she gathered around her people such as Kathy and Ted and Ann, who now carry on all of the programs which Sharon started.

Many professionals throughout this country and others currently perform family reconstruction as it is outlined here. I am certain that they will be as excited as I was to see this guide. The chapters on the star, the guide, and the reconstruction event precisely outline the essential steps in the preparation and performance of the reconstruction. As I read and re-read these chapters, I re-experienced the process which had transformed my life over 12 years ago. Their accuracy and thoroughness made me vividly aware of the intense effort which must be taken in the preparation phases. Similarly, I was aware of the awesome responsibility the professional assumes when he or she becomes willing to guide a person through such a magnificent experience, an experience markedly enhanced for the star through his or her total immersion in the process.

Reconstruction can leave participants other than the star open and hurting; their needs must be attended to also. The small-group work, Parts Party, and closing activities as addressed here are essential chapters in the reconstruction process.

It is an advantage to readers of a book such as this to know something of the experiences of the authors and others who have undertaken the journey. Here, the section on Journeys is an integral portion of the volume, making family reconstruction more real for the reader, more comfortable for the potential traveler.

This book truly is a guide. The information is not presented as dogma, but, rather, as a map. Lord Chesterfield said not only theory, but practice, and a map to ease our way. Our guides have given us such a map to assist us in our travels.

—James W. Keller, M.D.
Vice President, Medical Affairs
Southeastern Ohio Medical Center

THE EVOLUTION OF THE RECONSTRUCTION PROCESS

Open up your heart and let the sunshine in.

—*Old hymn*

Once I accept things as they are, I am free to create things as I want them to be.

—*Anonymous*

Family reconstruction is an action therapy technique developed by Virginia Satir. Both Virginia's model of family reconstruction and my own lead towards the same goals: a significant change in the understanding of one's history, the development of higher self-worth through the new understanding of that history, and a "re-capturing" of repressed feelings.

The lesson of the reconstruction model is that it is both structured and continually changing, forever evolving and integrating new ideas and styles to grow with the ideas and styles of the individuals who act as guides. It carries on the tradition of Virginia Satir to incorporate whatever works as a practical vision of therapy, and allows for an infinite amount of diversity.

For me, family reconstruction was never a static technique. Even early on, I primarily took Virginia's reconstruction model and began to adapt it to work with families suffering from some addiction, alcoholism, or drug abuse. During the 21 years that I have been doing reconstructions, I have continued to learn, and many people have learned from me. In the early days, of course, I taught what I knew at the time. I have learned so much more since, and I've continued to integrate these new models into the original reconstruction model. I appreciated Virginia telling me at one point that the reconstruction I learned from her wouldn't look at all like what I would be doing 10, 20, and even 30 years later. Fortunately, the model invites each guide to continue to learn and to change.

When I first began doing reconstructions, I worked with 24 people who were committed to the process, and to my role as the guide in this process, for a period of about two years. We did one reconstruction a month, with the members of the group rotating into position as the "star" or focus of the reconstruction, and the other 23 participants acting as role-players and audience. We would meet on Saturdays, and begin at around 9:00 a.m. We followed the schedule of choosing role-players and setting up the psycho-dramas, and we would end that afternoon at about 5:30 or 6:00 p.m. We would close in the evening with a pot-luck supper. This group stayed together for the full two years, during which I reconstructed each one of those people and learned some very important lessons which caused me to change the model.

One lesson was that working from 9:00 a.m. to 5:00 p.m. was too short a time. I found I needed about three or four additional hours, so I began starting at 8:30 in the morning and letting the reconstruction go until 8:30 at night, sometimes adding even one or two extra hours onto that. This allowed me to "do the job" in the most thorough way I knew. Currently at Onsite Training and Consulting we do family reconstructions in the context of week-long "Learning to Love Yourself" workshops. The reconstruction day occurs in the middle of the week, with the group spending time and working together both before and after.

Early on as a guide, I had learned a great deal from the work of Alice Miller about the concept of the "inner child." I learned that many people were emotionally wounded as children, with family situations that could not meet their needs and left them in a great deal of pain. Over the years, their bodies and intellects matured, yet their hurts, fears, and loneliness stayed with them. They kept a wounded "inner child" even though their "outer child" matured into an adult.

It became clear that using the inner child as an actual character (depicted by one of the role-players) on the day of the reconstruction event would allow the star to access earlier childhood memories and to get a clearer picture of the damage that had taken place as a child. It would also show that there were support systems or individuals in place, however damaged or weak, or this person never would have made it to adulthood. Finally, it would help the person be able to appreciate him- or herself, and to cherish the part of the self that was an innocent, vulnerable, and wounded child. We believe that people need to be able to accept themselves wholly, even when faced with the results of their adult behaviors, decisions, and choices.

In reconstructions we do today at Onsite, we refer to the role-player for this character as the *inner child stand-in* for the star. In this book, we will alternately use the terms "inner child" and "stand-in."

The inner child stand-in is depicted by a role-player throughout the day.

Another concept specific to my current version of reconstruction is the *family of choice.* The family of choice includes people the star has chosen to be in his or her inner circle of friends. It generally does not include primary family members. On the day of the reconstruction, the star will undertake a lot of work, and will make many realizations and decisions about lifestyle and relationships. The family of choice has been incorporated to demonstrate to the star that there is a safety net or security in place in his or her life. In this way, the star can begin to think about making decisions without fear of being alone. Many of our stars have had to make very difficult choices in terms of ending certain relationships that have been important to them, and have needed to know there was a strong system close at hand from which they could draw support. Sometimes, if a star is separating from a large, dysfunctional family, there are one or two people in the family he or she will want to retain in this family of choice, and of course this is acceptable. If most of the family of origin is supportive, then the family itself is kept together and understood as a separate support system. (Preferably, the family of choice and the family of origin don't overlap, and the star has *both* support systems in his or her life.)

The family of choice serves as a safety net or security system for the star.

In addition to the stand-in and the family of choice, a great deal of the work I do is with what we call *the current family.* In the case of someone who is married or coupled, this is the spouse or partner and any children the pair might have. Current families can also include ex-spouses and others who may not be living with the star at present but who retain strong emotional involvements, whether positive or negative. A much bigger emphasis is placed on current family in my work today than was in the work I did with Virginia, where the primary focus was on the family of origin. In my style of reconstruction, probably at least half of the work focuses on the current family; there we can see the present problems, the present "stuck spots," the locus of the pain today, what current relationships need to be looked at, etc.

(Current families can also include a work-related family. For example, when a physician is reconstructed, her office staff, her nurses, and the people around her in her professional life are also a very important part of the reconstruction.)

> ## *More than half of any given reconstruction is spent on the star's current family.*

The whole first half of the reconstruction event is used to identify current issues, and then the standard reconstruction pattern is used to go back and find out why a person stays stuck, to understand what happened, and to reach points of forgiveness and understanding.

Each reconstruction I do closes with a *primary self-worth celebration*. There are many types of celebrations; each reconstruction plans a unique vignette to celebrate the self-worth of its unique star.

I've never been really interested in a fixed model of working. In teaching, it's important for me to provide a flexible framework with concrete suggestions for adding creativity. For me, the therapeutic approach that works best is the recognition of ourselves and those we work with as whole people. This means that whatever model we use, we must recognize and heal all aspects of self: 1) the cognitive (thinking) part; 2) the emotional (feeling) part; 3) the behavioral (acting) part; 4) the spiritual (being) part; and 5) the social (relating) part.

Of course, some of the most valuable lessons I have learned have been rather simple ideas taught by wise and profound people, including Fritz Perls, the father of Gestalt Therapy, who taught that it is important to recapture and own the discarded and disowned parts of the self. Barry Stevens, a natural-born therapist specializing in Gestalt, taught me to use whatever is at hand, and I learned to pay attention to body language, voice inflection, and other modes of expression. From Norman Cousins, who wrote *Anatomy of an Illness* (Cousins, New York: Norton, 1979), along with many other books, I learned that personal responsibility must be taken by all people who want to become more fully healthy. Whether recovering from a physical disease or a spiritual, emotional disability, much depends on the person's willingness to take action. Sheldon Kopp, author, psychologist, and professor, taught me that there is a great spiritual journey we undertake, and that each of us is on a pilgrimage. We can stay at home in a familiar place of certainty or we can set forth and realize our dreams. Dag Hammerskjold, former Secretary General of the United Nations taught, "It's good to be a seeker and a learner, but sooner or later it's time to take what we have learned and begin to share with anyone who will listen." Virginia Satir's greatest lesson was integrating the need to grow healthy *in relationship* (sometimes with another person, sometimes within a system, but definitely within oneself). She taught me that we should attempt to heal current pain, reawaken old dreams, and give ourselves permission to develop new dreams. And from a friend, I once heard the following: "We must remember that to heal and to grow there are two processes that have to be accomplished: one is learning, and the other is unlearning."

I have five basic goals in mind for the person who is seeking help:

1) To reframe current thinking in order to see a bigger picture of reality.
2) To re-awaken and re-order the emotional and passionate parts of ourselves.
3) To break the power of compulsive behavior in order to provide freedom of choice.
4) To return to the precious worthwhile self that lived before becoming traumatized.
5) To develop safe and useful relationship skills.

My husband, Joseph Cruse, is a medical doctor who has shared some important information with me. He defines healing as equal parts science, skill, compassion, recovery, spirit, knowledge, humor, and mystery. Together, these can result in miracles.

Joe has also taught us a great deal about how important it is to know about the power of the brain in the development of our self-worth. We borrow from *The Manual on Experiential Therapy* (Cruse and Cruse, Palo Alto, CA: Science & Behavior Books, 1990) the following text.

> *Peace through mind/brain science was the theme of two conferences held in Hamatsu City, Japan. Discussion at these conferences emphasized new imaging technologies, including positive emission tomography (PET), that make it possible for the first time to relate human thought, emotions, and behavior to measurable chemical reactions within the living brain.*
>
> *At the conclusion of the second conference, the scientists and engineers who attended declared their intention to promote the scientific study of brain mechanisms involved in destructive and violent behavior, as well as those related to loving and creative behavior.*
>
> *The hypothesis is that peace through mind/brain science may be an idea whose time has come.*
>
> —Editorial, *Journal of the American Medical Association*, 262(5), August 4, 1989.

Ashleigh Brilliant spoke of the body and the brain in the beginning of his book, *I Have Abandoned My Search for the Truth* (Brilliant, Santa Barbara, CA: Woodbridge Press, 1980).

"[The body's] methods of feeding, eliminating and reproducing are almost too grotesque to be believed. . . . Most of these odd characteristics are apparently traceable to earlier times and conditions which our bodies have not yet learned no longer prevail. The learning which does take place occurs in a dense, unlikely and rather unlovely organ called the brain. Somehow, it seems there is more of us in our brain than there is anywhere else. In some mysterious way, thinking is the same as being."

Brilliant's suggestion that things about our bodies aren't so different from much earlier times, despite modern technologies, is not unlike the individual who brings childhood (primitive) behaviors, thought, and feelings into an adult world of higher functioning and sophistication.

Here is an exciting new paradigm. Consider the brain as a physical, functioning organ and the mind as a collection of measurable and observable events which occur in that organ. The brain has functions just as the heart has functions. The brain transmits impulses to the entire body, causing muscles to contract, glands to secrete, and body regulators to do their jobs; the heart sends our blood to carry oxygen to the entire body for nourishment. The brain and the heart receive back impulses and blood, respectively. The physical appearances of the brain and the heart have been evaluated by x-rays, scans, sonograms, etc. The function of the heart is measured in many ways: electrocardiograms, cardiac output, pulse rate, blood pressure, etc.; the function of the brain is measured by electroencephalograms, brain hormone levels, nerve transmission studies, etc.

The new paradigm suggests that the study of our thinking, feeling, and behavior are also measurements of brain function and dysfunction! Cardiologists study the heart. Psychiatrists and psychologists study the brain as well as the mind. (Perhaps they should call themselves "cerebreologists"!)

Many of the central ideas in this new view of the mind and brain were not popular even as recently as ten or fifteen years ago. Tension has developed between those defending the old paradigm that the brain is an electrically driven machine whose processes we will never be able to capture and measure exactly, and those who find themselves on a new shoreline, advocating a view that the brain is a hormonally and chemically modulated gland producing powerful mind-, mood-, and behavior-altering hormones and neurotransmitters. Advocates of this new paradigm find that confirmations in the research data are pouring out daily and have been for some time. Some clinicians and some programs are now using this data in patient care.

This new science has many different names, including neuropsychology, psychoneurobiology, and neurochemistry. In years to come, researchers will establish links between hormones and other chemicals of the brain and human behavior. This is a tremendous undertaking, but it is now within the realm of possibility. We will then know just how experiential therapy and other cerebrotherapeutic techniques can actually affect the function, chemistry, and anatomy of our brains. (Perhaps then the concept of world peace through imaging and meditation will become a reality.)

Jon Franklin succinctly sets forth the potential of the brain's ability to change in his book, *Molecules of the Mind* (Franklin, New York: Dell, 1987).

There are by some estimates perhaps as many as a trillion cells in the brain. Each one changes status and activity by the moment, exquisitely sensitive to the outside environment, storing, processing, changing, ever changing, ever embedded in the rich chatter of chemical messages that alter their meanings and context in accordance with complex behaviors, transformations and feedback loops. At any instant, a cell's variables offer choices more numerous than the total number of all the elemental particles in the entire universe! The result of this interplay is the multiplex structure of human thought and emotions (and behavior and spiritual connection) that we refer to as personality.

Structure, function, and behavior all affect one another. Actual structural changes in the connections between neurons and the working of certain centers in our brain can occur. Sometimes, the workings shut down and become atrophied because of overuse. At other times, the brain can change its functioning entirely because of new needs and new stimuli. We constantly adapt and change circuitry in our brains as we continue to cope with our environment. Other times we are "stuck" with our systems as they are and need an intervention to jog us free. We have to have our brains stimulated.

One of the most effective ways to provide this alteration is to direct the patient to establish and experience certain stimuli, thereby bringing forth renewed energy and renewed commitment to becoming "unstuck." This is the purpose of experiential therapy: to re-experience thought, behaviors, and emotions, and to deal with them in order to heal them and be done with them. Some thoughts, feelings, and behaviors may not heal as well as others and will need to be modified to cause us less pain. Finally, through understanding, some thoughts, feelings, and behaviors that have hindered us in the past can actually become positive parts of our lives as we encounter new circumstances.

> **With proper therapy, our lives become much more manageable.**
> **—Heather Ashton**
> **Brain Systems (Ashton, New York: Oxford Univ. Press, 1987)**

Therapeutic techniques and therapists must be versatile. Thoughts, feelings, and behaviors change the brain in a number of surprising ways. We previously believed that the brain was essentially unchangeable, and, so, what you had was all you got. But research shows that neurons, binding sites, control centers, and entire brain systems can be changed (Ashton, 1987).

Repetitive thinking, feeling, and behaving can change many of the brain's working systems. If a brain is constantly stimulated by anxiety-producing thoughts, emotions, and actions, eventually the brain systems change to produce anxiety in response to even the slightest stimuli. Repetitive thoughts, feelings, and actions can cause actual gain or loss in the number and size of certain brain cells, and can change the number and types of connections among our brain cells.

This is not so different from other ways in which the anatomy of the brain—and thus thoughts, feelings, and behaviors—can be changed, such as through surgery, head truma, brain tumors, etc.

Historically, psychologists and others in the 50s, 60s, and 70s were focused almost universally on the environment and behavior of the individual. There was tremendous conflict between the scientific community and the adaptive or humanistic community; this conflict continues today. The division between these approaches in our culture can be likened to the centuries-old differences between Eastern and Western medicine. Those in the West direct therapeutic efforts toward precise correlations as to cause and effect. Dealing in signs and symptoms, they set minimum criteria for diagnoses and expect continual re-evaluation. They expect to see measurable levels of recovery following intervention and certain treatment. In the East, however, healers go forward aware that new knowledge of the ebb and flow of chemicals within the body supports much of what has been their practice for centuries. For them, healing, religion, meditation, and prayer are needs whose source is the same.

Recently, the mainstream of scientific concern in this country and 12-step programs have begun to converge. This is perhaps just one indication that spiritual searches and scientific inquiries can teach and learn from each other. In any case, trends seem to indicate that the nature vs. nurture controversy is becoming the nature-plus-nurture dynamic, and that the historically rigid boundaries between and among medical, scientific, social, spiritual, and psychological disciplines are beginning to soften.

> **The nature vs. nurture controversy is becoming the nature-plus-nurture dynamic.**

Norman Cousins has often pointed out how holistic health and other deviations from the medical mainstream in our culture have been compelling and productive, yet non-specific enough so that the result has been confusion and division (see *Anatomy of an Illness* [already cited]). Parapsychology and a flood of new-age philosophies and practices have mixed bits of both Eastern and Western practices and beliefs. Many of these approaches claim to be "the only way." While such techniques may have their basis in fact and be validated through their effectiveness, their exclusive and exaggerated claims and usage are inappropriate and can result in highly unfavorable outcomes.

The implication that experiential therapy and re-experiencing emotions can actually change the function and structure of the brain can be overwhelming, but it is indeed possible. If a reconstruction can heal old and current feelings, it may just be possible that the star will have new behavior available over time, and that this will lead to actual structural changes in the brain.

Certainly the most redemptive of all experiences is when the human soul is reconciled with itself. We can use drama to heal. A human life is the most dramatic venture possible. No one can predict its course. We can develop fully, realizing our potential to its utmost, or we can lose our identities somewhere along the way. Because of the relentless unfolding of life, no creature needs healing as often or as deeply as do human beings. Sometimes we expect to be healed through doctrines, rules, or institutions, when really we are better off seeking healing through the art of honest contact, through the expression of the truth, and through heart-to-heart connections between and among people. We are taught—perhaps by God or some other Higher Power—through human struggles, whether our own or those of others. Sharing those struggles is a special kind of communion, and results in a special kind of community, whether in the privacy of one-on-one encounters with therapists, or in the larger audience of a reconstruction workshop.

People are called on from many directions to be whole and joyous rather than alone and isolated and sad. Yet one of the most difficult things can be simply knowing what that wholeness means, especially if we have come from emptiness and aloneness. But we are closer to wholeness when the sun shining means more than power, when children excite us more than do political wars, when we are more joyful in love than we are in affluence, when music and poetry fill our hearts more than does television, when we laugh and sing more often than we complain or whine, and when we weep not because we have lost something, but because we know how much we have been given.

Growth comes as we see ourselves on the wrong paths, as we decide to do only those things our inner selves believe in, as we go in search of ourselves to discover who we are and are not, as we find warmth of acceptance for ourselves as we are, as we learn that we are afraid of our true selves, as we recognize our need for others and the love they can give us, as we find ways to become closer to the people we need by sharing our deepest selves with them and letting them be free to need us back or not, as we realize that we get more love back from others when we are most honest with and about ourselves, and as we come to know that the more we are able to value ourselves and to see and accept our own limitations, the more we are able to accept others and to see a Higher Power at work. Growth comes as we realize that the only way to run our lives is to give up fighting for complete control, and to accept that Higher Power—in whatever form it takes for each of us— and let our lives unfold.

Transformation comes when we don't know how to go forward and yet we don't want to go backward, so we choose to seize the moment, to do what is necessary to be right with ourselves, and to let the change(s) happen.

Reconstruction is a transformation process.

Throughout the decades that I have been doing family reconstructions, many people have asked me to develop a book to contain my relevant body of knowledge, and to start a school to teach my model of reconstruction. Until two years ago, the only training I had done was informal, usually with therapists who would become group leaders after attending many weeks of reconstructions and learning by observation and informal sharing.

Then, two years ago, three people began a structured program of sharing and learning. Kathy Higby, Ted Klontz, Ann Rainey, and I have now spent countless hours together, with a wonderful, fluid give-and-take of sharing, teaching, and learning. I am thrilled to see them become "artists" in family reconstruction, and I welcome them—with all of their work's similarities to and differences from my own—as I believe Virginia Satir would, into the magical world of the family reconstruction guide.

I am proud to teach what I know, and to share with you the work of my friends and peers. Enjoy the adventure.

—Sharon Wegscheider-Cruse
March, 1995

Sharon Wegscheider-Cruse and Virginia Satir following Sharon's reconstruction.

BEFORE YOU BEGIN

We have written this book to help educate people about the powerful therapeutic technique known as "family reconstruction." We write about reconstruction as we currently practice it at Onsite Training and Consulting. But the technique is in no way static, and others may practice it differently to varying degrees.

This book has been written with text, graphics, and exercises, and though it is not a workbook *per se*, and the exercises suggested here can in no way substitute for the experience of undergoing or guiding or witnessing an actual family reconstruction, we do hope that they can begin to give the reader an understanding of the kind of work that reconstruction involves, and the kind of healing it can facilitate.

Educators may find this volume of great help to themselves and to their students. Professional therapists may be able to learn for themselves and thus better help clients, perhaps even by suggesting this book and using the exercises to guide them in both individual and group therapy. Those involved in group therapy or 12-step work will find it a great asset in providing clarity and understanding. Ultimately, *The Living Theater* is for anyone who is interested in further understanding of his or her "roots" in terms of family history and origin; anyone who would like to document his or her life, possibly to pass along to children or grandchildren; anyone who would like to record his or her own truth and use it to work with a counselor or therapist; and/or anyone who would like to grow in self-understanding and self-knowledge, and promote his or her own self-worth. This volume is also appropriate for any mental health or healing professional who would like to understand the reconstruction process; to use this volume as a text resource for learning more about family systems; to learn more about using certain kinds of tools (e.g., art, music, props, etc.) in working with clients; and/or to learn more about integrating the techniques of sculpture, psychodrama, group process, experiential therapy, etc.

The exercises contained here—some embedded in the text and others spelled out and clearly labeled as such—involve writing and imagining. They are intended to promote memories and feelings. Some healing can begin to take place simply by reading this book and doing the work suggested throughout. Some may want to do this work in conjunction with seeing a therapist who can help interpret the results.

We elucidate points of theory and technique as we go along in ways that seem to us to be germane to the context. Wherever possible, we refer the reader to other sections of the book (and even, occasionally, to other books) for further clarification of a particular idea. We try to provide a smooth reading experience, but we have not written this book in a strictly linear way because reconstruction is not a strictly linear process; to suggest otherwise would be misleading. It is our intention and hope, however, that a reader who finishes this volume will have a real sense of the intent and spirit of the reconstuction process as we undertake it at Onsite, as well as exposure to the techniques we employ in the process.

Throughout this book, we refer to specific terms with which the reader should become familiar.

Star — The person seeking a reconstruction. This is an individual who wants to explore his or her current and past relationships in order to have more manageability and increased self-worth in the future. This person is the focus of the reconstruction event.

Reconstruction Event — A 12-14 hour process lasting from morning through evening that will enable the star to heal from persistent pain that is rooted in the past, experience increased self-worth, and build confidence for future decision-making. The past, the present, and the future are all relevant time frames, and are all explored in relation to the star's life. Reconstruction uses a variety of techniques including, but not limited to, sculpture, psychodrama, Gestalt therapy, experiential therapy, guided imagery, group process, rage reduction, and grief healing.

Family Reconstruction Workshop — A 6-day process for 30-40 people that enables each participant to explore parts of current and former relationships. In the context of this process, the star experiences the reconstruction event, and others may participate as witnesses (audience) or as role-players. Throughout the week-long process there are smaller group meetings wherein all of the non-stars explore their own feelings about the events of the workshop, events in their own lives, and feelings they have lived with or are experiencing currently.

Guide — This is the therapist who directs the reconstruction event. The guide needs specific training in several therapeutic disciplines in order to conduct an effective event, and he or she must have both training and experience in order to have ready the appropriate tools to help an individual star. Each star has his or her unique history and issues that will need to be addressed throughout the week-long workshop and in the focused event itself. It is best if the guide is skilled in psychodrama, Gestalt therapy, and experiential sculpture techniques, as well as the use of imagery, music, group process, rage reduction, and grief healing techniques.

Sculpture — A technique that uses visual representation to re-create a scene representative of something which has occurred or which someone would like to occur. Sculptures are an efficient means to address scenes and issues from a person's past, present, or even future (in the case of a desired reality), and are used in reconstructions to facilitate and deepen a star's experience and understanding. Sculptures usually involve people role-playing characters from the star's life; most of the time props are also used quite effectively.

Psychodrama — This is a technique in which sculptures are "brought to life" and scenes are enacted among the players. All psychodramas begin with a sculpture, though not all sculptures result in psychodrama.

Note: We cannot emphasize enough that readers who perform the exercises included here will gain a sense of the process of reconstruction, and may begin to feel some clarity and perspective around their own family system and their place in it. But what the reader will *not* get here is a guide to give direction to the process, or an audience to give objective feedback, both of which are essential elements in any reconstruction. Again, use the exercises in this book for understanding; if you want to further your understanding and allow new feelings to surface, perhaps you can use the book with a therapist of your choice.

The feelings that will surface during this kind of personal exploration are often very intense and very private. We caution against using family or friends in the role of guide or support, and specifically suggest using someone professional such as a licensed psychotherapist.

CHAPTER ONE

WHAT IS FAMILY RECONSTRUCTION?

The more intensively the family has stamped its character upon the child, the more [the child] will tend to feel and see its early miniature world again in the bigger world of adult life.

—Carl Gustav Jung

In 1977, Sharon Wegscheider-Cruse attended a conference led by Virginia Satir, who shared in a distributed hand-out the following:

> Family reconstruction is one way to see our paths with new eyes and thus make the present and the future a new place to be. All of us were born little, without any little bag of direction about how to grow and develop as people. For all of us, our major resources were the people who were around and saw to it that we survived. The chances are good that the ways you learned to survive are what you are now using unless you have changed them.
>
> The methods by which we were kept warm and cool and fed and dry and held were our earliest learning in how to treat ourselves in the world around us. The many ways by which people interact with us, the touch of hands, the sounds of voices, the expressions of faces and the words used were even more powerful teachers for our education in how to be human beings. The people who assumed responsibility for our survival, our guidance, and our development were often very different, even to the point of giving very mixed messages.

Our minds being what they are, we made what sense we could, even if it was nonsense.

It seems to occur to few adults that a baby is human, like themselves, hearing, smelling, seeing, touching, feeling, and thinking. Because of this tendency, which comes out of ignorance rather than judgement, adults often focus on developing certain behaviors in children while neglecting the development of emotional tools. For instance, how many adults are aware of the emotional and intellectual significance of giving strong, opposing directions to a child, either noisily or quietly in blaming ways?

They learn also by witnessing such an activity between two people who have a survival relationship with each other. What kind of sense does a child make of that?

Further, adults often accompany their blue print with either stated or implicit rules for how and when the child may question or oppose the adult. An experience familiar to many children is noticing an expression of sorrow or sadness on the parent's face and asking, "Mommy (or Daddy), what's wrong?" Often the answer is, "Nothing." Or, "Everything is alright." Or, "Run along and play." In such cases, the parent is usually operating on one of three principles: 1) Adults should not burden children. 2) Adults should set examples of their idea of perfection. 3) Children are too young to understand.

Thus, the child is asked to believe nonsense. These kinds of principles are apt to be repeated since the principles are inadvertently part of the working parental design. The child has a mind and therefore has to make the best sense the child can. Since the child has no way of getting at the missing pieces, he has to explain much of the nonsense we have accepted as fact, which is then translated into the rules for how to be.

All human behavior is understandable when we understand the premises by which we operate, the internal experience we are having, and the goals we wish to obtain. The upshot of all of this is that children grow up with some very peculiar ideas about what motivates their parents and what explains their behavior. How many adults feel comfortable in telling their children what is really going on, that they are hurting or afraid or have made a mistake? The parent's hiding or withholding their own inner experiences is more likely to be the case. Under these conditions, the way is paved for both the child and the parent to misunderstand each other and therefore not meet as people. Perhaps the most unfortunate part is that the child puts together the discrepancy he or she experiences as a way of understanding self and others and this becomes the operating model for assessing oneself.

Family reconstruction is a method I developed to help a person go back and pick up the missing pieces. By understanding the missing pieces that created discrepancies, we can then develop a new model for ourselves by transforming the old model into something more in keeping with being a whole human being. Since great gaps often exist between us and our parents, we thus learn to develop new ways for a more nurturing relationship with our families as well as new feelings about ourselves. In short, family reconstruction brings everyone closer to being people. When what we have learned does not allow us to be free people, in charge of ourselves, then our current lives would probably have many unnecessary pains. When we come to the awareness that we are using outmoded ways of coping in new situations, we are then free to leave our compulsive loyalties to old ways such as rejecting, withdrawing, or destroying. Through understanding and realization, which means head, feeling, and heart, we are free to take on what fits for us now and act from choice rather than compulsion.

This is what family reconstruction is all about.

Family reconstruction is a vehicle designed to help individuals understand their historical family issues by means of an experience so powerful that they are then able to make new choices in the future, and thus change their lives. The goal of a reconstruction is to help a person develop increased self-worth and a genuine confidence about taking charge of his or her life. It is an experience of *empowerment*.

Let's explore in a bit more detail how family reconstruction has evolved from the techniques of Virginia Satir to those currently in use by Sharon Wegscheider-Cruse and the staff at Onsite Training & Consulting.

When Sharon first studied with Virginia, she was told that there was little involved in the selection of a star. The contract Virginia held with each star was as follows:

a)   There are no promises.
b)   You might be disappointed.
c)   There are no specific answers.
d)   I'll provide you with new light.
e)   The journey is up to you.

For many years, Sharon borrowed and used that same contract. She later added a few components:

f)   There is no Santa Claus or free gift.
g)   You are the Board Chairperson of your life and must demonstrate proactive choices.
h)   You cannot heal what you cannot feel, and you cannot feel what you medicate.

Over the years Sharon had learned more about substance addictions and compulsive behaviors. She learned that when people are affected with either a substance addiction (e.g., alcohol, drugs, nicotine) or with a specific compulsion (e.g., eating disorder, work addiction, gambling), he or she loses three very important basic freedoms: the ability to think clearly, the ability to feel emotions, and the ability to execute decisions and choices.

The four most difficult reconstructions she has facilitated over the years were with the following stars: 1) an alcoholic with only three months of sobriety; 2) an active cigarette smoker; 3) a workaholic (a psychologist!); and 4) an obese food addict. These experiences led her to add another extremely important criterion to her list of requirements for stars. After being assessed for "readiness" to do the intense work of a reconstruction, an evaluation is made to assess a potential star for addictive behavior. If the star is found to have any addictions, including nicotine, these must be treated in a primary addiction treatment program and/or a year's sobriety or manageability must be accomplished before the reconstruction process can occur. This makes each star's journey towards Virginia Satir's "Five Freedoms" (to which I was first exposed in a workshop with Virginia that took place in Mexico in 1975) much easier, and their fulfillment much more likely.

VIRGINIA SATIR'S FIVE FREEDOMS

1)   The freedom to see and hear what is here instead of what should be, what was, or what will be.
2)   The freedom to say what you feel and think instead of what you think you should feel and think.

3) The freedom to feel what you feel instead of what you think you ought to feel.
4) The freedom to ask for what you want instead of always waiting for permission.
5) The freedom to take risks on your own behalf instead of choosing to be only "secure" and not rock the boat.

The reconstruction event and workshop begins with extensive preparatory work between the star and the guide. (This work is thoroughly outlined and explained in Chapters Two and Three.) Together they will explore the star's current and past life, and plan new behaviors for the future. All of this work is recorded in writing in order to prepare for and facilitate the reconstruction event. On that day, it is the guide's job to take all of the extremely subjective information the star passed on about him- or herself and to present that information back to the star in an objective way so that the star can see new "pictures" and gain new insight. (For example, when Virginia was reconstructing Sharon, Sharon gave a tremendous amount of information about her mother having been absent in so many different ways that it came as a surprise to her when Virginia showed her in many sculptures all the instances in which her mother *had* been there for her. All day long, Sharon was getting a new look at her mother's presence in her life.) It is a powerful experience for the star, the guide, and everyone involved in the whole process.

Remember, the entire reconstruction process is but one event in a much larger recovery process, but one part of the journey of recovery from old wounds and a painful past. The process itself is diminished when either the star or the guide attempts to make it more than a step along the way.

The assumption is made that anyone ready to take this journey will not be a newcomer to therapy or personal growth. A reconstruction star must already have acquired a significant amount of self-study and insight before beginning to gather the information that is the first step in the reconstruction process. (More information about who makes a good candidate for reconstruction appears in Chapter Two.) The point to understand here is that a reconstruction is not an introduction to therapy, and is not appropriate for anyone who has never been in therapy.

On the most basic level, a reconstruction is the re-creation of a person's life through action therapy.

On the most basic level, a reconstruction is the recreation of one person's life through action therapy, in which significant events are role-played for further exploration and understanding. Reconstruction cannot be undertaken alone. To fully experience everything written about in this book requires working with a guide or teacher, someone trained in reconstruction, someone who can spend time doing all the preparatory work with you and then guide you through the entire process (which, again, at Onsite Training & Consulting is a workshop that lasts close to one week, although the actual reconstruction event takes only one day). There must be this partnership in the reconstruction endeavor—two of you must work together to understand a single life.

Reconstruction is a group journey, never solitary.

And there must be witnesses, fellow travelers, if you will. They are there to act as cheerleaders, as Greek chorus, as guardian angels, as audience, as support. Reconstruction is a group journey, never solitary. Thirty or more people watch the reconstruction event. This group may feel, identify, and understand along with the star; they may also, in turn, model the empathy, acceptance, and perseverance that the star cannot yet acknowledge or realize for him- or herself.

The group is also much more than witness to the process. For the group that gathers around a reconstruction, even the guide, will participate in a way unique to experiential therapy. They will do this by taking on roles as important people in the star's life. Standing in as mother, father, friend, lover, sibling, co-worker, boss, enemy, neighbor, etc., role-players pretend to be someone they do not know and about whom they have a minimum of understanding. Yet no prior acting experience or talents are required. People working together in the reconstruction process somehow seem to do and say the right things to facilitate the process for the star.

The business of acting in a reconstruction also enables the role-player to learn about another person. For example, someone playing an alcoholic parent might experience the shame, denial, and loneliness of being an alcoholic. This new perspective can be extremely valuable if he or she has ever lived with or loved an alcoholic because it can allow him or her to stand in that person's shoes, however briefly.

Action therapy involves all group members. The role players will be plunged into the reconstruction day in a more active way (moving around, talking, acting) than will non-role-playing audience members, but everyone in the room will have powerful feelings and thoughts as the reconstruction proceeds. It is virtually impossible to be in the room in which a reconstruction is taking place and not be engaged in the power of the process. Reconstruction is never boring!

ESSENTIAL HUMAN ELEMENTS FOR THE RECONSTRUCTION PROCESS

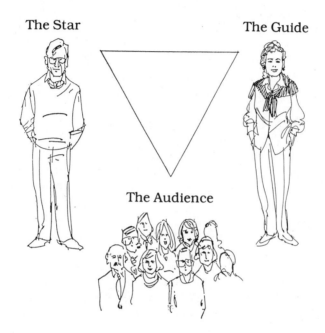

All three components are essential to the reconstruction process.

RECONSTRUCTION AS THEATER

Almost everyone who reads this book is familiar with the concept of drama—almost all of us have been to plays or seen movies or read stories. Reading this volume and using a bit of imagination, one can begin to understand the drama of one's own life. (Throughout this chapter, references to theater have been taken from *Theatre: The Dynamics of the Art,* by Bruce Hansen [New York: Prentice-Hall, 1991]).

A reconstruction is like theater in many ways, some of which are obvious. The process uses a lot of role-playing and psychodrama techniques. It takes place before an audience of onlookers. Imagination is a key element. There are costumes and props.

> **Even the most primitive and ancient cultures used some type of re-enactment as part of religious and social events.**

Even in the most primitive and ancient cultures people used some type of re-enactment as part of religious and social events—they acted the parts of animals or gods, dramatized famous battles, or used dance, music, and costume simply to tell the stories and ideas of their people.

The ancient Greeks developed the concept of theater that we understand in Western culture today. The word "theater" (or "theatre") comes from the Greek word *theatron,* which means *a seeing place.* The process of reconstruction is certainly intended to provide for all who are present "a seeing place." As the star of the reconstruction and other participants open themselves to learning and changing, they begin to see—with new eyes, heart, and soul—the stories of their lives.

From the Greeks to Shakespeare in Western culture, from the Eastern traditions of Noh and Kabuki, theater today serves many purposes. So does reconstruction.

1.   *A public event.* Reconstruction was designed to occur not in isolation, but as a social, interactive event. Telling one's story is important. It is also important that others hear it. When a group can hear, and witness, and empathize, much that is shameful and secret disappears, and self-worth and self-love can enter. Healing can begin.

2.   *To focus attention on issues and people.* In a reconstruction, topics of addiction, abuse, neglect, fear, hope, spirituality, regret, families, friends, authority figures, co-workers, and children are addressed. Any problem that is rooted in human pain can be a topic for reconstruction. No one topic is the singular focus.

3.   *To utilize the concept of a hero or heroine.* Reconstructions take as their subject matter the story of an individual person's life. This person is the "star" of that particular reconstruction workshop. Fathers, mothers, siblings, relatives, spouses or partners, lovers, co-workers, friends, children ... all of these people in a star's life are also characters in the reconstruction. The star becomes the hero or heroine of his or her own reconstruction.

4.   *To provide an emotional catharsis.* Aristotle believed that people could be purged of their deepest conflicting emotions by recreating those feelings and presenting them on the stage. This was 1500 years before the birth of psychology! A reconstruction process evokes many, many tremendously powerful feelings in its star. Vicarious feelings brought forth in other participants, whether audience members or role-players, are also powerful and healing.

5.   *To teach.* Reconstruction employs both direct and indirect approaches to teaching. Guides will be explicit and didactic when appropriate; role-modeling, rehearsal, and visual presentation may all be used to teach lessons such as decision-making, letting go of negative influences, etc.

6.   *To honor a Higher Power.* Although the religious or spiritual aspects of theater are associated more with the rituals of early tribes or societies than they are with most modern plays and movies, the idea is important to a reconstruction process. The acknowledgement of the power of the human spirit as well as some divine kind of Higher Power are always part of a reconstruction. Virginia Satir referred to this Power as "the life force." The spiritual nature of all people is honored in a reconstruction. Those who have participated can attest to the mysterious, inexplicable coincidences that occur, as well as the beautiful moments of healing and change that are decidedly spiritual in nature.

7.   *To celebrate.* Reconstruction uses many forms to celebrate the positive nature of any star. Dancing, music, parties, rituals, and games are all utilized to lift the self-worth of the star.

8.   *To create change.* Many dramas, whether plays or stories or novels, have been designed at least in part to promote or advocate for social change (e.g., Jonathan Swift's 18th century satire, *A Modest Proposal*; the 1970s movie, *The China Syndrome*; the 1990s play, *Angels in America*). The reconstruction process promotes internal change in feelings and attitudes about self and others. Old pain is changed through the discharge of feelings. Old rules come to be seen as outdated and no longer functional; they are replaced by new, more human and compassionate codes or credos for living.

Not to put too fine a point on it, but the elements of theater that Aristotle described thousands of years ago—plot, character, idea, language, spectacle, and music and dance—are all present in reconstruction.

Every reconstruction tells a story, the story of the star's life. This is more than a mere recounting of chronological events, it is the tragedies and triumphs, the losses and victories. The emotional meanings attached to events are very important. In a traditional play, the plot usually proceeds chronologically, building to a crisis and/or catharsis, and is followed by a denouement or a gradual slowing down of the action. A reconstruction begins in the present to establish the characters and issues of the star's current life, but follows a similar overall emotional arc by presenting psychodramas (that involve both the past and the present) and their associated catharses, and ending with a return to the present (and a celebration).

Full bodied characters, complete with motivations and goals, are a key element of any reconstruction as we try to explore and understand why the people we know and love (or hate) do what they do, and how we influence each other. Good guys and bad guys, heroes and villains, protagonists and antagonists—every drama has them. So does every life. So, therefore, will every reconstruction. The struggles between and among these people and the forces they represent help us understand the struggles inside ourselves.

Reconstruction embodies important ideas such as the triumph of the human spirit, the survival of people despite tremendous tragedy or against great odds, and the potential for recovery to win out over disease. The unconditional regard for all human beings and their right to self-actualize is an idea basic to all reconstructions.

The language of a reconstruction is not just the spoken, verbal language employed by the star, players, guides, and audience to communicate with each other, but the language of emotions and spirit as well—the language of *feeling.*

In theater, the audience expects to be entertained and moved. A reconstruction uses props, costumes, music, and drama to present a moving and memorable spectacle that shapes experience. The attention of the audience is held by the timing of events and the build of dramatic quality, culminating in celebration. And although music and dance are relatively new additions to the reconstruction process, they have been shown to be quite helpful—music can facilitate access to emotions in a powerful way, and dance can bring into the mix the participants' physical being.

Exercise 1.1: You in a Childhood Story

Think of your favorite childhood story. Cast yourself in the role of one of the characters, and re-tell the story as it relates to your own personal journey.

Exercise 1.2: You in a Grown-Up Story

Think of a favorite adult story, myth, play, television show, or movie. Cast yourself in the part of your favorite character. Write about the struggle of this character and the final result of the story.

RECONSTRUCTION AND OTHER THERAPIES

Over the past one hundred years, the study of psychology has developed many theories and methods. Those who have been thoroughly trained to work with others have learned both about the pioneers in the science of the human psyche and about the newest techniques. A good therapist is always studying "the masters" across eras in order to find the most effective tools for guiding people in pain who want to change their lives. Selecting appropriate techniques that will work for each client comes with much practice.

Various psychological therapies have waxed and waned in popularity. And, as in most fields, it has been easy enough for many in psychology to jump on the bandwagon of one idea or another. But recently the arena of psychotherapy seems to be more open to blended styles. Most good therapists identify themselves not with one idea or theory, but with an eclectic style that incorporates several ideas.

This is especially true of action or experiential therapies. However, many of these therapies were not respectful of people—by coercing emotions and catharsis through peer pressures, action therapies came under severe criticism. Following the excesses of the 60s and 70s, a more conservative view of therapy was needed, and most therapists stayed or moved away from action therapies. Yet from those action and experiential therapy techniques and ideas have come some powerful tools for healing. Perhaps now some myths associated with those therapies can be dispelled. We believe that action therapies *can* be taught and learned; we wouldn't have written this book if we didn't. In any case, it is important to understand how action therapy is used in an eclectic style.

One of the most powerful action therapies, reconstruction is the culmination of many processes, and incorporates what many believe to be the most important aspects of therapy and change. It has evolved and changed over time and now epitomizes an eclectic model.

The most obvious therapy used in reconstruction is psychodrama. In a reconstruction, the star will be the protagonist of the story. As mentioned in the Introduction, there will also be an inner child stand-in for the star. A reenactment of life events in role play will occur just as in psychodrama.

Borrowing heavily from Gestalt therapies, the reconstruction process attempts to unify or integrate lost parts of self by producing a "big picture." Using the idea that people are often unhappy because of unfinished business, and can heal when they reclaim lost parts of self, the basic assumption of Gestalt theory is that people are capable of dealing effectively with their life problems if they make full use of what is happening inside themselves and around them. Although it may appear that a reconstruction is past-oriented, the star is actually involved in a here-and-now experience, both on a feeling level and in the actual re-experiencing. A reconstruction uses past events and feelings to help change present and future behavior.

> *A reconstruction uses past events and feelings to help change present and future behavior.*

The process of reconstruction puts together pieces of the person's life as a 'whole event' or in context with many factors. Often in therapy a client may work on anger at a parent, abandonment issues, or the family system. However effective this work may be, it can acquire new power when explored in the concentrated wholeness of the reconstruction process.

Based on behavior therapies, a reconstruction uses action, decision-making, and modeling. Often in a reconstruction the star will have to make changes or commitments to change. Decisions made in a reconstruction are directed to behavioral change, moving from self-defeating to self-enhancing actions. A reconstruction often uses practice behavior techniques, asking the star to act out assertiveness or other unfamiliar behavior. Many new goals are defined along the way.

Based on cognitive theories, reconstruction often disputes old ways of thinking, and how these distortions drive irrational feelings and behaviors ("old tapes" or old family beliefs and myths).

Based on psychoanalysis, reconstruction values the early stages of childhood as a vital link to understanding the self.

From the work of Alfred Adler comes the concept of social context. Important aspects such as the events surrounding the star's birth, the star's birth order in the family, and sibling relationships are always explored as they pertain to the development of the star's needs and goals.

From Carl Rogers, reconstruction values and respects a person's ability to self-actualize. The guide and all the participants in a family reconstruction exhibit their belief in the star's ability to move toward an increased awareness of self, spontaneity, trust in self, and inner-directedness. Rogers emphasized the therapeutic relationship as primary in importance. In a reconstruction, the atmosphere of acceptance, warmth, and validation from the guide and participants is the corresponding vehicle for the star.

Virginia Satir's genius lay in her ability to take all of life's gifts—and any discipline or idea—and seem to put them to work to help people change. In her own work she admits to being influenced by biology, linguistics, theology, physics, learning theory, drama, history, art, and play.

Satir's brilliance was also evident in her effective use of the richest ideas of family dynamics (see the section on Family Systems, below). She was tremendously innovative, inventing her work over the 50 years she spent in the field in order to bring health and change and love into the lives of those she taught and counseled. Her knowledge of the concepts and approaches to psychotherapy, psychiatry, and social work was undeniable (see Satir & Baldwin, *Step by Step*, Palo Alto, CA: Science and Behavior Books, 1983). We suspect she also utilized her own life events, her thoughts and dreams, and the experiences around her to guide her in knowing how to work with people and perceive what tools and techniques would best expedite change. In other words, Satir knew that in a field about people, therapists bring their own selves to the people they work with. She felt that all of life, personally and professionally, was grist for the therapist's mill.

THE ECLECTIC FAMILY RECONSTRUCTION PROCESS

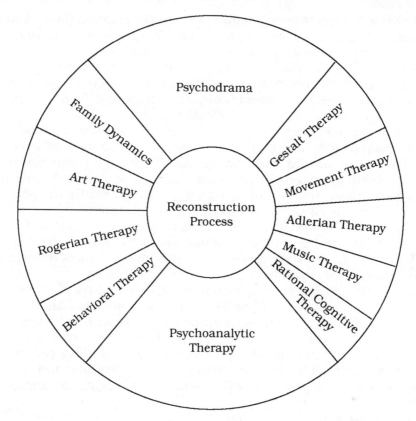

Many have adopted the Satir model for reconstruction over the years. Sharon Wegscheider-Cruse chose to add much more drama and Gestalt, working a great deal with present-day issues. Her model also adds music, humor, props, and audience participation in a more integrated and dramatic way.

For her part, Sharon says that she always felt Virginia's support for her work. Early on, they disagreed often on the issue of addiction. (Sharon still believes this exchange of opposing ideas was one of the clearest, best examples of having a healthy relationship with someone that she has found in her own life. "We could agree and disagree with utter companionability." Later, when Virginia visited Sharon and her husband, they took her to an addictions conference. She later told Sharon, "Now I see what you've been talking about.")

And when Sharon's peers questioned her work for being different from Virginia's, Virginia was always encouraging. It was important to Satir both that people added to her work and that she herself continued to learn.

FAMILY SYSTEMS: THE HEART OF RECONSTRUCTION

As civilized, social human beings, we operate emotionally and interpersonally in various human systems. We work in a system, we go to school in a system, we have family systems, etc. Systems, in general, are simply organisms. In this context: 1) they have a purpose for existing; 2) they are made up of people; 3) they have some kind of order (even if it seems to be disorder!); and 4) they require some kind of power or "fuel" for maintenance (food, air, water, intellect, feelings, affections, etc.).

There are open human systems and closed human systems. Open systems welcome change, recognize that self-worth is primary, exist in such a way that actions accord with reality, and encourage communication. Closed systems are reluctant to change, depend on law and order and punishment (there are a lot of "should's"), hold self-worth secondary to power and performance, and subject actions to approval from others. People *exist* in closed systems rather than *develop*.

Virginia Satir designed reconstruction primarily as an understanding of one's family system. It is a means of learning about oneself through the exploration of family dynamics and the review of one's personal history. Virginia believed that when people understood, they would feel better. With her experience in the addictions field, Sharon came from another perspective. She saw people medicating their feelings so heavily that they couldn't begin to understand. Much of the evolution of reconstruction since Sharon began practicing the technique is rooted in the perspective that first you heal the feelings and *then* you can understand and begin to deal with them. (This principle will be articulated repeatedly throughout this book.)

There are basically two different kinds of families. *Nurturing* families produce whole people who have high self-worth (we define self-worth as how good people feel about themselves or how they feel about their own goodness). *Troubled* families (which may be troubled for any number of reasons) produce troubled people who are in pain and who have questionable self-worth. Whether nurturing or troubled, a family itself has either high or low self-worth. And all families, whether nurturing or troubled, communicate. They share information and feelings, whether in healthy or unhealthy ways.

All families follow rules. Some rules are open and explicit so family members know what is expected of them and what the consequences will be if the rules are not followed. These are healthy rules that serve to make order out of chaos and meet the needs of the family community in which they are made. Other families follow rules that may be unspoken but are extremely rigid. These are rules of control rather than rules designed to make order out of chaos. The most controlling rules are very often made by the oldest or strongest or most dysfunctional members of the family. In these families there is often a great deal of punishment and indirect communication that reduces family members' self-worth.

FAMILY RULES

- Do it right.
- Boys don't cry.
- Your father is right.
- Don't talk.
- Don't trust.
- Don't feel.
- Children should be seen, not heard.
- Don't rock the boat.
- Don't question authority.
- Be good.
- You are stupid.
- Work first, play later.
- Blood is thicker than water.
- It's your fault.
- Keep family secrets.
- Be perfect.
- Do what we say, not what we do.
- Adults make the rules, children obey.
- Don't question.

Exercise 1.3: Your Family System

Answer the following three questions:

1) Does it feel good to live in your family right now?
2) Do you feel you are living with good friends whom you like and trust and who like and trust you?
3) All families go through difficult times. But is it generally a fun and exciting situation to be a member of your family?

As you may have guessed, answering yes to these questions indicates that you are involved in a nurturing family. Answering no to any of the questions may be a sign that your family is troubled. Many families fall somewhere in between.

Exercise 1.4: Your Family's Rules

Write down the rules from the family in which you grew up.

A few paragraphs above, we said that nurturing families produce "whole" people. What does it mean to be a "whole" individual? The list below should give you some idea of what it means to be whole. It is not intended to be exhaustive, nor is it ranked in any order of importance.

A whole person . . .

- is real and honest in thinking and communicating about self and others;
- is willing to take behavioral risks (such as telling someone you love him/her, changing jobs, choosing whether to have a child, etc.);
- is creative (this can mean problem-solving, learning a new language, taking up a new hobby, giving of oneself to another being, etc.);
- is competent in a selection of chosen areas;
- can change and be flexible when the situation calls for it;
- takes pride in his/her knowledge, beliefs, and values and remains open to new knowledge, beliefs, values, experiences, people, etc.;
- understands, values, and cares for his or her body;
- has some sense of meaning or belonging or spirituality in the world.

> **By raising our self-worth, it is possible to change all of our circumstances.**

In families there is a sense of self-worth that can be raised or lowered depending on the family's circumstances. By raising our own individual self-worth, it is possible to change all of our circumstances.

Communication can determine relationship and how a person fits into the world. By definition, all communication carries information. And whether there is simultaneous verbal communication or not, all that is communicated need not be verbal. Through our sensory systems we communicate with eyes, ears, skin, and touch. We also communicate with brain, logic, and thoughts. When people with high self-worth are communicating with each other, there is a sense of congruence. When congruence is in place, it is as though someone is saying, "I will tell you how I feel. I will take that risk. I may have to expose something of myself, my weakness or my lack of knowledge or whatever, but we will have an honest communication." This means that what you feel inside seems to match what is going on outside. The messages feel very clear.

CHARACTERISTICS OF A WHOLE PERSON

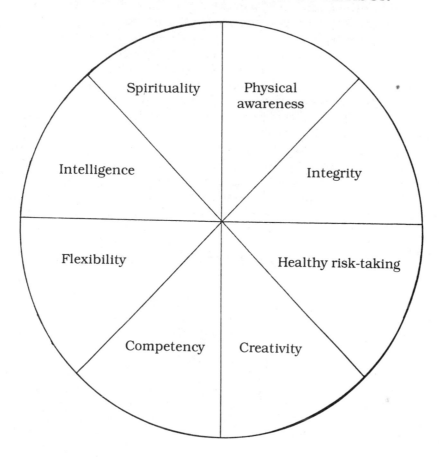

When congruence is in place, it is as though someone is saying, "I will tell you how I feel. I will take that risk. I may have to expose something of myself, my weakness or my lack of knowledge or whatever, but we will have an honest communication."

In contrast to the congruence that results form open communication are feelings that result from obscured communication styles. These are communication styles in which people "cover up" in an attempt to keep others from recognizing that their self-worth is shaky. They want to send the message that they are okay or competent or loveable, etc. in order to ensure that others respond favorably to them, and they will avoid being honest or straight in order to do this. There are a variety of techniques that all fit into this category of closed or covered communication. Virginia Satir used to say that in her work she found about 50% of people would people-please, about 30% would blame, 15% would try to be very logical and reasonable, and probably ½% would act silly and not even communicate. That leaves only about 4½% who communicate in a straight, open, vulnerable, way. But healthy relationships are dependent on congruent communication!

Life is always about one's current view of things. We can change our view and life can change. When things feel wrong, it's a signal that something probably is wrong. It doesn't help to waste time feeling sorry for yourself. Just pick up the signal and do something about it. There really are lots of things that people can change about their lives and about themselves. Good

TOOLS FOR FAMILY RECONSTRUCTION

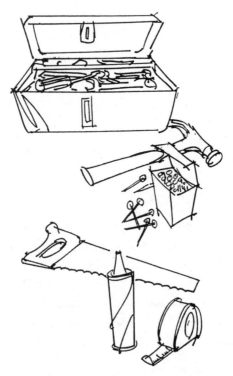

Knowledge of
connection to
a Higher Power.

Self-Knowledge.

Knowledge of
the world.

Knowledge about
others.

Family reconstruction is designed to explore and use the appropriate tools to increase competence in these four basic areas.

therapy is an exploration of oneself in an effort to understand that the healthiest, most caring people we can be are realized with the most open communication possible and the highest self-worth possible. It is important to bear in mind here that from the practitioner's point of view, therapy is not about solving problems, it's about nurturing people so they can solve their own problems.

> *Good therapy means that we explore ourselves as people and understand that the healthiest, most caring people we can be are realized with the most open communication possible and the highest self-worth. Therapists don't solve other people's problems, they nurture people so that they can solve their own problems.*

All people living in systems (family systems, relationships, schools, work settings, communities, societies) need four basic tools to cope with the world. Family reconstruction is about helping people find these basic tools: 1) knowledge about self; 2) knowledge about others; 3) knowledge about the world around us; 4) knowledge of some kind of God or Higher Power. (Virginia used to say we need to have knowledge *within, between,* and *among.*) These four basic tools help us develop the eight aspects of wholeness outlined earlier in this chapter.

SELF-WORTH

The ultimate goal of a reconstruction workshop is to bring the star to a higher level of self-worth. Surviving instead of living has a tremendous impact on a person. In a family in which a child's needs are valued and validated, the child learns to explore, take risks, and feel the joy of small steps toward growth and maturity. In a family in which the focus is on addiction, pain, loss, etc., the child's emotional growth is stunted. This child learns a distorted way of interacting with his environment and begins to make choices based on the unhealthy system in which he lives. This child doesn't have access to healthy choices.

For example, a kindergarten student from a nurturing, emotionally available family might be very open in sharing his family life with his class. A child from an emotionally distant family or a family with secrets (e.g., addiction, physical abuse, etc.) might be very quiet and not share about his family, or might invent elaborate fantasy stories rather than tell the truth.

At this young age, the child has already begun to carry his family's shame. He has no idea what this is about, he just knows that it's not okay to talk about what goes on at home and that it doesn't feel good. The vague sense that "something is wrong" continues to grow as the child grows. There is often also the feeling that he, the child, has somehow caused the problem and, therefore, should be able to fix it.

Young children are self-centered. They believe the world revolves around them. This is developmentally appropriate and healthy. But a child of an alcoholic may believe that he has been bad and that this is why his parent drinks. *It is important to remember that these thoughts may or may not be on a conscious level.* In another example, how many children, when being physically abused by a parent, have cried out, "I'll be good—"? If the beatings continue and the parent's behavior doesn't change, the child's beliefs that he or she is bad and to blame are embedded ever deeper. At some point—in most cases—the physical, sexual, and/or emotional abuse by the parents ceases. But because the child's shame was long before internalized and nothing since has happened to release it, it continues. The adult the child becomes continues to feel bad, and generally experiences poor self-worth. Such an adult may spend his entire life trying to prove his worth. He may gather prizes and awards in sports and school. (Alternatively, he may try to prove himself by rebelling and getting into trouble.) And each validation from the outside world may feel good—temporarily. To others, this person may even appear very accomplished—president of a big company, in an ideal relationship, a valued member of his community (or, alternatively leader of his gang, sexually accomplished, a valued member of his community...). We believe that these accomplishments are the manifestations of what is known as *self-esteem*, which is not to be confused with *self-worth*. At a conference in Howell, Michigan, the therapist Jerry Moe presented this distinction: *Self-worth comes from the inside; self-esteem comes from the outside.* In other words, self-esteem is the pursuit of honors from the outside world to fill the emptiness a person feels inside. But this doesn't change a person's self-worth. The old feeling of not being good enough persists and erodes the good feelings that come from accomplishments.

We're not suggesting that someone who does well and wins awards must be a victim of abuse or alcoholism or some other grave dysfunction in his upbringing. But when there is *compulsive* behavior, even around seemingly positive pursuits, there is often a link to deep hurt or pain originating in childhood. Of course, not all accomplishments are achieved as attempts to prove anything at all. Sometimes it can help to have a therapist help you determine where along this continuum of experience and perception you may be.

Exercise 1.5: Self-Esteem vs. Self-Worth

At this point, the reader is invited to "fill in" the chart below. In the section labeled "self-esteem," write up to five events in your life that have positively affected your self-esteem. In the section labeled "self-worth," list up to five events that have negatively affected your self-worth. Follow the examples for each category, and note the feeling associated with each entry.

Self-esteem	**Self-worth**
1. Good grades	1. Mom's compulsions
2. Soccer trophies	2. Sexual abuse
3. 3 major job promotions	3. Brother's chronic illness
4. Winning Mother-of-the-Year award	4. Dad's message: "You're stupid."
5. Elected to community office	5. Religious teachings of a punishing God

Self-esteem	**Self-worth**
1.	1.
2.	2.
3.	3.
4.	4.
5.	5.

It begins to become apparent that high self-esteem does not necessarily lead to high self-worth. In fact, low self-worth may prevent a person from fully internalizing the good feelings that come with accomplishments.

The chart below lists 10 characteristics of low and high self-worth:

Low self-worth	**High self-worth**
1. Poor hygiene	1. Respect for one's body
2. Weight or food problems	2. Good boundaries with others
3. Addictions/compulsions	3. Willingness to feel feelings without medication
4. Vague sense of hopelessness	4. Ability to experience joy
5. Depression	5. Optimism
6. Anxiety or fear of loss	6. Ability to face challenges and walk through fear
7. Inability to achieve or sustain intimacy	7. Capacity for achieving and sustaining intimacy
8. High sensitivity to criticism	8. Ability to tolerate and respond to criticism rather than reacting
9. Problems with authority figures	9. Respect for authority, yet ability to question when appropriate
10. Feelings of shame ("I'm not good enough")	10. A sense of gifts self has to offer the world

Exercise 1.6: Doing Something Positive for Your Self-Worth

The reader is now invited to make a list of five of his or her own low self-worth characteristics. On the high self-worth side, list how you would like to be or feel instead. Then think of one thing you could do to help yourself move in the direction of increased self-worth. An example is provided:

Low self-worth

Always tired; don't want to get up in the morning

High self-worth

Wake up full of energy and ready to go

Suggestion: At night list five things that made it worth getting up that day (they can be little things, e.g., nice weather, a good cup of coffee, your pet licking your face, the client you hate didn't call at work, etc.). Do this for one month.

For the reader:

Low self-worth

High self-worth

Suggestion:

CHAPTER TWO

THE STAR: CRITERIA AND PREPARATION

I learned how to survive, but not to live with peace, comfort, and joy.

—Anonymous

When a person chooses to be a star, there are often many months, and sometimes even years, between the time of application and the time that the reconstruction takes place. Much preparatory work is required of an applicant.

CRITERIA

The criteria for selecting a star has changed quite a bit over the years. In the beginning of family reconstructions, almost anyone who was in therapy and applied to have Sharon plan and guide a reconstruction was accepted. (She can even remember a time when she and Virginia would pick a star right from the audience, do a brief interview then and there, and begin the reconstruction on the spot!) But the model has evolved and changed

We now perform a much more intensive inquiry into any potential star's life and history, and we have had to change the criteria for being a star in a family reconstruction.

23

dramatically over the years, and we now do a much more intensive inquiry into any potential star's life and history. We have had to change the criteria for being a star in a family reconstruction.

Because we work both cognitively and emotionally, it is important that the star has a certain basis of information before beginning the reconstruction process. It's preferable for the star to have a basic understanding of family systems, addictions, and compulsive behaviors. It is also helpful to have had enough private or group therapy that he or she understands something about therapeutic processes and family-of-origin issues. We like stars to be familiar with the concepts of role play, the inner child, sculpture, and guided imagery. A working knowledge of these ideas and theories makes the star's preparation for the reconstruction—and the guide's execution of the reconstruction—much easier to understand. (For the reader, these concepts are described more fully in Part II of this volume, in the chapter focusing on the reconstruction event.)

With respect to family systems, in her own work Sharon likes clients to understand how roles function within a family. She uses the roles of *family hero, scapegoat, lost child,* and *mascot.* You can learn more about these roles by reading Sharon's book, *Another Chance* (Palo Alto, CA: Science and Behavior Books, 1981, 1989) or by attending a family systems workshop in which such roles are explained and explored. A brief discussion of family roles also appears towards the end of this chapter.

It's also tremendously important that any star be able to access his or her feelings throughout the preparation exercises and interview as well as during the reconstruction event itself. Sometimes a potential star is emotionally medicating with one or more substances such as drugs, alcohol, nicotine, excessive food or sugar, etc. Sometimes a potential star is engaged in other compulsive behaviors such as workaholism, sexual addiction, or gambling. We know that someone who is medicating with substances or behaviors is going to have a very difficult time accessing feelings. Remember, Sharon's credo on this topic: *You cannot heal what you cannot feel, and you cannot feel what you medicate.*

It is absolutely imperative that a star address any kind of primary addiction well in advance of the reconstruction event, and have eliminated that behavior from his or her life *for at least one full year* before beginning the work of reconstruction. Once sobriety and abstinence are in place over a period of months, an addictive or compulsive person will begin to experience current feelings in a powerful new way that can often trigger past feelings. Only when feelings are truly accessible is someone ready to embark on the kind of work that can be achieved through reconstruction.

It is also important that a potential star be assessed by a qualified therapist for readiness to do this work. Timing is key. For example, undergoing a reconstruction too soon following any kind of major loss is not a good idea because the person is still acutely involved in the grief process. Attempting a reconstruction with someone who has never been able to share intimately with a therapist or a large group is also not a good idea, nor is working with a person who is in the midst of a clinical depression.

We ask potential stars to attend and become involved in at least one family reconstruction workshop in which someone else is the star before becoming stars themselves.

If a therapist evaluates a person and concludes that the timing is appropriate, we ask the person to take the Millon Clinical Multi-Axial Inventory II (MCMI-II). The MCMI-II is a well accepted, written, multiple-choice survey used as a personality and mental illness assessment tool. The MCMI-II provides further confirmation that this is, in fact, a reasonable time for the candidate to undergo a family reconstruction, and gives the guide additional information about the candidate which can contribute to the process.

REASONS AND ISSUES

It is important for each of us periodically to review our motives for continuing along the path of recovery. Each person who requests a reconstruction is asked to submit a list of *reasons* why he or she wants to undergo this process. Potential stars must decide which are the most compelling reasons why they are driven towards a deeper understanding of themselves, where they came from, and how they want to proceed from this point forward. These questions are often difficult to answer and seem to require having an idea of how the outcome will feel once the work is done. But forming a list of reasons can provide focused goals for the stars to work towards.

Below is a list of possible reasons people may choose to take an in-depth look at their pain and the legacy of their pasts.

- To be free from past pain, loss, anger, and guilt.
- To be more at ease with self and to have more peace of mind.
- To have a deeper sense of spirituality.
- To feel closer to one's inner child and to forgive oneself for past mistakes.
- To learn to develop a closer relationship with family and friends.
- To learn how to live freely and happily.
- To let go of compulsive behavior and stuck feelings.
- To let go of shame and give it back to its source (e.g., the victim of abuse feels shame that properly belongs to the perpetrator of the abuse).
- To move forward in making life decisions.
- To learn to lighten up and not take oneself so seriously.
- To feel a greater sense of self-worth.
- To achieve deeper levels of intimacy.
- To learn how to get personal needs met.

- To learn to trust others, self, and a Higher Power.
- To finish grieving the loss of childhood and to live in the present.
- To relinquish the role of victim.
- To break the chains of the past for the sake of one's children's freedom.
- To experience a new beginning.
- To develop more self-confidence.
- To stop repeating old patterns.
- To access feelings that have been buried.
- To change negative attitudes, beliefs, and patterns, to positive ones.
- To learn how to give and receive healthy nurturing without falling into dependent caretaking or neediness.

Exercise 2.1: Reasons List

Review the list above and create one of your own. Using the reasons in the sample list as a guide (you may very well come up with other reasons that don't appear on this list), write down the five main reasons you would choose to undertake an in-depth exploration of yourself such as family reconstruction.

Potential stars are also asked to provide a list of five major *issues* they would like to work on during the reconstruction process. This list allows stars to let their guides know the areas in which they feel the most "stuck." It also encourages prospective stars to narrow their focus, and provides them with a gauge—following the reconstruction they can evaluate to what extent their needs were actually met by the process.

Below is a list of possible issues a star may wish to address during the reconstruction process.

- Guilt.
- The need to always be in control.
- Grief and loss issues arising from deaths or voids.
- Feelings of abandonment.
- Unresolved feelings around parents.
- Shame and a sense of being less than okay.
- Fear of taking risks.
- Fear of failure (this is a good one for perfectionists).
- Conflicts around authority figures.
- Fear of confrontation.
- Conflicts in relationship(s) with partner and/or children.
- Blocks to sexual intimacy.

- Feeling overwhelmed with rage.
- Feelings regarding siblings.
- Setting boundaries.
- Food problems and body image.
- Handling anger.
- Work issues.
- Making healthy life choices.

Exercise 2.2: Issues List

Review the list above and create one of your own. Using the issues in the sample list as a guide (again, you may very well come up with others that don't appear on this list), write down the five main issues you would hope to address during a reconstruction event.

Again, to clarify, these lists of reasons and issues are as important for the guide as they are for the star. They give the guide "maps" to follow. Together with the star, the guide will take these lists and formulate a distilled list of goals for the reconstruction, and areas to address during the process. This list, in turn, is used to plan the "script" for the reconstruction. (There isn't an actual script with dialogue—rather, we work from a scene list or outline to help us remember what sculptures and psychodramas from the star's life are going to be most important. Other exercises may also be planned ahead or may arise organically and spontaneously out of the sculptures and psychodramas.) The list is also written on a board at the front of the room in which the reconstruction occurs. The guide can check the list periodically throughout the course of the day to evaluate the progress of the event. At the end of the reconstruction, both the guide and the star can review the list to assess what was achieved. In this way the list is helpful not only as a map and agenda before and during the process, but as a tool for follow-up evaluation once the event has concluded.

OTHER PREPARATORY MATERIALS AND EXERCISES

A selected star who has been assessed for readiness by a qualified therapist, taken the MCMI-II, and provided lists or reasons and issues, is then asked to submit even more information, including a family map, a completed workbook called *Learning to Know Yourself*, a family chronology, a family-of-origin history, family rules, and a gratitude wheel. These are additional "data tools."

(A sample family map template appears on the following pages. A detailed explanation begins on the next page of text.)

A SAMPLE FAMILY MAP TEMPLATE

FAMILY OF BIRTH

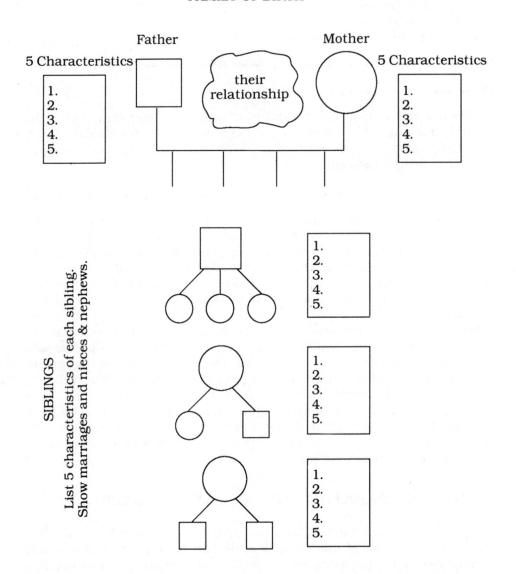

Symbol Code: x =deceased, ⚮ = divorced, $ = money or property issues,
〰 = conflicted relationship, □ = male, ○ = female, ALC = alcoholic,
ED = eating disorder, DA = drug addition, S = smoker.

1. Collect the names of parents, grandparents, and all of their siblings and children.

A SAMPLE FAMILY MAP TEMPLATE *CONTINUED*

NUCLEAR FAMILY

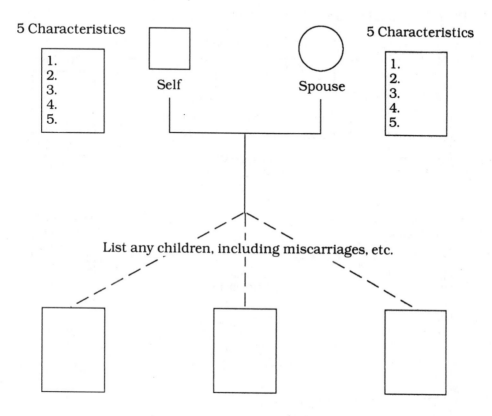

5 Characteristics

1.
2.
3.
4.
5.

Self

Spouse

5 Characteristics

1.
2.
3.
4.
5.

List any children, including miscarriages, etc.

5 adjectives for each child
List marriages, grandchildren

2. Add dates of birth, dates of death, causes of death, illness, and other major life events (include suicides or suicide attempts, cancer or other chronic diseases or disabilities, and identify practicing or recovering alcoholics or drug dependents, miscarriages, still-births, abortions, etc.), as well as a few identifying characteristics and/or memories.
3. Go back as far as you can provide information that is as complete as possible.
4. Complete the map for your family of origin and then include your own current nuclear family (spouse or partner, any children, sons or daughters-in-law, grandchildren, etc.)

A SAMPLE FAMILY MAP TEMPLATE *CONTINUED*

FATHER'S FAMILY

Birthdate of oldest Great Grandparent: _____

Great Grandparents

Heritage

Married:
(date _____)

Married:
(date _____)

Heritage

Put great
aunts & uncles
in order

5 Characteristics
or memories

1.
2.
3.
4.
5.

Grandparents
married:
(date _____)

5 Characteristics
or memories

1.
2.
3.
4.
5.

Father

1.
2.
3.
4.
5.

5 Childhood
Characteristics
of father

Put all aunts
and uncles
here.

A SAMPLE FAMILY MAP TEMPLATE *CONTINUED*

MOTHER'S FAMILY

Birthdate of oldest Grandparent: _____

Great Grandparents

Heritage

Heritage

Married:
(date _____)

Married:
(date _____)

Put great
aunts & uncles
in order

5 Characteristics
or memories

1.
2.
3.
4.
5.

Grandparents
married:
(date _____)

5 Characteristics
or memories

1.
2.
3.
4.
5.

Mother

1.
2.
3.
4.
5.

5 Childhood
Characteristics
of mother

Put all aunts
and uncles
here.

The *family map* traces a minimum of three or four generations, moving from the family in which the star was raised back through parents, grandparents, and great-grandparents. We ask the star to do his or her best to provide information about names, nicknames, birth dates, birthplaces, occupations, marriage dates, children, ages at time of death, causes of death, etc. We like to know if there have been any addictions in the family, including nicotine. We want to know if there were any divorces, and if so, whether there were new marriages or additional children or step-children. All of this information becomes very valuable as we get ready to do the reconstruction. The map should be filled out by the star as completely as possible.

Exercise 2.3: Family Map

Begin with the birth date of your oldest great-grandparents. Write their names and ages at the time of their deaths in squares or circles—men are drawn in squares and women in circles. Write their geographic locations—both where they were from and where they lived. Set the map up on the page like a family tree, noting marriages, divorces, separations, affairs, births (and any unusual circumstances surrounding them), miscarriages, deaths, formations of new or combined families, etc. Note the dates of these events.

Note to prospective guides: Later on, you may want to color code diseases and dysfunctional behaviors such as alcoholism, drug addiction, eating disorders, mental illness, chronic or acute physical illness, sexual abuse, verbal abuse, etc.

Learning to Know Yourself is a workbook consisting of a series of questions for the star to answer. When complete, the workbook functions as another kind of database for the reconstruction. It assists the guide in planning for the pre-event interview as well as the actual reconstruction event. (The workbook is not included here, but is available for ordering through Science & Behavior Books. The address and phone and fax numbers are found at the end of this volume.)

You may be getting a sense of how much work goes into the preparation for the reconstruction process. People apply to be stars a long time in advance (often one - two years) of when they will actually be reconstructed.

We then move into the *family chronology*. We like to have the star provide brief paragraphs with simple sentences about important events that occurred at certain times in his or her life. These do not need to be too detailed. The time frame is outlined in the following example:

"SAMPLE FAMILY CHRONOLOGY"

AGE	SHORT REMINDERS OF INCIDENTS, UNFINISHED BUSINESS, HURTFUL/ PAINFUL TIMES
0-5	Grandpa died Left in the grocery store
5-Jr. High	My dog died We moved to the farm Sister was born
Jr./Sr. High	Overweight Sexual abuse (Brother) Dad drinking Played basketball well Felt ugly Hated dinner table
College Yrs.	Was afraid Started smoking First love affair Started drinking Car accident
20's	Got married Had a son Drank more Tired all the time
30's	Mom died Fight with my sister—estranged

etc.

Again, we like to see a *brief* identification of important events that took place during these time periods, such as moves, divorces, deaths, reunions, sexual abuse, alcoholism, job changes, bankruptcy, war(s), or anything else that seemed important to the star or to those around the star (e.g., mother had a miscarriage . . . brother went to war . . . star gave birth to beautiful, healthy twins . . . aunt committed suicide). When finished, this should also cover important educational events, losses, illnesses in self or others close to self, and traumatic events for self or others close to self. The chronology will function as a guide-for-the-guide.

Personal history, which is to say *memory*, is stored in our senses as well as in our brains, and will emerge for every star in different ways throughout the preparation process as well as during the reconstruction process. As you develop the family chronology, use whatever resources you have in terms of records of births, deaths, illnesses, geographic moves, job changes, a sense of economic circumstances, etc.

Often stars worry about not being able to remember. They even worry about talking to relatives about childhood events and chronology. Gather what information you can and trust the process. Be as specific as possible about times, places, content, etc., but go ahead and intuit what you don't know for fact. We're not asking you to lie or to be purposefully false, but, rather, to explore. Use your hunches. If the essence of your guess is accurate, people at your reconstruction will generally know it. If your guesses are inaccurate, they'll likely know that, too. **(Note: Hunches and guesses are for creating a sense of atmosphere and for capturing essences. We do not *ever* use hunches or guesses around serious topics such as abuse, violence, or other trauma in which accuracy is paramount.)**

Exercise 2.4: Family Chronology

Briefly outline the following:

1.   Events and circumstances around the time of your birth.
2.   Your early childhood.
3.   Your teen years.
4.   Your young adult years.
5.   Your 20s.
6.   Your 30s (as appropriate).
7.   Your 40s (as appropriate).
8.   Your 50s (as appropriate).
     etc.

> *Even if you don't have very clear memories you will be surprised at how much of your own information will simply surface in this process.*

Virginia Satir always believed that we could tap into unknown data about our lives. It doesn't matter if it's not completely accurate. What is most important is that if we have as many facts as we can, and we are working with the true perceptions of the star, we will have everything we need to proceed because we are not about *proving* the objective truth of what actually took place. We are about *healing* whatever needs to be healed based on the star's perceptions of what took place.

> ***We are not about* proving *exactly what occurred; we are about* healing *whatever pain exists based on the star's perceptions about what occurred.***

For a more fact-based history, we ask the star to give us a *family-of-origin history*. This consists of factual information about the star's family of origin, but it too allows for memories. After indicating facts about grandparents, we ask for brief recollections of what it was like to visit with them; how often visits occurred; where they took place; what, if anything, the star remembers about the grandparents' house(s); how others in the family felt about them, etc.

SAMPLE FAMILY-OF-ORIGIN HISTORY OUTLINE

MOTHER'S SIDE

Grandfather's Name: _____ Grandmother's Name: _____

Birthdate: _____ Birthdate: _____

Birthplace: _____ Birthplace: _____

Date of Death: _____ Date of Death: _____

Cause of Death: _____ Cause of Death: _____

Geographical places they lived (cities, states, etc.) _____

_____

_____

Your recollections of these:

Visits: _____

_____

Holidays: _____

_____

Their Home: _____

Their Religion: _____

Personalities and Characteristics: _____

_____

_____

_____

_____

Siblings of each one: _____

_____

Children of the couple: _____

_____

_____

_____

_____

_____

Additional Comments: _____

_____

_____

Occupations: _____

_____

My grandparents' roles in and out of the home: _____

_____

_____

What I know about them: _____

_____

_____

How my parents felt about them: _____

_____

_____

What I know about them, from memory or from stories: _____

_____

_____

_____

_____

_____

_____

Provide as much of same information as possible for your great-grand-parents on your mother's side. Do the exact same exercise for your grand-parents and great-grandparents on your father's side.

Exercise 2.5: Family-of-Origin-History

Complete a Family-of-Origin History for your family of origin.

Family rules are also requested. As discussed in the previous chapter, what were the rules in the star's family when he or she was growing up? The star should list separately those that were explicitly stated and those that were tacitly implied.

One of the most interesting things Sharon learned from Virginia Satir was how to take family rules and transform them into affirmations. All of us grow up with many different kinds of rules that have been explicitly spoken, such as "If you can't say something nice, don't say anything at all," and "Boys shouldn't cry." Many of us also grew up with implicit rules that were not directly verbalized but which were somehow clearly imparted. Examples include knowing it's best not to ask your parents about sex, doing as your parents say instead of as they do, and observing the idea that older people are more important than younger people.

Whether the rules are spoken or implied, they have a strong impact on children's feelings of self-worth and on their behavior. But something any-one can learn is to take an old family rule, for example, "If you can't say something nice, don't say anything at all," and consider what message you would have preferred to receive instead, such as "Sometimes it's necessary to say things that people aren't going to want to hear." Say the new rule over to yourself a few times, and then maybe write it on a sheet of paper and hang it on the mirror where you get ready every morning, or stick it on the refrigerator so that you see it many times throughout the day. Let that new message in. Next time you're tempted to hold back with someone, relying on the old rule which tells you to keep quiet if you can't say something nice, you will have ready a new message for yourself, which says that it's okay to say things someone might not want to hear. *This way, you have the option to choose.*

So, again, we can't always get rid of old messages and old rules easily, but we certainly can add new, neutralizing messages that give us a choice. It's a good idea to sit down every once in a while and write down perhaps five different old rules, and transform them into new rules you would have preferred to have been taught. (This is a great exercise for a therapist to do with a client or for someone to do on his or her own.) Once we teach ourselves these new rules, then, over time, the old rules and messages have much less power to control our behavior. We are able to choose to behave according to a different message.

Finally, we ask the star to fill out what we call a *gratitude wheel.* This is a list of people who have been important to the star, or influential, or simply trustworthy, people who are part of the star's core support system. The list can include (but does not have to) people outside of the star's family to whom he or she is grateful and with whom he or she feels a close kinship.

THE INTERVIEW

The interview is an opportunity for the star and guide to get to know each other and to review the star's preparatory materials. It also gives the star a chance to learn more about the reconstruction process that will take place, and should serve to put him or her at ease prior to the workshop and event.

The interview takes place in the days just prior to the beginning of the week-long reconstruction workshop, and lasts about eight hours. The star and guide may need to ask many questions of each other, and share thoughts and feelings. The interview begins the personal relationship between the two people who will go through the intimate process of reconstruction together.

Often things have changed in the interval between when the star submitted lists of reasons and issues and the time of the interview. This is an opportunity to revise and make current those lists and any other aspect of the materials that warrants updating. Sometimes the star will simply want to change a reason or add an issue. The interview is an opportunity to ensure that the reconstruction is relevant to the star's current life. For example, it is in reviewing with the star his or her family map that the guide will have a chance to color-code any diseases, dysfunction, suicides, etc. so that the map becomes an even more useful resource for the reconstruction process.

The therapeutic value of the star's research in preparation for the reconstruction event should not be underestimated. This process covers ground full of family secrets and previously unawakened memories, so even during the interview the star will experience many feelings. These need to be honored in the moment, but not dealt with at length. The guide will note feelings expressed throughout the interview as areas to emphasize during the reconstruction event, but the interview is not, as a rule, the arena for tackling this work.

So, in addition to introducing the star and the guide(s) to each other, main purposes of the interview are for the guide to check out "hot spots" (i.e., locating those places where the star has a lot of emotional energy), and for the star and guide together to fill in blank spaces in the star's material and/or update it. The guide makes notes about key events and issues, and begins a list of potential roles and props for the event itself.

The interview begins with a "check" on the star's feelings. Then the star is given information regarding the purpose of the interview. Following this, the schedule for the interview day itself is outlined. The star is instructed to "bookmark" any feelings that arise during the interview, saving the feeling for work during the reconstruction process itself. The guide then walks the star through the goals for the day. Because the star has been working on plans for some time, there may be some additions to or deletions from the written work in order to be current. The goals are flexible; they provide everyone involved with a kind of ruler by which to measure the process and progress throughout the day to ensure that the star's needs are being met.

The preparatory materials—reasons and issues lists, family map, *Learning to Know Yourself* workbook, family chronology, family-of-origin history, family rules, and the gratitude wheel—have already been reviewed by the guide and are the documents he or she uses to interview the star. Prior to the interview, the guide may wish to make notes about anything in the materials that seems unclear. Such preparation on the guide's part can significantly smooth the interview process itself. (For example, perhaps the star mentioned anger towards a particular person somewhere in the materials, but never clearly stated the source of the anger. This kind of missing information can be supplied during the interview.)

Here is a general outline of the interview.

1. Check star's general feelings.
2. Clarify preparatory materials.
3. Clarify family of choice.
4. Clarify current family or current living situation.
5. Clarify current situation of family of origin.
6. Walk through the family chronology.

7.   Discuss process of reconstruction and how role-player selection will work.
8.   Answer any questions.

UNDERSTANDING FAMILY ROLES

Family roles are very helpful in planning for a reconstruction. When we speak of "family" in this context we are referring to any family system (ideally this wouldn't apply to the star's family of choice, but it sometimes does in subtle ways). Sometimes we are able to get a better picture of a situation faster if we have a good understanding of the family roles involved.

In her work, Virginia developed four particular roles: *The super-reasonable one, the placater, the blamer,* and *the irrelevant one.* As Sharon began working with families, she made use of different roles. As mentioned earlier, those that were most helpful to her were *the family hero, the scapegoat, the lost child,* and *the mascot.*

Every drama has its *hero.* Often, so do families. The hero is frequently the oldest child; it can also be an only child. Of all the roles in any family, the hero is most determined by birth order. This is the person who is very helpful inside the family, and very successful outside the family. The hero provides those times of hope and pride that even painful families can experience. So the hero is used to bring self-worth to the family, particularly when other sources are more limited. From the outside, the hero sometimes seems to have it made and to be very together, and doesn't show the kinds of visible traumas, conflicts, and scars that many of the other people in the family display. Most of this, however, is simply on the surface, because inside, the hero, too, feels miserable. Sometimes, because the hero is so successful, he or she receives the least amount of attention and sympathy for what is going on inside the family system.

If the hero is the oldest child or an only child, then right from the beginning, he or she is part of the original family triangle. This is a particular role in the family that no one else will ever occupy because this child is the one born into the relationship between the parents. (Every other child in the family has another child to whom he or she can relate.) The hero will also feel a lot of family stresses, and take on much of the pain that the parents aren't confronting. Many times the parents actually communicate with each other through the child who plays the family hero. And for his or her part, the hero feels just enough outside the parents' relationship that he or she ought (or so the hero feels) to be able to do something to help it, to correct the problems between the parents, to make up for their struggles. In some way, it is to this impossible task that the hero tends to dedicate his or her life.

THE HERO

This is an adult role assumed by a child in the family whose job is to provide self-worth, hope, pride, and success for the entire family. This child assumes this role because one or more of the parents is not emotionally available due to their own dysfunction.

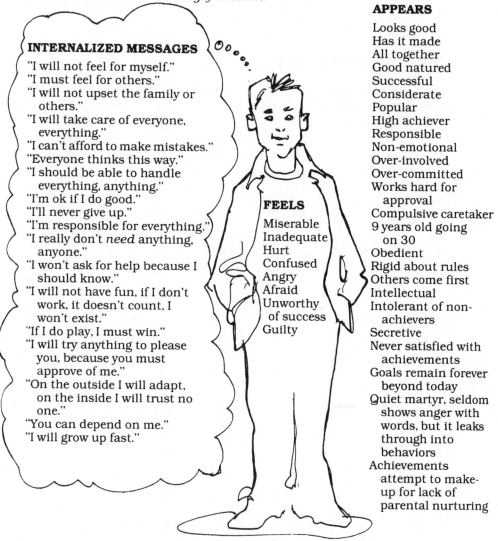

INTERNALIZED MESSAGES

"I will not feel for myself."
"I must feel for others."
"I will not upset the family or others."
"I will take care of everyone, everything."
"I can't afford to make mistakes."
"Everyone thinks this way."
"I should be able to handle everything, anything."
"I'm ok if I do good."
"I'll never give up."
"I'm responsible for everything."
"I really don't *need* anything, anyone."
"I won't ask for help because I should know."
"I will not have fun, if I don't work, it doesn't count, I won't exist."
"If I do play, I must win."
"I will try anything to please you, because you must approve of me."
"On the outside I will adapt, on the inside I will trust no one."
"You can depend on me."
"I will grow up fast."

FEELS

Miserable
Inadequate
Hurt
Confused
Angry
Afraid
Unworthy of success
Guilty

APPEARS

Looks good
Has it made
All together
Good natured
Successful
Considerate
Popular
High achiever
Responsible
Non-emotional
Over-involved
Over-committed
Works hard for approval
Compulsive caretaker
9 years old going on 30
Obedient
Rigid about rules
Others come first
Intellectual
Intolerant of non-achievers
Secretive
Never satisfied with achievements
Goals remain forever beyond today
Quiet martyr, seldom shows anger with words, but it leaks through into behaviors
Achievements attempt to make-up for lack of parental nurturing

Family *scapegoats* tend to be middle children. They "arrive" once the action has started, and they feel the impact of both parents and sibling(s). The scapegoat notices early on that being good seems to bring some kind of

THE SCAPEGOAT

This role is designed to provide a focus of attention away from the real source of family dysfunction and to provide a target for all of the pain the family members feel.

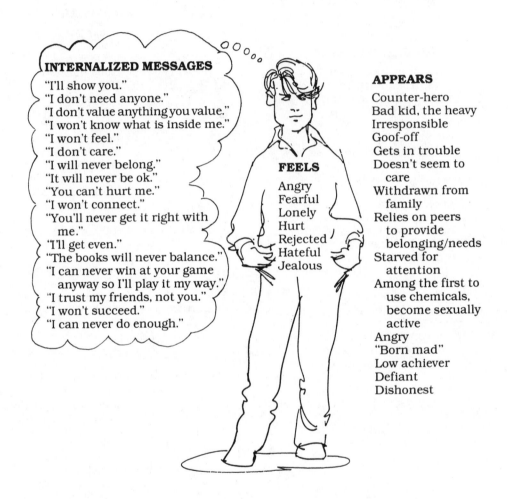

INTERNALIZED MESSAGES

"I'll show you."
"I don't need anyone."
"I don't value anything you value."
"I won't know what is inside me."
"I won't feel."
"I don't care."
"I will never belong."
"It will never be ok."
"You can't hurt me."
"I won't connect."
"You'll never get it right with me."
"I'll get even."
"The books will never balance."
"I can never win at your game anyway so I'll play it my way."
"I trust my friends, not you."
"I won't succeed."
"I can never do enough."

FEELS

Angry
Fearful
Lonely
Hurt
Rejected
Hateful
Jealous

APPEARS

Counter-hero
Bad kid, the heavy
Irresponsible
Goof-off
Gets in trouble
Doesn't seem to care
Withdrawn from family
Relies on peers to provide belonging/needs
Starved for attention
Among the first to use chemicals, become sexually active
Angry
"Born mad"
Low achiever
Defiant
Dishonest

glory to the hero, so he or she will try that. But it usually doesn't work out as well for this child, and the hero continues to be labeled as the special, prized one. After a while this other child feels somewhat excluded, like an outsider in his or her own family. The child will tend to gravitate even further outside to get attention from others (usually starting out with other children or playmates, and then later peer groups; later still, the attention sought is often negative, at least on the surface). This child feels a lot of frustration, but finds no place to express these feelings inside the family. Thus, fleeing the family is the most frequently seen behavior among scapegoated children. When the child is young, he or she may actually run away. Slightly older children may run in a different way as well, joining a strong (but not necessarily positive or healthy) peer group, or abusing substances. In a dysfunctional family, there are plenty of stresses and strains. As the scapegoated child begins to act out, the family suddenly has a focus for blame. Pretty soon the family is blaming this child for much of what is wrong with the family. Because of the scapegoat's lack of verbal expression and storehouse of bottled-up feelings, he or she will often gravitate towards others in similar positions in their families. Trouble-making can emerge from situations such as this, whether at school, in the neighborhood, or elsewhere. As the hero brings pride and self-worth to the family, the scapegoat brings the family shame and pain. The attention this gets the scapegoat is negative, but desperately needed just the same. Another irony is that although the satisfaction is superficial and short-lived, the means used to get that attention are often dangerous, and generally bring child long-term complications and pain.

The *lost child* also tends to be one of the middle children in the family. This is a child who "acts in" rather than "acting out" (which is what the scapegoat does). With the hero getting lots of positive attention and the scapegoat getting lots of negative attention, the family doesn't have a lot of attention left for this child, who tends to exist without staking a claim in the family system. This child is often shy and withdrawn. He or she may become preoccupied with solitary pursuits. This might be the child who gravitates towards the television or the computer, spending lots of time alone. This child may also be more vulnerable to eating disorders, either attempting to seek some control and developing restricted eating habits that can lead to anorexia or perhaps doing a lot of binge, comfort eating and experiencing weight problems at an early age.

Lost children become loners, tending to stay out of everyone's way. The parents, for their part, almost welcome this behavior as a relief because there is usually plenty of activity going on with the hero, and enough chaos going on with the scapegoat, and they like to have at least one child they "don't have to worry about." This child sort of takes care of him- or herself. But at the same time, this child is growing increasingly limited in terms of social skills. As the lost child lives in isolation, he or she is more likely to build a fantasy world. Thus the isolation becomes problematic in the context of school and natural social development. This child simply has too little experience expressing feelings or handling the expressed feelings of others.

Lost children are often forgotten children. People forget to praise them for their achievements, or reassure them around their fears, or even offer companionship. The neglect isn't necessarily intentional, but it does send a

THE LOST CHILD

Their role in the family is to offer the family relief from the problematic situation that having another child in the dysfunctional system would cause. They offer this relief by becoming invisible.

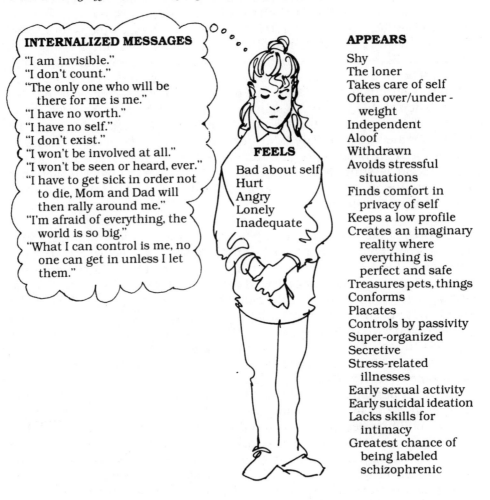

INTERNALIZED MESSAGES

"I am invisible."
"I don't count."
"The only one who will be there for me is me."
"I have no worth."
"I have no self."
"I don't exist."
"I won't be involved at all."
"I won't be seen or heard, ever."
"I have to get sick in order not to die, Mom and Dad will then rally around me."
"I'm afraid of everything, the world is so big."
"What I can control is me, no one can get in unless I let them."

FEELS

Bad about self
Hurt
Angry
Lonely
Inadequate

APPEARS

Shy
The loner
Takes care of self
Often over/under - weight
Independent
Aloof
Withdrawn
Avoids stressful situations
Finds comfort in privacy of self
Keeps a low profile
Creates an imaginary reality where everything is perfect and safe
Treasures pets, things
Conforms
Placates
Controls by passivity
Super-organized
Secretive
Stress-related illnesses
Early sexual activity
Early suicidal ideation
Lacks skills for intimacy
Greatest chance of being labeled schizophrenic

message to the child that says he or she isn't important, and doesn't have enough worth to command the family's attention, as does the hero, or cause enough trouble to command attention, as does the scapegoat. So the lost child's self-worth is often minimal at best. Moving into adulthood, he or she frequently suffers from depressions and compulsive behaviors or addictions that first arose in childhood as a coping mechanism to alleviate pain.

Finally, the *mascot* is a role often, but not always, played by the youngest child in the family. Gender, disability, and age are probably the three strongest contributing factors to a child's potential for adopting the role of mascot, with age being the most powerful of all. This child is often not taken very seriously by the family and is, for whatever reason (age, gender, disability), excluded from receiving information or from being involved in family situations (e.g., a family will decide where to go on vacation without asking the youngest child for his or her preference; or the only daughter in a sports-oriented family, although not the youngest child, never quite

THE MASCOT

Their role in the family is to bring good feeling to the family system. They are to provide comic relief, fun, and humor to an otherwise grim environment.

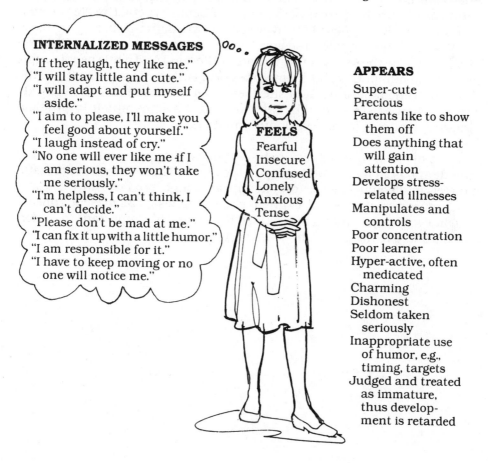

INTERNALIZED MESSAGES

"If they laugh, they like me."
"I will stay little and cute."
"I will adapt and put myself aside."
"I aim to please, I'll make you feel good about yourself."
"I laugh instead of cry."
"No one will ever like me if I am serious, they won't take me seriously."
"I'm helpless, I can't think, I can't decide."
"Please don't be mad at me."
"I can fix it up with a little humor."
"I am responsible for it."
"I have to keep moving or no one will notice me."

FEELS

Fearful
Insecure
Confused
Lonely
Anxious
Tense

APPEARS

Super-cute
Precious
Parents like to show them off
Does anything that will gain attention
Develops stress-related illnesses
Manipulates and controls
Poor concentration
Poor learner
Hyper-active, often medicated
Charming
Dishonest
Seldom taken seriously
Inappropriate use of humor, e.g., timing, targets
Judged and treated as immature, thus development is retarded

"enters" the family system; or a sickly child is not "bothered" by being included in what are perceived to be physically or emotionally stressful activities). The family treats this child as someone who is fairly helpless and fragile. Sometimes the family even "protects" this child from knowing how much pain and stress there is in the family; throughout life, the adult this child becomes always seems a little more fragile and a little less mature than might be appropriate for his or her age. Thus, protective impulses around a child can prove a handicap. In unhealthy families there are lots of secrets and things going on to cause people pain. Very often this youngest child is simply not made aware of what is actually going on in the family. But if a child doesn't know what's going on, he or she will inevitably have a lot of fears. Some of these fears will be justified and others will not, but because they aren't addressed or discussed, the child carries a lot of anxiety. This anxiety creates tension in the family; this same child will often provide some external behavior that relieves the tension, such as clowning around and being distracting, even to the point of being hyperactive. (Many children incorrectly diagnosed for hyperactivity are actually just trying to relieve some of their family's tension. Tranquilizers given to these children may prove to be the seeds of future drug addiction.) And while people enjoy the fun and humor this child sometimes brings, it is often ultimately to the child's detriment because he or she doesn't get taken seriously. If not sickly already, then as stress builds, this child may also escape into physical illness. Sometimes fears develop into phobias.

Each of the four roles results in a child who appears one way on the outside and is, in fact, another way on the inside. The hero looks successful but feels inadequate. The scapegoat appears tough, but feels hurt. The lost child appears reclusive but is filled with loneliness. The mascot appears outgoing and entertaining but is filled with fears. It's important to understand what is really going on.

CHAPTER THREE

THE GUIDE: QUALIFICATIONS AND PREPARATION

The more fully I live, the more I grow, the more able I am to help others.

—Anonymous

The role of the guide is absolutely key in the reconstruction process. It is very important for the guide to be professionally qualified; personally, physically, and spiritually healthy; cognitively insightful and creative; emotionally available; free from compulsive behaviors; and clear about his or her own identity. A lot of the qualifications and skills we require of guides would be present in any good therapist. These attributes bear out in the reconstruction process in various ways. Let's take a closer look.

QUALIFICATIONS AND SKILLS

Firstly, we presume that the guide will be a certified or licensed therapist in at least one of the following areas: Gestalt therapy, counseling, psychodrama, social work, psychology, or psychiatry.

Secondly, we have learned the hard way that if the guide has not healed his or her own current or past relationships and family issues, this will contaminate each reconstruction process in which he or she is involved.

IMPORTANT COMPONENTS OF A GUIDE

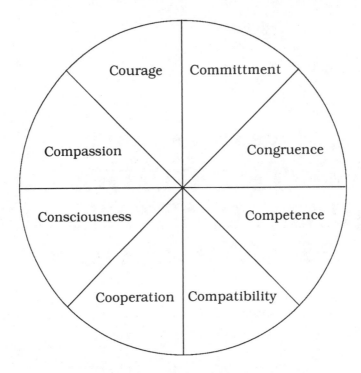

VIRGINIA SATIR'S 8 C'S

> ***The guide must heal his or her own past and current relationships and family issues, or the pain and conflicts will contaminate any reconstruction process in which he or she is involved.***

A therapist is most ready to guide others to wholeness through family reconstruction when he or she has undergone his or her own reconstruction. This is not unlike more "conventional" therapies in which it is often assumed and generally preferred that a therapist will have undergone treatment as an integral part of professional training. A healed individual who has been through sufficient therapy to work through his or her own pain and conflicts is going to be a much more effective therapist for others than will someone who has by-passed this work.

Reconstruction is designed to empower the star; in order to do this effectively, the guide must already be empowered so that the needs of the star are the primary focus of the day and the guide can stay in the background, doing the work on the star's behalf.

And again, to bring about the kind of reconciliation and forgiveness and healing we attempt, we need a guide who has already done his or her own healing. Otherwise the star can get stuck in anger, resentment or other feelings that do not facilitate healing.

In terms of cognitive insight and creativity, the guide needs to remember as much as possible from the written material and the interview. This will not be enough, however. The guide will also need to be able to think quickly on the spot, to make connections, and to lead the star and the audience to greater understanding. It will be important to be able to create spontaneous sculptures in order to make a point, and to discern when and how to probe for further information or deeper emotion. It's very important for the guide to be historically aware and to bear in mind during a reconstruction what else was going on in the world at any given time under examination (wars, assassinations, economic trends, etc.). Some external influences have a tremendous impact on personal lives. Did the star's parents live through the Depression? Did the star's father go to war?

The guide has to be a talented detective, watching for clues and signs, and not lettings things go by unnoticed. In order to be as vigilant as is necessary, the guide needs to be experienced enough personally so that nothing the star says will either shock or bore. The guide also has to have enough confidence to be able, as Virginia would say, to follow an instinct and not always need all the facts. "Why dig for all the facts," she would say, "when a hunch would work just as well?"

It's important for the guide to remember what Virginia taught Sharon: that 95-98% of the time people try to do their best, and that they are healthier than they think they are. This has been of primary concern to Sharon as she has worked with some group leaders and therapists who get caught up in the down side of things, worry that people can't handle certain issues or feelings, and have a tendency to see people's limitations.

Sharon has since operated with this principle in mind. Guides need to know that each person has what is necessary to heal him- or herself, and that guides guide, but they don't fix anything. The guide also has to know that a star's tendency to act out is defensive, and must be able to avoid taking it personally, getting embroiled in it, or letting it turn into a fight of any kind.

It's important for the guide as well as the star to know that there is not going to be a major miracle that occurs in one day. The importance of the reconstruction in the entire process of healing must never be exaggerated. Many other things affect and influence a star. We always require that the star be in therapy with a professional therapist — this ensures that the star will have someone to return to after the reconstruction event, someone with whom he or she can continue to work and to process as he or she begins to effect the changes committed to through the reconstruction.

The guide's emotional availability in terms of being able to empathize with the star is crucial to the process. The guide guides the action, but follows the feelings of the star in so doing. Again, the temptation to over-direct the star cannot be indulged; the guide must resist the inclination to imagine this will expedite the process because it only serves to hinder it.

> **The guide guides the action, but follows the feelings of the star in so doing.**

And as we require sobriety of all stars, we likewise require it of all guides. Any guide who has been medicated by food, alcohol, drugs, nicotine, work-aholism, or other compulsive behaviors would have extreme difficulty con-ducting a reconstruction, and any star undergoing a reconstruction with such a guide would be at an extreme disadvantage.

The reconstruction process requires the guide to be on his or her feet sharing great energy for 12-14 straight hours. It takes tremendous good health and alert energy to do this kind of highly focused therapy. In addi-tion, skills of music, dance, humor, and physical stamina are all important to the process.

Conducting reconstructions is such a powerful way of doing therapy that it's easy for the guide to develop an unhealthy "inflated" ego, or for the work to appeal to individuals already suffering from an unacceptable level of narcissism. Because it may appear during the process that the guide has more power than he or she actually does, and because stars and audiences are sometimes in awe, it's important for the guide to remember that recon-struction is a process brought to life by virtue of many people interacting and the insights and energies of the star and audience, as well as a spiritual dimension. The guide is simply a guide.

Again, the guide is not taking the star where the guide wants, but leading the star along his or her own path. The guide supports the star; the guide helps the star to more fully understand where he or she is by exploring where he or she has been; and the guide offers the star opportunities and directions to lead him- or herself to new places.

The star has given the guide a great deal of subjective information. As noted in Chapter One, the guide takes this subjective information and returns it to the star in a more objective way. Sometimes this is done through sculpture, sometimes by adding information. The goal is to help the star get a bigger, clearer picture, and develop more ways of seeing that picture. The guide takes what he or she has learned about family systems, relationships, and addictions and makes some new points, adds some information, and suggests alternative ways of viewing things that give the star more options.

THE QUALIFIED GUIDE

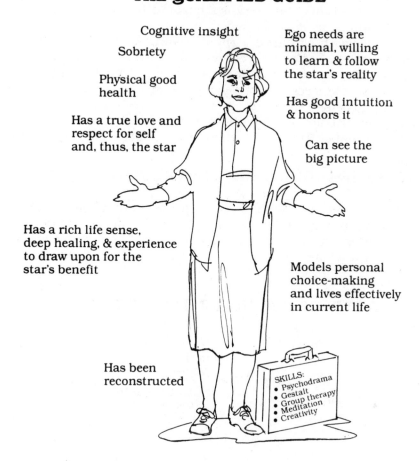

Cognitive insight

Sobriety

Physical good health

Has a true love and respect for self and, thus, the star

Ego needs are minimal, willing to learn & follow the star's reality

Has good intuition & honors it

Can see the big picture

Has a rich life sense, deep healing, & experience to draw upon for the star's benefit

Models personal choice-making and lives effectively in current life

Has been reconstructed

SKILLS:
- Psychodrama
- Gestalt
- Group therapy
- Meditation
- Creativity

The guide tries to help the star learn how to communicate more directly instead of hinting about things or avoiding conflict. The guide tries to provide a language for sharing oneself honestly in relationships with others.

Many times, stars will want to skip over certain events or feelings; usually these are extremely important events or feelings. Once, during an interview, Sharon was talking to a star about the fact that the star had had an abortion. The star very quickly said that this was somethng she had already processed, and that she felt finished with it. But during the reconstruction, when Sharon set up a sculpture with the baby and the abortion clinic, it turned out to be a pivotal point for this woman. This often happens with deaths as well. Someone will say, "Well, my father died when I was twelve years old, but I don't have a lot of feeling about it; I hardly even remember him." Then when we set up a sculpture showing other children having their fathers alive and present all through high school, or when we re-create the death scene, this star will discover feelings he or she didn't even know existed. As in all kinds of other therapies, paying attention to resistance is extremely important.

Being familiar with cathartic ways of dealing with emotions is very important. We teach 21 or 22 different ways to express anger and do anger reduction work. It's very important to use lighting and music and whatever it takes to have people access their grief. It's not uncommon to spend a very long time letting a person cry quietly or even sob. Anger and grief are pivotal points in any reconstruction. Helping someone access and express his or her feelings is as important as imparting any instruction or information.

PREPARING TO GUIDE A RECONSTRUCTION

The guide has several decisions to make before the reconstruction begins. Where the reconstruction will take place is an important consideration. Who will attend, what props will be used during the day, and whether music will be utilized (and if so, what music) also must be decided.

A FEW OF THE GUIDE'S DECISIONS

Setting. Reconstructions have taken place in all kinds of settings. Sharon has done them in the basement of a college, in the attic of an old house, in someone's living room, and in retreat centers. Today she does them primarily in a setting that is specifically designed for reconstructions. Certainly it's optimal to have a setting that is conducive to the process—this makes it easier for the guide, the star, and the audience.

The setting we use today is a big, empty room measuring approximately 25′ x 40′. Both movable chairs and pillows are present for the comfort of the audience. The room is equipped with a stereo system, speakers, and lighting that can be adjusted to fit the particular action taking place. It is very important to have a very comfortable, easy setting so that most of the attention can be given to the work at hand. A small room off of this big room is fully stocked with props, costumes, wigs, papers products, jewelry, and make-up, as well as the artistic tools necessary to create specific props for each reconstruction. There are 3-4 small rooms in addition to this which are used for small-group activities.

Outside the rooms themselves is a natural setting that is beautiful and peaceful and healing. It is also important that the setting promote natural healing, that people have time to reflect and connect with nature. Sharon says that in the early days, she didn't really appreciate how important setting was, and conducted reconstructions just about any place she had the opportunity to do so. Today she values setting as an integral factor and says she now knows that the more people are able to be in a place that meets the needs of the body, mind, spirit, and soul, the more powerful the healing process.

Exercise 3.1: The Importance of Setting

Understanding that both an outdoor and an indoor space are required, think of a setting that would be conducive to meditation and exploring your inner self. Describe the following:

External location:
Internal room:
Where to sit or lie down:
Time of day:
Lighting:
Music:
Special effects to create proper atmosphere:

If possible, go to that place, and spend about 15 minutes there. When you return, write about how it felt and how significant the appropriate atmosphere was.

Allowing Family and Friends.   The question of whether a star's spouse, significant other, family, or friend(s) can attend the reconstruction is an important issue which must be addressed by the guide and star. The star initially decides whether he or she would want to have such people attend. A request for this is then made to the guide in writing. In this letter, the star should:

1.   Describe the person, focusing on how the star sees his or her relationship with this person.
2.   Describe how he or she feels with this person.
3.   Provide some history that demonstrates the other person's support of the star's recovery process.
4.   Provide historical evidence of the commitment this person has made with the star to recovery in their relationship.
5.   Provide evidence that this person has experienced a similar reconstruction workshop or other recovery therapy.
6.   Agree to have this person attend someone else's reconstruction before attending the star's.

The guide will then evaluate this information and examine the relevant issues in order to make a decision.

Several things must be considered in such a decision. First, it is important that there be no major obstacles in the relationship what would interfere with or take focus away from the reconstruction. This is not the place to "drop a bomb" and see how the other person handles it. It is also necessary that the invited person be emotionally healthy enough to realize that attending is going to be personally intense and perhaps difficult, but that the reconstruction event is a day for the star, and it is not a place to do therapy for invited guests.

The purpose of having a family member or friend attend a reconstruction is three-fold: it may serve to support the star on the day's journey and add an even deeper level of the reality to the experience by virtue of the presence of someone "from home"; it may offer a wonderful opportunity for the star to thank someone who has played a significant role in his or her life; and it may allow this particular relationship to be clarified. This last possibility bears some explanation. Boundaries in this relationship may need to be set or reinforced, an old wound in the relationship may need to be explored, or the relationship may need to change or even end. Having this person present at the star's reconstruction provides a real first-hand opportunity for the star to experience the kind of work that will need to be done at home.

Having a spouse or significant other at a reconstruction presents a special set of opportunities for growth, solidification, and change. Over the course of the day, the star's partner may begin to gain a whole new understanding of the star. This person has a unique chance to see his or her relationship with the star in a new way as well. As the star's perspective unfolds, the star's partner can experience new feelings, and perhaps develop a deeper level of understanding than previously existed.

A partner's presence at the reconstruction also presents a challenge to the star, to the partner, and to the guide. The star may be hesitant to bring up some of the more painful coupleship issues because he or she is concerned about protecting the partner. Alternatively, if there is a lot of anger in the relationship, the star may use this as an opportunity for revenge by focusing painful feelings that surface on the partner. There may be concerns on both the star's and the partner's side that if the star does all of the reconstruction work in an open and honest way, he or she will eventually (or immediately!) leave the relationship, or there will be negative repercussions in the relationship. Ultimately, in order to have a partner attend a reconstruction, the star's level of trust must outweigh his or her level of fear. (This is not to say that if a star never raises this option of having his or her partner attend, that this means he or she is working more out of fear than trust. We only mean that if the desire is there, the star will need to be very trusting in order to be fully honest throughout the process in the presence of a person with whom he or she is intimately involved "in real life.")

Keep in mind that the partner has his or her own set of fears, and may attend with an "agenda." The challenge of the day for the partner is to feel the feelings, absorb the experience, let go of the agenda, face the fear, trust, and move through it. This is difficult because the partner has not only the same fears as the star, but the additional fear that he or she has no control over what the star will expose. The partner must wonder, "Will I look like the villain? What will the rest of the participants think of me when the workshop is all over? Do I have to act strong and be supportive and forget *my* feelings? Is there something I don't know about the relationship that will hurt me deeply? Is the star going to use this experience against me? What will happen to the relationship, and to me, as a result?"

The major challenge for the guide is to be aware of the fears of both the star and the partner. The guide needs to know the potential problems and be prepared to deal with them as they may arise. Some of the problems can also be minimized, or perhaps even eliminated, by exploring fully the dynamics of the couple's relationship and understanding the star's motives for having the spouse present. The guide should be sure there are no major obstacles in the relationship that could turn the focus on the day from the star to the couple. Again, this is not a day to do major couples' work; this needs to be very clear to all involved. Goals, possibilities, realistic and unrealistic expectations, and guidelines all need to be made clear to both the star and the partner.

Again the decision to give permission for a partner's attendance at a reconstruction workshop involves several factors. The star needs to have demonstrated a willngness to do his or her work and not hold back if the partner is present. The partner must be at a level of emotional health and/or

PEOPLE IN STAR'S LIFE MAY WANT TO COME TO THE RECONSTRUCTION

recovery such that he or she can handle the intensity of the event, practice self-care throughout the week, and have appropriate support at home to deal with the aftermath. Both the star and the partner must accept the guidelines and be willing to let the process unfold. The couple's relationship must be stable and not in any major crisis. Lastly, the star needs to want the partner to be present, and not be bidding for this because it is the partner's (or anyone else's) wish.

If the partner attends the star's reconstruction workshop, he or she is reminded that the events portrayed are from the star's perspective, and that this will not necessarily match his or her own. The partner will be reminded that the reconstruction is for the star, not for their relationship. The partner is also reminded that feelings and observations about what they see throughout the event may arise, and that the appropriate place to express these feelings and thoughts is in the context of small group activities on the day following the reconstruction event. The partner will be attending the reconstruction as an audience member, and so will have the same access and obligations to small group activities as do all audience members. In other words, this is the star's day only, and not a day for couples' work. This cannot be emphasized enough. On the day of the reconstruction, the partner will be directed to sit out of the star's line of vision. The partner will also be encouraged to find his or her own support system to rely on during the day's events.

In all cases, the primary concern is to maintain the integrity of the star's experience. The partners, family members, or friends who may attend a reconstruction should be able to offer unconditional support for the star throughout the process. If the guide determines that this is not possible, permission for attendance should be denied.

Exercise 3.2: VIPs in Your Life

Make a list of people you would trust enough to have present at a major event in your life such as your own reconstruction. In a second column, list your feelings about each of these people, and in a third column, the reasons you would choose him or her.

Whether you undergo a reconstruction and invite these people to attend or not, you may wish to find a way to thank them for what they mean to you.

Props.   One of the important tasks of the guide is the preparation of props for the reconstruction event. This involves creating a list and gathering whatever will be needed for sculptures and psychodramas.

The word "props" is a theatrical term that is slang for "properties." It generally refers to any item from the enviroment of the character which is displayed on stage. Set props include objects such as furniture or other stage dressing that may serve in the background and may or may not be used by the actors (or, in the case of reconstructions, by the role-players). A personal prop is an item particular to a character and is usually worn or handled by the person playing that character.

The selection of props generally begins following the guide's review of written materials submitted by the star, the interview, and the planning of scenes or vignettes. As the props are a kind of "finishing touch" to the planning, they will be gathered, invented, constructed, and laid out the

SOME SAMPLE PROPS

night before the reconstruction event. It is the guide's job to carefully decide what props will help the process of a given star's reconstruction. Some discretion and experience is required in this task. In general, the guide should be thinking about heightening the drama through the use of the props. But guides should be cautious, also. Props can help or hinder a reconstruction.

> **Guides should be cautious when choosing props. They can be highly effective in telling the star's story, but they can also be a hinderance.**

In theater, the term "stage business" means two processes are going on, one for those on the stage, and one for the audience. The audience can get bored if things on stage are not going smoothly. To avoid this problem, props must be enhancing rather than distracting. They must be easily accessible to the guide, and easily used by the role-player. If a prop is too unwieldy or takes too much time to locate or use, some of the momentum of the experience is lost, as is the intention of the prop itself. In making too much of a production out of a reconstruction, props can get in the way of a good story. Yet props can be used lavishly and to excellent effect if they aren't too cumbersome.

The real purpose of props in a reconstruction is not to increase the drama but to aid the star in *seeing* (and thus understanding) something or someone in his or her life. Use props to present a picture, to present a truth, to access emotions, to add emphasis, to control the presentation of action, and to make a point.

One of the things a prop can do is present a powerful picture that says more than words can. A role-player depicting the character of an alcoholic could sway or slur his speech, but he will make an even greater impact with a bottle of whiskey in his hand, because this reminds the star how much of a role alcohol played in this person's life.

Because props let the star see the important pictures of his or her life, the selection of these pictures is a crucial choice made at the guide's discretion. In general, the guide should keep in mind what the star needs to see. Perhaps the star has some denial about certain aspects of his or her life that were revealed to the guide through the written material or in the interview. The guide can help the star and the audience to see this reality in an effective way through the use of props. (For example, a bag of heavy rocks to suggest guilt is a prop we often use. Watching someone carry this bag around represents the oppressive effects of guilt quite succinctly.)

In one reconstruction we did, the star did not seem to think there were any problems of alcoholism in herself or in her children. Rather than argue the point, the guide simply placed a liquor bottle in the hand of anyone in the star's life whom she had described as a heavy drinker. The guide also had the star's stand-in carry a liquor bottle in any scene in which alcohol was a presence. These visual pictures helped the star surrender to the reality of her disease.

Sometimes a prop can be used as a shortcut. A crown placed on the head of a favorite child or the person who is always the center of attention can convey what might take five minutes to describe. Props are good to use with teaching sculptures or picture sculptures of a current situation so that the star can simply recognize a problem in that moment of the process, and know that the problem will receive more attention and work later in the reconstruction.

People can play in place of props. A line of people can represent a wall or barrier or a physical structure such as a house. Role-players can also represent family pets, objects, or abstract ideas or characteristics.

And whether represented by an object or a role-player, a prop can be used to access feelings. It is the drama of a reconstruction that leads the star to re-create or reexperience feelings that occurred in the past. The star will need enough visual presentation to tap into those feelings.

One of the most graphic props is an ordinary man's leather belt with a metal buckle. The belt will be recognized by virtually everyone as a symbol of parental discipline. Some equate it with violence because they were hit with belts in anger. But even those who did not experience a belt in this context will grasp the concept because the image is part of our society's collective understanding. People who were hit with a belt as children can recall the powerlessness, the physical pain, and the fear they felt in anticipation of being struck. They remember the rage they felt, and the shame. The prop will be even more effective if the sound or auditory effect of the belt is also represented. The jingle of the buckle, the sound of a belt being taken off through the belt loops of a pair of pants, the slap of the belt popped against itself in threat—these will evoke powerful feelings in almost anyone.

Props are used in a way akin to Jung's theory of archetypes. There are certain cultural connotations and associations that belong to certain objects. Some span a long period of time, some work in this way for only a specific era or generation, some are cross-cultural and in this way universal. (Perhaps in the future there will be a generation that doesn't "get" the meaning of the belt, but for now its significance is profound.)

Props are often metaphorical. The objects-as-props represent important aspects of the star's life. One star of a reconstruction was embarrassed by his rural background when he went to school. He always had sheep shit on his shoes. Inventing a prop of brown feces (made of construction paper) helped the star to understand the symbolic meaning of the manure as it related to the shame of being different from the others, and of being poor. Props are also an excellent technique to use with a star who is too cognitive or overly verbal. The props transform the working mode for the star and help him or her get to the emotional work at hand.

Some reconstruction stories necessitate a sense of space or setting. This may require a very elemental presentation of scenery: a sign denoting town, a paper column to show a large house, a table and chair for a family kitchen. Sometimes a family is shaped by its residence, whether mansion or hovel. Props are especially helpful in representing themes in the family system or in an individual history. One of the important tasks for the guide during the planning stage of a reconstruction is to listen for and anticipate these patterns and themes. Some of the most commonly seen themes in the lives of potential stars are disease, addiction, shame, grief, oppression, neglect, deprivation, enmeshment, and over-achievement. These are just a few—every star is unique.

Noting themes.   Perhaps the largest task of the guide in preparing a reconstruction is to find the themes in a particular star's life.

Sigmund Freud referred to the "repetition compulsion" as that tendency in our adult lives to replay the unresolved subconscious issues from our childhood. These can be noted in anyone's history. It will be vital to healing and change for the star to see and feel old patterns. This is part of the process by which he or she becomes empowered to make new choices.

During the preparation process, the guide must be extremely alert to the star's patterns, and should choose props that can emphasize or illustrate themes (those the star is aware of as well as those about which the star is still in denial).

For example, a very large trash can attached to a rope and then loosely tied around the star's waist illustrates the disease. The star could carry the trash around as a burden, throwing away the good things in life. The trash can also becomes thematically representative of the shame around related self-destructive behaviors.

Music.   As with props, following the review of written materials, the interview with the star, a conference with the rest of the guiding team, and the planning of sculptures and vignettes for psychodramas, it is very helpful to plan for music that can be played at key times during the star's reconstruction event.

Sometimes the star will have mentioned a song or piece of music that has been important, perhaps a reminder of a certain time or event. There may have been a favorite popular song associated with a romance or relationship, or with the loss of a relationship. There may have been a song from childhood that a grandparent sang or a mother constantly played on the stereo (the associations to such music might be positive or negative). In one reconstruction, the star remembered the theme song from a favorite television show that was part of the nostalgia of her childhood. Some music can have cultural significance. Pieces of music important to the star are often noted in the *Learning to Know Yourself* workbook.

MUSIC AS AN EFFECTIVE TOOL

Most frequently, on the day of the reconstruction event, music will be used to note a major event in the life of a star, to accent certain important feelings, to help set the tone of a particular event or period in the star's life, to help the star grieve or celebrate, and to bring the group gathered for the reconstruction into a cohesive emotional place.

Music is important also to access the auditory senses of the star and other participants. The reconstruction will inevitably have a major visual impact. Music seems to touch a different part of our emotions. Perhaps this is because we have ingrained a kind of receptive posture where music is concerned. Music is a remarkably collective experience, even accounting for various tastes and preferences. It speaks to higher concepts and somehow raises us to spiritual planes.

One obvious way music can be vital to a reconstruction is to add tone to moments of poignancy, loss, victory, celebration, romance, and turns of events. After all, this is often the purpose music serves in our daily lives!

Music should accompany the most dramatic moments of a reconstruction such as the deaths of family members. Grief work often requires some attention in the course of the reconstruction. This is a time for the star to cry, to mourn, and to be held and comforted. Just as loss is an almost mystical experience that touches us all in a kind of universal way, music can enhance the feelings that arise at such a time.

Often loss is metaphysical rather than bodily. In other words, a parent may still be living, but the star has "lost" the relationship with this parent to the disease of alcoholism or to the distance that sometimes follows a divorce or other family upset. Perhaps the star simply never felt close to a parent to begin with. Whatever the actual circumstances, music helps grief work.

Music is also an integral part of transitions. Births, graduations, moves, separations from job or family . . . transitions such as these mark the most stressful and intense times in a person's life. The stress can be present whether a change is good or bad, positive or negative. People often review things (their lives, themselves) during times of transition, and transitions themselves are markers along a person's journey. Music can enhance the recognition of this aspect of a star's life.

Music is a wonderful component of so many human rituals. In a reconstruction, ritual is often used to celebrate or make an impression. We will no doubt want to use music in these moments.

Music enhances the spiritual connections in the reconstruction process— recognizing miracles or "angels" (more on the blessing of "angels" can be found in Chapter Four) in our lives, honoring the amazing fact that we have survived against adversity, etc.

One additional way to use music is to use the same song or piece whenever a pattern in the star's life comes up. The repetition can facilitate recognition of the pattern(s). Also, when the mood of the reconstruction is depressed or lacking in energy, music can be used either to emphasize the prevailing feeling or to counteract it, and can be chosen depending on the intention.

Remember, like the props, the music needs to be ready for use during the event. It will need to be easily accessible to whomever is controlling the sound system. That person should be aware of which selections may be used when. The guide should have communicated with this person so that there are no clumsy delays, and so that when the guide asks for a certain piece of music it can almost immediately "appear" as an added element.

Below is a lengthy list of possible music a guide might want to use during a reconstruction workshop or event. The selections have been categorized for ease, and wherever possible, we have included label/artist information to facilitate location.

Exercise 3.2: Meaningful Music

Think of some music that has been meaningful in a positive way in your life. List the song or piece titles. Collect this music so that you can have ready access to it for your own comfort and/or pleasure. You might want to make a personal tape containing this special music.

RECOVERY

SONG TITLE	ARTIST	ALBUM	ADDRESS
	Michael Brase	The Sounds of Recovery The Sounds of Recovery Vol II	P.O. Box 121671 Nashville, TN 37212
	Michael Byers	You Are My Friend	Insight Productions P.O. Box 4459 Glendale, CA 91202-4459
Tip Toe Thru the 12 Steps	Greg Tamblyn	Single Release NCW How Could I Be Better Than This? Shoot Out at the I'm OK Corral	Greg Tamblyn P.O. Box 45258 KC, MO 64111 316-757-7250
The Impossible Dream	Movie Sound Track	Man of La Mancha	MCA Records 70 Universal City Plaza Universal City, CA
	Artie Ripp/Ron Koslow	Beauty and the Beast-of-Love & Hope	Capitol Records Hollywood & Vine St. Hollywood, CA
Wind Beneath My Wings The Rose	Bette Midler Bette Midler	Beaches "The Rose" Soundtrack	Atlantic Records 75 Rockefeller Plaza NY, NY 10019
Amazing Grace	Judy Collins	Colors of the Day	Elektra/Asylum Records 75 Rockefeller Plaza NY, NY 10019
Someone Was There	Michael Byers	That Kid Can Fly	Insight Productions 1346 N. Columbus Ave., #8 Glendale, CA 91202
Windows and Walls	Dan Fogelberg	Windows and Walls	EPIC Records 1801 Century Park W. LA, CA
Right Here Waiting For You	Richard Marx	Repeat Offender	Capitol Records Hollywood & Vine St. Hollywood, CA

Come From the Heart	Kathy Mattea	Blowin in the Wind	Polygram Records NY, NY
Love Can Build a Bridge	The Judds	Love Can Build a Bridge	BMG Records NY, NY
The Return Home Is Where The Heart Is Let Em Go	Sally Fingerett	Unraveled	Amerisound 1331 Chesapeake Ave. Columbus, OH 43212
Imagine	John Lennon	Imagine	Capitol Records Hollywood & Vine St. Hollywood, CA
If Tomorrow Never Comes The Dance	Garth Brooks	Garth Brooks	Caged Panther Music Liberty Records 3322 West End Ave. Nashville, TN 37203
Show Me The Way	Styx	Edge of the Century	A&M Records P.O. Box 118 Hollywood, CA 90078
Shower the People You've Got a Friend	James Taylor	In the Pocket Greatest Hits	Warner Brothers Records 3300 Warner Blvd. Burbank, CA 91510
Trouble Me	10,000 Maniacs	Blind Man's Zoo	Elektra/Asylum Records 75 Rockefeller Plaza NY, NY 10019
Point of Light	Randy Travis	High Lonesome	Warner Brothers Records 3300 Warner Blvd. Burbank, CA 91510
The River	Garth Brooks	Ropin The Wind	Capitol Records Hollywood & Vine St. Hollywood, CA

SONG TITLE	ARTIST	ALBUM	ADDRESS
All By Myself	Eric Carmen	The Best of Eric Carmen	Arista Records 6 West 57th Street NY, NY 10019
I Want to Live	John Denver	I Want to Live	RCA Records
You've Got a Friend	Carole King	Tapestry	CBS Records 51W 52 St. NY, NY
I Will Stand Fast Light in the Hall	Fred Small	I Will Stand Fast Jaguar	Flying Fish 1304 W. Schubert Chicago, IL 60614
An Eagle When She Flies	Dolly Parton	An Eagle When She Flies	Columbia Records 666 5th Ave./P.O. Box 4455 NY, NY 10101-4455

DEATH, GRIEF AND LOSS

SONG TITLE	ARTIST	ALBUM	ADDRESS
Tears In Heaven	Eric Clapton	Unplugged	Reprise Records 3300 Warner Blvd. Burbank, CA 91505-4694
I'll Be There	Escape Club	Dollars & Sex	Atlantic Records 75 Rockefeller Plaza NY, NY 10019
Goodbye My Friend	Linda Ronstadt	Cry Like a Rainstorm	Elektra 75 Rockefeller Plaza NY, NY 10019

FAMILY

SONG TITLE	ARTIST	ALBUM	ADDRESS
Family Tree	Lionel Cartwright	Chasin the Sun	MCA Records Universal City, CA 91603
Forefathers	Dan Fogelberg	Wild Places	EPIC Records 1801 Century Park West LA, CA 90057
Family Tree	Tom Chapin	Family Tree	Sundance Music Box 1663 NY, NY 10011
Seeing My Father In Me	Paul Overstreet	Sowin Love	RCA Records BMG Music NY, NY
He Walked On Water	Randy Travis	No Holding Back	Warner Brothers Records 3300 Warner Blvd. Burbank, CA 91505-4694
Your Mother & I	Loudon Wainwright III	More Love Songs	Rounder Records One Camp St. Cambridge, MA 02140
Where Are You Flesh & Blood	Wilson Phillips	Shadows & Light	SBK Records 1290 Ave. of the Americas NY, NY 10104
Put it There Mama's Girl	Paul McCartney	Flowers in the Dirt	Capitol Records Hollywood & Vine St. Hollywood, CA
Fathers Song	Fred Small	No Limit	Roundie Records One Camp Street Cambridge, MA 02140

DISEASE

SONG TITLE	ARTIST	ALBUM	ADDRESS
Is That All There Is	Patsy Cline	12 Greatest Hits	MCA 80 Universal City Plaza Universal Plaza, CA
I Miss Billy The Kid	Billy Dean	Billy Dean	Liberty Records 3322 West End Ave. Nashville, TN 37203
Toy Soldiers	Martika	Martika	CBS Records
End of the Innocence	Don Henley	End of the Innocence	Geffen Records 9130 Sunset Blvd. LA, CA 90069-6197
Therapy	Loudon Wainwright III	Therapy	BMG Records NY, NY
Cowboy's Born With a Broken Heart	Boy Howdy	Boy Howdy	Curb Records 47 Music Sq. E. Nashville, TN 37203
Everybody Hurts	R.E.M.	Single	Warner Brothers

INNER CHILD

SONG TITLE	ARTIST	ALBUM	ADDRESS
A Child Is Born	Barbra Streisand	Disney-For Our Children	Walt Disney Records Burbank, CA 91521
	Priscilla Herdman	Star Dreamer	Herman, RC #2 Box 78 Pine Plains, NY 12567

Artist	Title	Publisher / Address
Joanie Bartels	Lullaby Magic	BGM Music/ Discovery Music, 5554 Calhoun Ave., Van Nuys, CA 91401
Pamala Ballingham	Earth Mother Lullabies	Earth Mother Productions, P.O. Box 43204, Tucson, AZ 85733
J. Aaron Brown	A Child's Gift of Lullabies / The Rock A Bye Collection	Someday Baby, 1508 16th Ave. South, Nashville, TN 37212
C. Kaldor & C. Campagne	Lullaby Berceuse	Music For Little People, P.O. Box 1460, Redway, CA 95560
J. Aaron Brown	A Gift of Songs for Sweet Dreams	Someday Baby, 1508 16th Ave. South, Nashville, TN 37212
Sheila Ritter	Playtime & Sleepy Time	Becanada Music, 2326 Easy Street, Ann Arbor, MI 48104
Julie Barnett Smith	The Child Within	T&J Troubadour Productions, 3118 S. Los Altos, Mesa, AZ 85202
Columbia Music	Til Their Eyes Shine	Columbia Records, 666 5th Ave./P.O. Box 4455, NY, NY 10101
Marlo Thomas	Free to be a Family / Free to be You & Me	Arista Records, 6 West 57th Street, NY, NY 10019

The Child Within Holds The Keys

COUPLES

SONG TITLE	ARTIST	ALBUM	ADDRESS
I Will Be Here for You	Michael Smith	Heart of Stone	Geffen Records 9130 Sunset Blvd.
How Can We Be Lovers That's What Love is All About Back On My Feet Again	Michael Bolton	Soul Provider The Hunger Soul Provider	CBS Records 51 W. 52nd St. NY, NY
I Will Always Love You	Whitney Houston	Body Guard Soundtrack	Arista Records 6 W 57th Street NY, NY 10019
And So It Goes	Billy Joel	Storm Front	Maritime Music 200 W. 57th St. NY, NY 10019
Love of a Lifetime	Firehouse	Firehouse	EPIC Records 666 5th Ave./P.O. Box 4455 NY, NY 10101-4455
Don't Hold Back Your Love	Hall & Oates	Change of Season	Arista Records 6 W 57th St. NY, NY 10019
He Talks To Me	Lorrie Morgan	Leave the Light On	BMG Music NY, NY
I Forgot That Love Existed	Van Morrison	Poetic Champions Compose	Poly Gram Records NY, NY
One Friend Left	Dan Seals	The Best	Capitol Records Hollywood & Vine St. Hollywood, CA

ENERGIZING MEDITATION

SONG TITLE	ARTIST	ALBUM	ADDRESS
Coming Around Again	Carly Simon	Greatest Hits Live	Arista Records 6 W 57th St. NY, NY 10019
Eye of the Tiger	Survivor	Eye of the Tiger	Scotti Brothers 2114 Pico Blvd. Santa Monica, CA 90405
	Bob Seger	Nine Tonight	Capitol Records Hollywood &Vine St. Hollywood, CA
	Kitaro	Silk Road	

Using the star's chronologies.   At some point between the ages of 12 and 30, many people develop a disease of compulsion or addiction (alcoholism, drug addiction, nicotine addiction, sexual addiction, workaholism, etc.). If someone has developed either the seeds of such a disease or a full-blown addiction or compulsion, it can help to have him or her develop a complete chronology, as near as possible, between the time the addiction started and the time sobriety began. This is important because addiction is the opposite of freedom, and when doing a reconstruction, it is important to place the addiction in the proper, fullest context of the star's life. There is much to be learned in this. In times of massive addiction, for example, there are going to be patterns of self-defeating behavior and crazy-making situations. When people can learn to accept this portion of their lives as diseased, then some of the work becomes about dealing with the fact of the addiction rather than going back and working piece by piece with the crazy-making information. For example, a spouse or child of an addict is living in a very predictably chaotic setting. We may not have to walk through every piece of the chaos to deal with the rage, confusion, and pain that came from it.

Detailed chronologies are also helpful for all marriages, and for any period of abuse. (Very frequently sexual abuse is not in the consciousness of someone who suffered through it, but it will surface over the course of the reconstruction event.) Also in the chronology, we ask for a work history and/or a military history. Stars are asked to prepare a list of all the people in their family of choice, the key people in their personal lives, and the key people in their work lives. All of this becomes part of the family chronology.

> *Reconstruction is the fastest and most powerful therapeutic process in which some therapists have ever been involved.*

Reconstruction is so powerful that the guide has a tremendous responsibility to establish a safe setting for the process. The Gestalt, group therapy, psychodrama, sculpting, guided imagery, music, props, and humor are all supporting a theoretical family systems framework as well as a belief in the larger spiritual aspect to the process. This belief holds that every person is special and that self-worth is the power that heals.

Any star undergoing a reconstruction was not able to acknowledge his or her pain while growing up. The star's spirit, or sense of self, was effectively suffocated out of existence or put "on ice." For some this was the result of trauma, for others it was the result of neglect. Plans for the reconstruction event should include provisions for the type of star who will be working that day. A star who easily accesses feelings should be encouraged to be cognitive; a talkative, cognitive star should be encouraged to use only a word, phrase, or single sentence to respond to a particular scene or situation. Yet the reconstruction itself must be balanced. If, as a guide, one has too much fear, for example, reconstruction will be too hesitant and the new awareness too safe to be helpful. If one is too cognitive or intellectual, reconstructions will be too heady and lack the affect or emotion powerful enough to facilitate change. If one is too dramatic, reconstruction will be a show to demonstrate the flair of the guide and the star will only be an instrument to reflect the guide's creativity—there will be no internal, lasting impact for the star.

There are many similarities among reconstructions, and this book discusses many consistencies within the process. It is important to keep in mind, however, that each reconstruction is different. Each star brings to the process a unique set of experiences, a unique outlook on the world and on the reconstruction process. Reconstructions are a specialized framework in which we can accomplish work that is highly individualized. The more reconstructions we witness and participate in, the clearer this has become.

One way to begin to break down the difference in types of stars (and so to begin to think about various guiding styles that may be appropriate depending on the star) follows the idea of the four roles played in families.

The chart below lists each role and some of the characteristics a person who has played this role may bring to the process of reconstruction. It is essential that the guide be aware of both patterns to expect and strategies for intervention.

HERO

CHARACTERISTIC	STRATEGIES
1. Controlling - They take charge and may become defensive.	Allow star to do less talking, more feeling.
2. Analyzing - Figuring things out.	Allow star to do less talking and more feeling.
3. Want to look good - Want A's.	Praise for risk-taking and letting go of control. Have them carry symbols of their accomplishments until they grow weary and feel the pain.
4. Perfectionists.	Same as above.
5. Caretake others.	Point this out as it occurs and give permission for self-care. Also point out control in caretaking behavior.
6. Deny their anger.	Encourage anger work, get audience feedback.

7. Smile through their pain.	Allow inner child to show this and tell how it feels.
8. Loyalty.	Sculptures and pictures which show reality of addiction and powerlessness.
9. Shame - They could not fix the family, may try to rationalize.	Sculptures and pictures which show reality of addiction, powerlessness.
10. Tendency to be compliant.	Encourage decision-making and boundary-setting.

SCAPEGOAT

CHARACTERISTIC	STRATEGIES
1. Often present w/anger, may hide pain.	Offer affirmation, point out positives.
2. Don't trust, may try to sabotage.	Be consistent, point out patterns of sabotage.
3. Very low self-image, may fight worthiness.	Use audience to affirm. Validate star's reality of family system.
4. Shame about pat behaviors.	Do work on forgiveness of self, point out positives, perhaps a forgiveness award ceremony.
5. May try to get the guide angry at him.	Point out sabotage. Have inner child verbalize feelings, offer positive regard and clear choices.
6. Difficult to move to pain.	Build trust, allow rage work, add affirmations, move to losses.
7. May get stuck in blame.	Show hopelessness of holding on to resentments - Use a towel pull exercise - Keep arguing and pulling until tired.
8. Lonely inside.	Do exercises all day to connect star with inner child and with audience.

LOST CHILD

CHARACTERISTIC	STRATEGIES
1. May tolerate large amounts of pain without reacting.	Expect the reconstruction to move slowly at the beginning. Allow the pain to build to the point that the star feels it and begins to get empowered. The audience may get impatient but this is essential for a lost child.
2. May dissociate or disappear physically or internally during reconstruction.	Keep star in center stage and develop a signal to help him reconnect when he isolates internally - affirm.
3. May have low energy.	Plan energy builders, active scenes, into the script.
4. Audience may begin to feel star's pain before the star does and get angry.	Let audience share what they see - not critically but in an encouraging style. Let audience affirm worthiness.
5. May have few social skills for building new relationships and setting boundaries.	Do teaching around this area and encourage star to start slowly and build.
6. Day may proceed slowly.	Best for the guide to relax and go with the star.
7. Huge grief, covers anger.	Allow grief to come. Will most likely precede anger. Then revisit places of anger.
8. May want to please, not make waves.	Give affirmation for self-care and allow inner child to share needs.
9. May have trouble getting help, used to doing it on his own.	Do trust-building exercises. Use angels to help. Let him see contrast and relief in learning.
10. May be quiet and shy.	Help star develop a voice, a loud scream, or wailing tears.

MASCOT

CHARACTERISTIC	STRATEGIES
1. May joke and try not to get serious.	Allow inner child to carry a symbol of clowning and express the pain of always performing.
2. May get distracted.	Treat star seriously. Guide can notice and call attention to distracting behaviors and also call star back as necessary.
3. May be very needy, dependent, try to get guide to do all the work.	Allow the star to participate in the directing of the sculptures. Ask for input. Back off when appropriate.
4. May try to distract guide by fidgeting, joking, being annoying.	Stop. Ask star to take a deep breath and feel.
5. May perform for audience.	Audience feedback. Affirmation of being himself.
6. May fight taking responsibility for own actions.	Encourage boundary-setting and limits with others. Do some teaching around choices, perhaps a growing-up ceremony.
7. May not know how to take independent action.	Encourage support system. Let star practice making choices.
8. Fearful.	Set up his fear and let him face it.
9. Wears a mask.	Allow star to show and tell audience who he really is. Affirm.
10. Depressed-sometimes suicidal.	Allow anger to be expressed instead of depressed. Validate his reality.

Exercise 3.3: Your Family role(s)

Review the chart above and choose the role(s) and up to five characteristics that identify you. Take a sheet of paper and write the first characteristic at the top. List all the ways this has helped you in the past, and all the ways it has harmed you. Below this, write three strategies you can use to reduce the harmful effects of this characteristic. Here is an example:

ROLE: Lost child
CHARACTERISTIC: Isolation

POSITIVE EFFECTS:

1. Learned to be by myself.
2. Active imagination.
3. Independent.

NEGATIVE EFFECTS:

1. Lonely.
2. Few social skills.
3. Inability to play.

STRATEGIES:

1.   Make one social phone call each day.
2.   Raise hand to speak at each support group meeting I attend.
3.   Find one outgoing friend and observe—learn how to be social.

Follow your strategies for 1-2 weeks and then go on to the next characteristic.

Spirituality.   We wish to end this chapter addressing the issue of a guide's spirituality and how this connects to the reconstruction process. Virginia Satir frequently said that when one views human life as sacred, one has to recognize that there is a spiritual dimension to every reconstruction. There are many kinds of spirituality we work with in reconstruction. We work with the spirit all of us share. We work with people's very committed beliefs to a certain deity. We work with those who have been abused by spirituality. Sharon believes that reconstructions work best when the guide genuinely believes in such sacredness, and genuinely believes that there is spirituality in every person.

> *While it's absolutely key that the guide is able to experience a soulful connection with the star, and is able to use information to access emotion and can share emotion, he or she ideally understands that something larger is connecting us all.*

The guide needs to have some sense of spirituality because he or she needs to be able to honor the star. Reconstructions demand that there be some sense of awe and respect for the value of each person's life.

PART II

THE EVENT

When I was young, I set out to change the world. When I grew older, I perceived that this was too ambitious, so I set out to change my state. This too, I realized as I grew older, was too ambitious, so I set out to change my town. When I realized I could not even do this, I tried to change my family. Now as an old man, I know I should have started by changing myself. If I had started with myself, maybe then I would have succeeded in changing my family, the town, or even the state—and who knows, maybe even the world.
                         —A Chassidic Rabbi on His Deathbed

CHAPTER FOUR

RECONSTRUCTION DAY: THE EVENT

Let us run with patience the race that is set before us.
—Hebrews 12:1

AN OVERVIEW

The schedule for reconstruction day can only be approximate. For any number of reasons, the sequence of events within a reconstruction may take a different order with any given star and/or guide. Certain sections may be short in one reconstruction and long in another. Any reconstruction will take at least 10 hours, excluding breaks. The schedule we present here is simply intended to show a general flow.

9:00 a.m.	Warm-up trust exercise for the large group; Introduction (history and evolution of reconstruction)
9:30	Reasons & Issues (30 minutes)
10:00	Family of Choice (1 hour—sculpture)
11:00	Current Family (1 hour—sculpture)
Noon	LUNCH BREAK
1:00 p.m.	Family of Origin (1 hour—sculpture)
2:00	Chronology (4-6 hours—psychodrama)
6:00	DINNER BREAK
7:00	Generational patterns (1 hour—sculpture)
8:00	Celebration and Closure (1 hour—sculpture)

On reconstruction day, people have gathered together and are ready to start this process they have heard so much about. We begin with a sharing about some of the ground rules for the day.

One of the important things for people to know is that they are embarking on what is primarily an emotional healing journey together. Up until this time, they have had a chance to do some learning, to hear some lectures, to find out more about the therapeutic process. This day, though, is not for taking notes or for doing a lot of thinking. This is a day to let feelings emerge. Most people will have a particular part and/or role to play during today's process. All in all, maybe two or three participants choose not to play a role. It's of the utmost importance that no one at a family reconstruction workshop or event be forced to do anything he or she is uncomfortable with. This will be a day of feeling and re-feeling, a day for re-living memories. There will be times of surprise, hurt, anger, sadness, excitement, grief, anguish, joy, and gratitude.

The reconstruction experience will combine guided imagery, Gestalt therapy, psychodrama, group therapy, music, positive reinforcement, and self-worth exercises.

The reconstruction experience will combine experiential sculpture, guided imagery, Gestalt therapy, psychodrama, group therapy, positive reinforcement, and self-worth exercises. By the time the day is over, each person will have a more complete picture of him- or herself.

The reconstruction event is a 12-14 hour session that allows one person to re-experience his or her past, take a look at the present, and make plans for how it can be in the future. The goal on this day is to use specific therapeutic methods that will allow this star to move beyond thoughts, feelings, and behaviors that are self-defeating in order to heal. In this way will the star be able to see and make new choices in life.

Reconstruction is a powerful, reality-based form of therapy. The experience will help the star and others present to resolve some relationship issues within their family of origin as well as in their current families. They will start to realize their core self-worth and begin to understand why and how they are trapped in self-defeating behaviors.

The psychodrama of the star will be recreated all day, afternoon, and evening. Once selected, the star has begun to amass information about his or her family of origin and current family. If the job has been done well, the star has a family tree, anecdotes, stories, and memories.

Morning Events	Afternoon Events	Evening Events
Present	Past	Future
How is life today in every area?	What has happened in my life that impacts on who I am today?	What kind of future do I want for myself?
"MAP"	"CHRONOLOGY"	"CLOSURE"

1. Reasons for doing a reconstruction
2. Family of Choice
3. Current Family
   Possible Other
   Families
4. Professional Family
5. Ex-Family(ies)
6. Family of Origin
	1. Establish conditions at "birth" of the star
	2. Face old wounds and re-experience feelings; find celebrations and re-experience feelings
	  - Childhood
	  - Young Adult Years
	  - Adult Years
	    a) Relationships
	    b) Family
	    c) Career
	    d) Trauma
	    e) Addictions
	3. Experience and Heal Feelings
	    a) Grief
	    b) Sadness
	    c) Hurt
	    d) Anger
	    e) Abandonment
		1. Understand generational patterns
		  a) Mom's family history
		  b) Dad's family history
		2. Re-establish Family of Choice with Blood Family
		3. Celebrate
		  a) Certificates
		  b) Poster
		  c) Sharing of Group

GOALS		
1. Establish Inner Child Concept 2. Identify Current Problems and Painful Relationships 3. Establish the People in the Star's Life	1. Heal Inner Child 2. Connect with Oneself 3. Confront Denial 4. Establish Inner Power 5. Learn to Love & Appreciate Oneself	1. Increase Belonging 2. Increase Self-Worth 3. Experience Joy
METHODS USED		
SCULPTURE & TEACHING	PSYCHODRAMA & GESTALT	SCULPTURE & TEACHING

For many stars, reconstruction day is a day of forgiveness, of letting go, of experiencing forgotten love, and of remembering sadness long imagined to be buried and anger that has been difficult to face. The day will bring up many issues the star probably thought were no longer present. But from all of this re-experiencing and re-feeling, new healing will come.

Workshop participants will be playing specific roles all day long that are connected to the star's generational history. As mentioned earlier in this book, the "casting" experience can often be mysterious because somehow the person playing a particular role will turn out to have good reason in his or her own life to learn about that role. For example, if the star is a man who has cast someone in the role of his daughter, it may very well be that the woman cast as the daughter has issues with her father which she came to the workshop to explore.

For most people, memories will come flooding back. Little vignettes and dramas are reenacted all day long, punctuated with pauses when the group gives feedback on various scenes. Participants are asked not to analyze events, but, rather, to concentrate on the feelings that are coming up. Often the participants are able to work through as much or almost as much as the star can. We have often enough called the reconstruction process "emotional surgery"—it is the beginning of the true healing of the inner self.

There will be a great deal of inner-child work done on this day, and a very important role will be the development of the star's inner child, who will find and claim the part of the self that was abandoned in order to survive in a dysfunctional family. The voice of the inner child will gain power and strength and be able to express many things that were left unexpressed. A spontaneous voice that feels free to question what it doesn't understand, this voice may cry or express anger or learn to ask for what it needs or grieve many, many losses. Traumas will be faced, re-experienced, and healed. It will be a powerful day of therapy for all present.

THE ROLE OF THE GROUP PARTICIPANTS

There is, as Virginia used to say, a universal connectedness, a spiritual thread. She believed, as do we, that anybody can play any role. Yet it is important that those selected to play roles in the star's process throughout the day are meaningful somehow to the star. There should be some connection for the star with these people, either positively or negatively— whatever works to allow the star to do the work he or she needs to do.

Guides always give participants the option to decline playing a particular role, but they should encourage them to role-play because there are things to learn in playing a role. And though any role-player mostly just needs to be willing to express any feelings that arise while playing a role, there are also a couple of other guidelines.

1. Once a person is established as a character in the star's life, it is important that that person stay with that role throughout the entire reconstruction. Good reasons for declining a role include tiring easily, or being uncertain about one's own emotional state.

2. It has not been a good idea to have people switch genders in being assigned a role to play. Males must play males, and females must play females. There were a number of times before we made this a strong guideline in which role-players were often able to take on opposite gender roles in a reconstruction without difficulty, but then at a later date, after the workshop was over, they would have some difficulty around identity and relationship. Issues of sexual abuse can be tied into issues of gender identity; in any case, doubts and conflicts around gender-identity questions that may be arising for any number of reasons is something that is not necessarily readily apparent to staff. We have resolved that it is best if men play male roles and women play female roles. If the group is short a role-player of a specific gender, a chair with a sheet draped over it or life-sized dolls made specifically for reconstructions can be used.

GROUP FEEDBACK AND SHARING

It is very important to the reconstruction that group members share their perceptions. It's not so important to analyze or figure things out as it is to keep the role-players and the star in a setting that is most helpful for them to access feelings. We like sharing and feedback to be communicated in "I" statements that are attached to perceptions—"I see..." "I feel..." or "I hear..." This keeps people very connected to their feelings.

Many times the role-players are able to sense that something is happening inside the star, and can feel as though they themselves are feeling the star's feelings, sometimes even before the star does. The input of these people is extremely important.

> **The audience plays a very active role.**

Throughout the entire day there are going to be opportunities for vignettes and times when the whole audience will have a chance to share some grief or do some anger reduction. These should be followed by a "time-out" during which each person can share a little bit about what's going on for him or her at that point. In this style of reconstruction, the audience plays a very active role.

EMOTIONAL CATHARSIS

Throughout the day there are going to be moments of intense emotion. Examples of this include the star grieving the death of his mother. The guide will set up a funeral scene with the actual specific details of the star's mother's funeral. Perhaps ten or twelve people in the audience are also quietly crying to themselves because they, too, have lost someone significant. As the guide finishes the specific work with the star and his mother, the group can have what is called a "time out" or a "magic time." Allow the people who are feeling grief to file by a "coffin" made from chairs and blankets in the front of the room. Let each one in his or her own way have a very cathartic experience around the grief being felt.

Another example of a kind of collective catharsis that is frequently appropriate is a "magic" time between a grandparent and grandchild. This is a very touching, warm time. It's easy to pick up on it when there are a number of participants in a workshop who have or have had wonderful supportive relationships with their grandparents. If a star chooses to re-experience his or her loving relationship with a grandparent at some point in the reconstruction, invite any participant who is relating to approach another participant and be held for a bit while each one recalls and shares a moment of a certain kind of love and appreciation as they remember what it was like to be tenderly and affectionately loved by their grandparent(s).

In this way, throughout the day, the audience is woven in and out of the work and can experience their own cathartic moments. This is bonding for the entire group, including the star.

EMOTIONAL BLOCKS AND FAMILY SCULPTURES

Many of the more traditional forms of therapy include discussing issues, achieving insights, and deciding to make changes. These are very important aspects of recovery and are necessary for growth. Another dimension of healing is equally essential.

Throughout life, people repress numerous painful experiences that they are emotionally unprepared to handle. These experiences may range from verbal teasing and schoolyard shaming to the painful violation of sexual abuse. Like many other kinds of therapy, one goal of experiential therapy and the reconstruction process is to explore these events in a safe environment, to re-experience or recreate the helplessness of the past events, and to reclaim one's personal power—this opens the door to new choices, which in turn result in growth and change.

Reconstruction is a fast, intense process that can save time and spare people pain. And while the goals are the same as in other therapies, the process is often experienced as more powerful. Its medical analogue would be the agressive treatment choice for a given condition. Reconstruction is a kind of aggressive treatment of the psyche.

> ### *Reconstruction is a kind of aggressive treatment of the psyche.*

One powerful way of uncovering and unleashing long-buried memories and feelings is with family sculpture. Family sculpturing is done through role-play. As already discussed, various members of the star's life are cast with role-players from the workshop participants. Name tags identify the roles being played. The star informs the role-players briefly about the characters they are supposed to portray by sharing verbal or nonverbal messages he or she received from these people, and pertinent details about their relationships, circumstances, or events. Roles to be played can be selected from all areas of a star's life. Examples of sculptures include the family of origin, work family, support groups, extended family, and parts of self. Each member of each of the sculptures will have a role in helping the star walk through fear to move towards choice.

We often call these sculptures "teaching sculptures" because we are looking at the reality depicted through the sculpture and learning from it.

THE EVENT PROCESS

The reconstruction event begins with the guide setting up sculptures to depict each of the family configurations listed in the overview (the current family of choice, the current immediate family, and the current family of origin.) The guide will use all of his or her skills in reaching the goals of 1) establishing the inner child concept, 2) identifying current problems and "stuck" spots, and 3) establishing all of the important players in the star's life.

This portion of the event usually takes about 2-4 hours and begins to be educational when the star demonstrates feelings and the guide uses Gestalt, rage reduction, music, questions and answers, psychodrama, or whatever tools are necessary to bring the star to the depths of those feelings.

After a sculpture is in place, a guide works with the star using Gestalt, questions and answers, and maybe some psychodrama to elicit all the feelings the star has about the sculpture. A detailed discussion of psychodrama is presented later in this chapter, within the section on Family Life Chronology (this is the portion of the day devoted to learning and healing through the use of the psychodrama technique). It is up to the guide to determine when the sculptures in the first part of the day merit further work by exploration through psychodrama. If the star can learn a great deal by observing the teaching sculptures, then they will be serving their purpose. If the star is filled with anger, grief, sadness, or some other powerful emotion, then the guide may choose to move into a psychodrama in order to provide the star with an opportunity to express those feelings before moving on.

INNER-CHILD CONCEPTS

The inner child stand-in will appear in every sculpture. Sometime in the afternoon or evening on this day, the inner child and the star integrate, and the person playing the role of the inner child is through working in that way as the star can now act on his or her own behalf.

Still, the concept of an inner child can be difficult to grasp. It often provokes fear and resistance.

Each human was born a tiny, innocent being, open to the world around him or her. Each human being is also born into a particular environment, with a certain set of personality characteristics, and will undergo certain experiences. A developing child incorporates all three of these aspects of being to form his or her own picture of the world.

When a child is very young, caregivers are gods. The child depends on them utterly for his or her physical well-being and safety. This makes the caregivers tremendously powerful. The child also looks to primary caregivers (most often parents) for emotional stability and nurturance. Their approval or disapproval makes an indelible impression.

Information given to a young child by caregivers is completely absorbed. A child doesn't have the ability to analyze information and accept or reject various components of it depending on their "fit" with his or her own personality. (In painful families, the process of critical thinking is never taught or encouraged.)

Children begin to respond to similar kinds of information similarly, and this pattern can continue well into adult life.

Some examples of messages learned as children and carried through to adulthood are listed below, along with likely behavioral adaptations (which, in these examples, are usually pretty maladaptive).

Message:	Possible Behavior:
"You're stupid."	No motivation or workaholism
"Don't cry."	Cold aloofness; shame around feelings
"You're nothing but trouble."	Argumentative or perfectionistic
"Best little boy [girl]"	Can't take risks; must please

Message:	Possible Behavior:
"Something bad is going to happen"	Negative thinking, critical; cautious; fearful
"Family comes first."	Lack of intimacy; enmeshment with family of origin; guilt
"Work first, play later."	Busy-ness; tension; workaholism; emotional unavailability
"It's not okay to touch."	Sexual inhibitions or sexual acting out; touch-starved

If one considers the term "defense" in light of its definition around the notion of providing protection, it seems positive enough. In psychology, *defense mechanisms* are developed by people in order to survive. Each of us learns our own special behaviors and beliefs that allow us to survive the painful circumstances in which we may grow up; in this way, our defenses are to be applauded rather than scorned. The problem is that circumstances change over time, and more often than not, our defenses become so rigid over time that they don't change; in this way our defense mechanisms prove to be obstacles in our path towards freedom.

Trauma can interrupt the development of a "free" child. If a child grows up with illness, abuse, death, poverty, addiction, etc., he or she will develop a whole set of beliefs about the world based on these experiences. Based on traumas or traumatic circumstances, a child makes unconscious decisions that affect his or her entire life. For example, if a child grows up in poverty, there can be several ways in which the adult the child becomes may still be reacting. Workaholism may develop in order to gain material wealth believed necessary for a sense of security; a lack of ambition might develop because the person's sense that he or she will always be poor can lead to little, if any, exertion towards accomplishing anything; or earlier deprivation might push the person to obtain material goods at any cost, including taking from others, embezzling, income tax evasion, etc. In another example, if a child loses a parent at an early age, the adult this child becomes might seek early parenting behaviors from all relationships as he or she grows older. This can interfere with later primary relationships and adult friendships.

Somewhere within each adult is the innocent child who came to the world open to all it had to offer. This child knows the pain, the joy, and the truth of what came to pass. This child has been wounded and has been waiting to be released for a long time.

The inner child is simply the concept by which we understand who we would have been had all the messages and trauma not shaped our belief systems. The goal of therapy is to let go of our "characters" or facades and our set of absolute responses. It is to heal the wounded child and to set ourselves free. Often when a person first begins to get in touch with his or her inner child, a doll or stuffed animal is chosen to make the connection. Such an object may be necessary for a while, but it becomes important to make clear that this child is part of any adult's personality and not a separate entity. Much growth takes place with the acknowledgement of this integrated interpretation of the self.

FAMILY SCULPTURES

Whatever "family" is being sculpted, there are different kinds of sculptures and sculpturing to make a visible picture of a scene in order to understand a concept of system. The different kinds of sculptures are: 1) "taking a photograph"; 2) doing a living sculpture; and 3) entering a psychodrama.

A STILL SCULPTURE

1) *"Taking a photograph."* Ask the star to describe different members of his or her family system (this can be the family of origin, the current family, a work family, etc.). Have the star describe each member of the family using very specific adjectives to suggest appearance, behavior, and personality. Is the person happy? Blaming? Passive? Strong? Controlled?

    The star will ask someone in the group to play each part, and bring these people up front. From the description given, the guide will position the role-players into a configuration that best protrays the essence of the star's experience. The guide can keep checking with the star to make sure they're getting it right. Exaggerate the positions until the point is made. Make sure that the positions of characters and the distance between people is correct.

    Again, it is wise to use an inner child role-player for the star so the star can stand back to get a clear picture of the whole system. There are many ways to symbolize truths about people through the sculptures. Someone kneeling on the ground is playing a victim or martyr. Another role-player can point his or her finger to depict someone who is very blaming. Use lots of props and costumes, body language, and facial expressions. Everyone holds position until the role-players begin to feel very absorbed in their roles. So far, there is no talking. If role-players are still in their positions, a "picture" or "photograph" begins to emerge for the star, and a great deal can be learned.

2) Words can now be added to transform this into a *"living sculpture."* The star may talk to the people in the sculpture and the people in the sculpture may respond so that a dialogue takes place. The guide can take the star around and have the star express feelings towards each of the people in the sculpture. It's important, in any case, for the guide to stay close to the star in order to begin to sense or feel what is happening for the star, perhaps before he or she knows. Role-players share with the star their feelings from the perspectives of the characters they're playing. The guide, too, adds perceptions and asks for feedback from the group members not participating as role-players in this sculpture.

3) Thirdly, take the sculpture another step into *psychodrama.* Actually set up a scene where all of the role-players begin to interact with each other. Sometimes Sharon lets the star just watch and observe and feel; other times she finds it more appropriate to put the star right in the middle of the action, letting him or her become involved as one of the people in the sculpture. If the star is able to identify and express his or her feelings, then there is no need for the inner child stand-in. If the star is being introduced to a new way of understanding a situation, then the inner child stand-in can be used to demonstrate so that the star can see a new picture.

A LIVING SCULPTURE

This exercise is an example of a family sculpture. A family-of-origin sculpture has been chosen for illustration. This is a fictitious family, although parts of it may be very familiar to the reader.

First, each family member is described with pertinent details.

Mom:
Overweight; drinks; critical; "Do it right."

Dad:
Drinks a lot; angry; busy; "I'm tired."

Star:
Youngest; shy; scared; loner, in choir

Sister:
Oldest; nice; helpful; good in school

Brother:
Middle child; busy; angry; not home much; loves sports

To set up the sculpture, a workshop participant is chosen to play each role. A scene or age would be selected by the star or the guide (e.g., the dinner table). A dining room table would be created using various props for the table, chairs, plates, etc. Each person would be seated in the appropriate position at the table. The star would give a brief description of the scene, suggesting what might be happening, and who would be saying what to whom. (As above, the inner child stand-in can be used if the guide thinks it might be more useful.)

A FAMILY-OF-ORIGIN SCULPTURE

Then the sculpture would be brought to life. The role-players would speak what they feel in the roles they are playing. The star would be encouraged to feel, to confront, to make connections as to how these old patterns translate into present-day behavior, and to decide what changes need to be made.

FAMILY-OF-CHOICE SCULPTURE

The initial sculpture of the reconstruction is, in most cases, the current family of choice. This simply means all of the people whom the star has *selected* to be in his or her life (i.e., not usually family-of-origin members) and who are important and supportive at the present time. This can include friends, support groups, sponsors, therapists, intimates, fellow club members, or anyone that gives all the necessary love and support possible in the context of an adult relationship. People in a family of choice give at least as much as they receive from the star. These are the people who are "there" through thick and thin; they are healthy enough themselves to be available when the star needs them.

Work families are often part of families of choice. These include co-workers, peers, employers, employees, supervisors, or any other special people who are supportive in the work setting.

Another element in a family of choice are the people we consider "angels." Angels are a special category of people who have entered the star's life to bring some message or gift. It may be the neighbor who brings cookies or a person who offers financial help or a person who encouraged and praised the star at a low point. This kind of love often comes from unexpected sources. From a spiritual standpoint, children could not survive without love and nurturance. A star has already survived, so the assumption can be made that some angels have passed through his or her life. It is the decision of the guide to use a sculpture of angels within the family of choice—it may be better to wait until a low point in the reconstruction when the star could benefit from being reminded of those who have given special gifts.

Angels are those very special people in our lives who have touched us in a profound way. They may have crossed our paths only briefly; they may have known us since we were born.

> **Angels are those very special people in our lives who have touched us in a profound way. They may have crossed our paths only briefly; they may have known us since we were born.**

Sometimes an angel is a family member (an aunt, a grandfather, a long-lost cousin) who loved us unconditionally. Maybe this relative reminds us from time to time that we are special, or might have validated our experience of the family as problematic. Perhaps they just thought we were cute or funny; perhaps they just *listened* to us.

An angel can be a teacher who noticed our sparkle or our pain. Maybe he or she encouraged us to keep going when we wanted to quit, or noticed a special talent and nurtured it. A pet can be an angel in our lives. Perhaps as a child the only one who really "understood" was the family dog. The only place we got hugs may have been the family cat. The only one who forgave us instantly when we did something wrong may have been the animal we loved so much.

Our cluster of angels can be filled with people from our past or present. Sometimes our angels are just people who have been very special in our lives. They may have died, or we may have otherwise lost contact with them. Sometimes they are people we see often. Brief encounters can also be very meaningful; sometimes an angel is someone who seems simply to "pass through" our lives fleetingly, but bestows upon us some gift or grace. Angels are special gifts from our Higher Power, and need to be cherished and acknowledged. Without angels, many of us might not have survived the traumas in our lives.

Exercise 4.1: Your Angels

Make a list of up to five angels in your life. Remember that their gift(s) can be ongoing or may have been fleeting. Write about why each one is an angel for you, and the effect each one has had on your life. When you're through, share the list with a friend. You may wish, wherever it's possible, to contact these angels and thank them.

It is important to begin the reconstruction by recognizing one's already-existing safety net. The family of choice reflects the support available to the star. This family will be present during the reconstruction and they will appear later, at the end, to celebrate.

The family of choice is also indicative of the star's ability to choose healthy relationships beyond family or marriage. It shows the star's capacity for reciprocal caretaking, good boundaries, getting needs met, having fun, learning, and finding healthy substitutes for parents or siblings.

> **It is important to begin a reconstruction by recognizing the safety net of one's family of choice.**

There is, on the other hand, the possibility that the family of choice may demonstrate patterns that are not so healthy. Even the very first sculpture may bring up many issues (e.g., poor boundaries, a limited ability to get one's needs met, etc.). Sometimes the family of choice is a place for a lot of work and change. In any case, there will usually be at least one or two people in the star's family of choice who are genuinely supportive for the star, so it's hardly ever a negative effort.

Occasionally, emotional "discharge" work (i.e., demonstrating the feeling being experienced and not just talking about it) is done during these sculptures. This work also occurs at other times when the guide may determine that it's appropriate.

The goal of this sculpture is to provide an opportunity for the star to acknowledge supportive relationships, to identify problems and/or problematic relationships which are currently present in his or her life, to practice setting appropriate boundaries, and to formulate plans to address those problematic relationships which are identified.

The guide will use sculpture guidelines to spatially situate all members of the star's family of choice. This is usually the time when the star will bring up the role-player for the inner child stand-in for the first time. This role-player may begin by standing in the center of the room. The guide will identify where the star lives so that the participants will understand geographical distance if some of the star's family of choice are located in different cities, states, or even countries. The guide identifies each person in the family of choice, and then gives some brief description of both the person (e.g., what he or she does for work), and his or her relationship to the star.

After placing all of the family of choice, the guide brings up the star to look at the sculpture. The guide instructs the star to choose a person to address first. The star begins, "I feel ..." and describes any feeling about this person—it could be gratitude, love, laughter, joy, etc. In this case, the guide will coach the star to express the meaning of this person in his or her life, and then to position the person in relation to the inner child so that the approximate distance reflects the emotional closeness the star desires. If that closeness does not currently exist, the guide will help the star explore how to achieve it. Maybe a letter or phone call following the reconstruction is suggested. If so, this goes into an after-care plan. (Remember that a staff person is assigned to make notes over the course of the entire day about all agreed-upon tasks for the star's after-care [what the star will do after returning home]).

Sometimes the star needs to express some negative feelings to members of his or her family of choice. Anger, hurt, or fear may be revealed. Sometimes the guide needs to help the star to recognize the necessity for this. This could be done through direct talk, decision-making, or discharging feelings. In any case, the implication will be for some work when the star returns home.

The guide may wish to help the star decide if this person should be included in the family of choice. And while probably most of us have people who are healthy for us in our lives, certainly there are some who never want to let go of anyone, and never relinquish any relationship. But this can be like putting on too many coats, because while the joys are many, the burdens of relationships are also heavy. And too many are too heavy. We do naturally "outgrow" certain relationships, or our lives change in ways (work, primary relationships, children, geographical location, etc.) that demand our attention elsewhere. In any case, good-byes are part of life. We cannot keep every good person who has ever been meaningful to us.

One parent tells a story about his three-year-old daughter beginning pre-school. He asked if she had made any friends. She said yes, her best friends were Heather and Cassie, but not Joey and Betsy. He said to her that she could have a lot of best friends. She replied, "No, when we hold hands in the circle, I can only have two best friends because I only have two hands!" What this child instinctively felt and expressed was the reality that we each have a limited ability to "hold hands" with others. Relationships require energy and time, so adults must be selective. We may have room for more than two, but we may become overwhelmed when numbers grow too high.

Some people have relationships in which they take care of everyone. These people tend not to be assertive; they do not ask for what they need, but are, instead, more comfortable meeting the needs of others. There can be a lot of denial around relationships and how well they may or may not be functioning. Family-of-choice sculptures help sort, cull, and negotiate until there is a supportive, manageable network around the star.

CURRENT FAMILY SCULPTURE

It's also extremely important to look at the people with whom the star lives. This may include the family of origin or other relative(s), roommates, or the star's own family (partner and/or children). The star may be living alone, in which case we often include dating partners, neighbors, or pets (who often turn out to be very significant and, if present, will be included regardless of the make-up of the human members of one's current family!). For those who are not involved in an ongoing, committed relationship, the current family may also look somewhat different. In the current family sculpture, however, we are trying to look at the people who are physically closest to the star, and to whom the star is closely connected, whether positively or negatively. In any case, this sculpture will reflect the way the star's life looks at the present time.

This sculpture will also include people from the past who might still be tied to the star. For many stars, by the time reconstruction actually takes place, there may be a history of previous relationships or marriages. There are often ongoing feelings associated with these ties, some of which may even be current (financial arrangements, children, etc. can be means by which relationships that might otherwise be completely "over" are not over at all, but have transformed). Grief over the death of a loved one may not be fully resolved.

It is important to include any person who is a significant part of the star's current life in the current family sculpture.

So, a "current family" may include an ex-spouse, a deceased spouse, children from a previous relationship, an ex-in-law who still has close contact with the star's children, an ex-lover who may still be calling or to whom the star still runs when things are rocky in his or her present relationship, etc. It is necessary for the star to see that these ties remain, to assess the necessity of these ties, and to put these relationships into proper perspective, because it is possible to avoid intimacy in one's current primary relationship (or as manifest in the absence of such a relationship) by complicating it with over-involvement with the past. Again, the feelings may be positive or negative.

The star is invited to examine the relationships he or she has with each person or animal represented in the sculpture. The way we structure our lives is an indication of our emotional state. This sculpture reveals something about our current life structure, and, so, our current emotional state. It is important to show the problems each of the members of this sculpture might have, and any diseases or compulsive medicators. Grown children who have moved from home and possibly married or had children of their

FAMILY-OF-CHOICE SCULPTURE

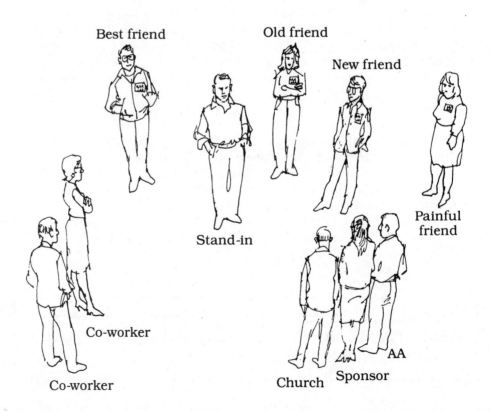

A CURRENT FAMILY SCULPTURE

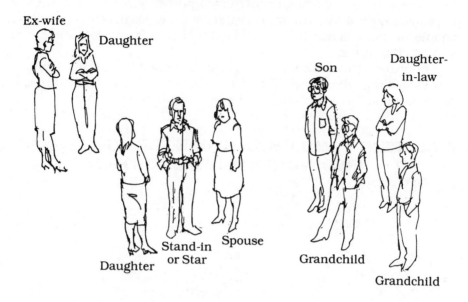

Ex-wife

Daughter

Son

Daughter-in-law

Daughter

Stand-in or Star

Spouse

Grandchild

Grandchild

A SINGLE PERSON'S CURRENT FAMILY SCULPTURE

Friend

Date

Stand-in or Star

Neighbor

own are still described in detail. The star should examine the relationships he or she has with each member of the sculpture, feel the feelings surrounding each, say good-bye in some cases, set boundaries in others, thank some people for the roles they have played in his or her life, feel rage about others, and reclaim power.

The goals of this sculpture are to establish the star's family members, to express feelings about these family members, and to establish patterns for psychodrama(s) to occur later in the reconstruction.

A CURRENT FAMILY SCULPTURE FOR A PERSON WITH INVOLVEMENTS FROM THE PAST

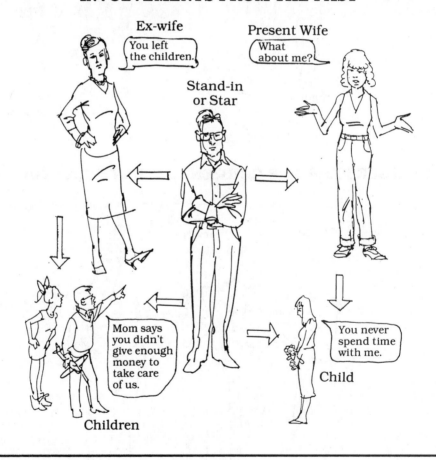

Exercise 4.2: Your Past Relationships

Examine your own "ex-" relationships. Are there any leftover attachments that keep you from being fully available for intimacy with others? If so, write about your feelings concerning your part in this present tie with the past. Then decide what action(s) you need to take in order to reach resolution. Finally, make a list of resources you will use to help you proceed (e.g., counseling, a sponsor, writing, making amends, etc.)

CURRENT FAMILY-OF-ORIGIN SCULPTURE

The third and final sculpture of the first phase of reconstruction is the present-day picture of the star's family of origin. This includes parents, step-parents, and full, half-, and step-siblings, their spouses, and their children.

The purpose of this sculpture is to establish the characters in the star's life, to describe the relationship for the star to members of his or her family, to elicit even more patterns of pain or dysfunction as noted in the previous sculpture, and to elicit the expression of any current emotions surrounding the star's relationship to his or her family.

As in the other sculptures, role-players for the necessary relatives should be placed in relationship to the inner child stand-in for the star. Use props such as bottles of alcohol, work-related items, sport items, aprons, crowns, money, etc. These can introduce or remind us of many of the relevant dynamics within the family of origin. Remember that props are used throughout the entire reconstruction process. The amount and type of prop(s) will be indicated by the star's story. In some reconstructions, a large number of props are indicated; in others, fewer are used. Some families are very colorful and involved in a varity of activities which makes it easy to visualize and create props. Other families are very drab and non-involved and it is difficult to imagine even a few props. In any case, each segment of the reconstruction has many possibilities.

The guide introduces the family members to the participants by describing their characteristics, their locations, and their current circumstance. Adjectives, provided by the star during the in interview, are given. Marriages and/or children are mentioned, as are any significant addicitons that might make these people emotionally unavailable.

The loss of any members of the star's family of origin may be dealt with at this time. If a parent or sibling has died, the star may do significant grief work at this time, or it may be delayed until the Chronology portion of the day if the star is not yet ready. This is also a good time to note relationships with in-laws, marriage partners, nieces, and nephews. These relationships, and possibly relationship patterns, may show the damage done in a dysfunctional family or may reflect a growing, healthy support system.

After placement of the family, the guide will let the star look at the situations and characters represented. He or she will need to express grati-

CURRENT FAMILY-OF-ORIGIN SCULPTURE

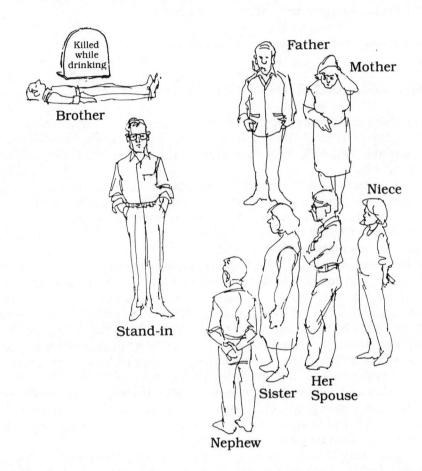

tude, anger, disappointment, or love at this point. This piece can elicit many feelings for stars; it is customary to discharge these feelings vocally or, if appropriate, with bataka-bat work.

Often key family issues will be established through this sculpture (e.g., emotional unavailability, neglect, the effects of abuse). This is the first scene in which the star will address family members and those painful patterns or unresolved feelings. The timing of work can be tricky at this point. Usually not much resolution takes place after feelings are expressed. Later in the reconstruction, the star will work on early life events and the family dynamics; this may include the setting of boundaries, or acts of acceptance and forgiveness. The work for the star gets more refined as the reconstruction moves into psychodrama.

WORK/PROFESSIONAL FAMILY SCULPTURE

The patterns we learn in childhood follow us throughout our lives, with the original dramas playing themselves out in many areas. One arena in which people may be less aware of this occurring is in work or professional families. On the day of reconstruction, there is also often a sculpture to explore the star's work history or work family. (Whether to include and develop such sculptures will be decided between the star and the guide. We simply adjust the schedule as needed. The same is true of ex-families. One of the creative and useful aspects of the reconstruction process is that it can be tailored to meet the needs of a given star.) Let's use the family roles to try to understand how this can be.

A *hero*, for example, may be overworked and underpaid. She just wants the approval and the awards. And no sooner does she win one than she focuses on the next. She may also be trying to keep everyone happy and smooth all the wrinkles. Unfortunately, the hero never allows much, if any, time to appreciate her own efforts. The "bag of prizes" (and this may be dramatized with props) is always being carried in an effort to prove self-worth. There is, however, quite often an uneasiness about being unworthy, and an insecurity about what has been built or established thus far. Trust is low, and fear is high. Ulcers, anxiety, heart conditions, hypertension, and colitis often plague the hero in his or her work setting. There is a need to please and a generalized feeling of hopelessness. If this person came from an alcoholic family, for example, and all of his or her striving, achieving, and awards did not change the family, the feeling of failure persists and it will be difficult for the hero to relax and enjoy any accomplishments.

The *scapegoat*, on the other hand, proceeds through life with a different set of rules. She is often angry, may have trouble holding a job, or may feel persecuted. She is rebellious, with a great capacity to "push buttons" of superiors, and often will have to pay the price. She generally doesn't receive the awards a hero strives for, and may, in fact, mock or ridicule the system that gives them. In the family, the scapegoat got attention by breaking rules, causing trouble, and fighting the system. When this is transferred to the work place, it can be very painful. She has real difficulty following rules and conforming. She may feel chronic dissatisfaction with her job(s) and have a vague sense of goals and aspirations for herself if she has any at all. If she does pursue awards, she may choose an unconventional means or route, and this can also get her into trouble. The scapegoat is angry on the outside and fearful on the inside. After all, if she does try to join the work family, she may once again be second-best to her hero co-workers; this is pain to be avoided at all costs. The result is often a stormy, painful history with superiors and co-workers.

The *lost child* has often learned to be quiet and complacent. He may be overlooked for promotions although he will most likely be a very competent worker. He will usually work quietly, independently, and responsibly. As in the family of origin, the work family may forget this person is around. Fitting in socially will most likely be a sensitive, if not painful, issue for this person. His role has not prepared him to be part of a group—any group—even if he wants to join. Fear may dull his aspirations to excel. In order to achieve, he would have to take the risk of allowing others to get to know him, and he simply doesn't know how to do this. There may be some repressed anger about not getting the job(s) for which he is qualified. Depressions may persist, which can be interpreted as lack of motivation. The work family may thus serve to reinforce the feelings of abandonment he carried from childhood.

The *mascot* may be outgoing, fun, easy to get along with, and still have trouble forming deep committed relationships, even in his work world. He may be very dependent and need constant guidance and approval. He may lose interest easily and never finish projects on time, or at all. Often he doesn't have the ability to switch from socializing to serious business, and may miss cues to settle down to hard work. Although charming, and often able to interview well, superiors and co-workers can tire of this person's inconsistencies and lack of seriousness. The mascot may have many goals and start towards all of them, from education to promotion, but he may not achieve any of them. Inside, the mascot is afraid that if he sets aside his mask, everyone will know that he doesn't understand the plot. He missed it in his family of origin by being born into the middle of the drama, and he feels the rest of his life is the same way. He continues to withdraw at his own expense.

The important point to all of these examples—and they are just examples—is that there is no escaping the pain we feel. Words won't do it, acting out won't do it, hiding won't do it, and charming won't do it. Many have tried chemicals, and they don't do it either. All of these ploys may work temporarily, but eventually we pay the price, which all too often is devastating and increases exponentially the pain we were attempting to cover in the first place.

The following sculpture was actually performed at a reconstruction, although we've changed the star's name for purposes of confidentiality. We offer it to the reader here as an illustration of how messages from the past can be carried to work choices and work environments.

Art grew up in a home where his mother was a compulsive overeater and his father was a workaholic. It was a quiet home. Anger was never expressed. Art and his brother were well-cared for physically. Art's father was kind, but too busy to spend time with him. Art became the focus of his mother's attention, to the point that she was overprotective and smothering. Because his brother was older and pretty much on his own from the time Art can remember, he always felt like an only child—a hero. His mother was often ill and Art felt responsible. He tried to be the best little boy, and he did very well in school. He tried to please his parents. He worked hard, and asked for little in return. Some of the messages he internalized were: *Be perfect, be a nice guy, work hard, please others, don't make waves, don't be angry, allow others' needs to control you, your needs are not as important as others'.*

Art became a physician! His issue was the work-race, so it was important to show how the messages learned in his family of origin influenced his job choice, work patterns, and response(s) to authority. To do this, he was asked (you can let the star do this or use the inner child stand-in for the star) to take a place in the middle of the room. A different person was asked to represent each of the different aspects of Art's work patterns or present work situation. Art was asked to run from one to the other, trying to feel the feelings around this aspect of his work, and to allow his feelings expression as they arose.

Art was asked how he felt about his work situation before and after the sculpture. Before, he used the terms "okay ... reasonable ... balanced ... best of all worlds." Afterwards, he used the terms "cumbersome . . . busy . . .

ART AT WORK - EXAMPLE OF A HERO CHILD'S ADULT PROFESSIONAL LIFE

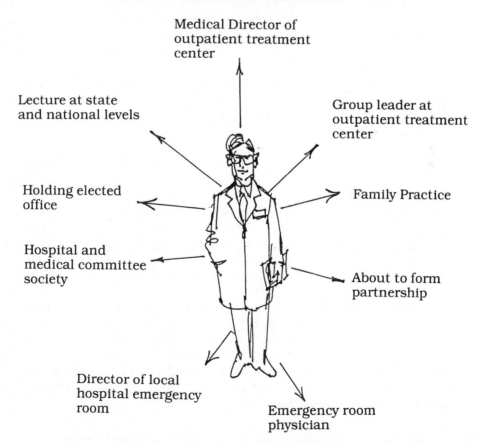

Medical Director of outpatient treatment center

Lecture at state and national levels

Group leader at outpatient treatment center

Holding elected office

Family Practice

Hospital and medical committee society

About to form partnership

Director of local hospital emergency room

Emergency room physician

suffocating . . . draining." In order to clear the way for change, Art was encouraged to set boundaries and to make new choices concerning these patterns or situations, his family of origin, and his grief and anger about repeating old patterns.

FAMILY LIFE CHRONOLOGY

With all of the roles now established, it is time to move into the chronology. This will be 4-6 hours of psychodrama, carefully moving the star through the important events of his or her life—re-living situations and re-experiencing feelings—that leads to healing (see note below). This is a very intense experience that touches each person in the room. Healing occurs for the star and the participants. Sometimes there is so much emotion in the room (e.g., if people in the audience are really angry that their parents are alcoholics, etc.) that it's important to stop the work with the star and do a "large group theme Gestalt." This may involve rage reduction, listening to music, or having a comforting, nurturing moment. The guide is constantly aware of the emotional pulse of the large group, and knows when to add such experiences.

For example, perhaps the star had been grieving the loss of a loved one and the audience members are feeling grief over their own lost loved ones. We might have the guide sit with the star while another guide or group leader shares with the audience ways to grieve, or reads a poem about grief, or, very often, plays a song that expresses grief. This can allow the whole audience to grieve simultaneously. When the group grief work is finished, the guide returns with the star to the reconstruction process.

Creating dynamic pictures of the star's life is an important part of the reconstruction process. Following the exact chronology of events in the star's life is not as important as supporting the themes that the guide has determined the star needs to see. For example, if the star's chronologies as submitted in preparation for the reconstruction event are filled with abandonment issues, the themes of abandonment would become more important than the straight listing of chronological events, and may be best addressed through theme pieces rather than psychodramas based on the family chronology outline. We discuss both techniques below.

Note: While we employ the technique of psychodrama largely to elicit feelings, we do not intend to re-traumatize anyone in the workshop, star or participants. Abuse issues are often important to address somewhere in the childhood pieces. Whether focusing on physical, verbal, or sexual abuse, a good rule of thumb is to do enough to allow the star to feel feelings, discharge fear and rage, and take back power, but not to do so much that the star feels re-traumatized.

Events around the time of birth. Often the first *psychodrama* of the chronology section involves creating a picture of the events preceding and attending the birth of the star.

As mentioned earlier in this chapter, although not every sculpture concludes with a psychodrma, every psychodrama begins with a sculpture. This scene will introduce the star's parents as a couple and, unless the star is the oldest child, this sculpture will also show any siblings and their ages. The guide may wish to describe for the participants the generational business of family history for each parent e.g., issues of poverty or wealth, trauma, death, etc. will all be mentioned. Were grandparents happy when the two people met and got married? Was there shame or conflict at the time of their courtship and marriage? Were these people married for a reason other than love?).

It is helpful to put the marriage of the star's parents and the birth of the star into historical context. War or the Depression or the turmoil of the 60s

SCULPTURE FOR THE STAR'S BIRTH

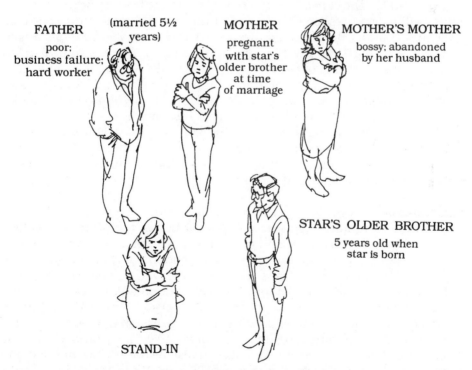

Every star's birth is unique; every star's family is unique. Understanding the star's family at the time of his or her birth can be helpful. Some families have a lot to offer a new child; others have very little. The guide may decide to move from a still sculpture into a psychodrama if appropriate.

or other pressing historical circumstances can greatly affect the events surrounding marriages and births. It is also helpful to know the cultural backgrounds in the two families the stars parents came from. Similar backgrounds may have made for an easy adjustment to a new life together. Differences in socioeconomic groups, religions, or ethnicities is sometimes a cause for friction.

Any unfinished business of either parent can be pointed out with a still sculpture or a psychodrama. The transition of a young adult into marriage and parenthood is one of the most important in life. A person's ability to differentiate and leave his or her family of origin can have a powerful impact on the next generation (e.g., some people cannot disconnect from their families of origin and remain enmeshed; sometimes a star's parents have been previously married and may not have successfully ended those prior relationships).

Usually a scene will describe how the couple met and got together; the status of their love, finances, family involvement(s); and any current addictions or compulsions. This is a time to assess the birth order of the star, and associated expectations. The oldest child brought into the world is often an "experiment" in the sense that the parents may try hard to be perfect. The child itself may be expected to be everything the parents couldn't be, to do what they couldn't do. Some children carry the unresolved shame, anger, hurt, and grief of the family of origin. Middle children are hard pressed to live up to the standards of the first child, especially if there is competition stemming from the first child being the family hero. If a child is born into an already established family wherein the parents are perhaps tired of child-rearing, he or she may feel unimportant or neglected.

This scene will describe whether the star was, as a child, wanted or unwanted, and how available the parents were to parent at the time of the birth. The guide may add movement, props, and talking to this sculpture, or simply use this as a teaching sculpture.

Childhood to age 5. As these are important formative years, it is important for the star to see, sense, and feel what early childhood was like. Issues of love and nurturance vs. neglect will be explored here.

This is a time when children are most dependent on primary caregivers. Children of this age form feelings of trust or mistrust, autonomy or dependence, initiative or guilt and shame. Early abandonment, unresolved fears, and misunderstanding about power and love are also determined at this time.

Psychodrama will often be used here for expression of feelings and for new learning. If any trauma or abuse took place in early childhood it will be acted out in the first piece or two. This will also be descriptive of the home atmosphere for the star during these early years. Were parents available, loving, and attentive, or distracted, demanding, and strained? The guide will use anything identified in the star's written material as important about this age.

SOME SAMPLES OF EARLY CHILDHOOD PIECES

ABANDONMENT

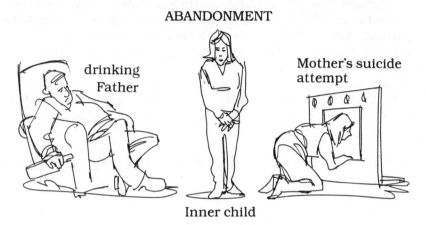

drinking
Father

Mother's suicide
attempt

Inner child

CARETAKING AT AN EARLY AGE

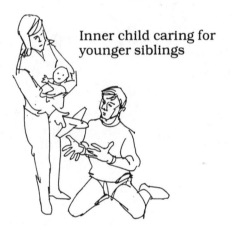

Inner child caring for
younger siblings

Middle Childhood.   Ages 5-12 will often be about moving into a larger social arena and going to school, making friends, and beginning to learn about the world. Younger siblings may be born, and older siblings may leave home.

Note: Again, in terms of abuse issues at this age, it is important to remember that the goal of setting up abuse psychodrama is not to push the star to re-live the event but to feel enough of the old feelings and yet be able to change the scene by re-claiming the inner child. The star must see and act as a victim no more, but as an adult who can claim victory over the abuse; leave shame behind by knowing it was never the fault of a little child; and be freed of repression.

Reconciliation of the star with his or her inner child, which was mentioned earlier, generally takes place around this time in the Chronology portion of the day. The guide builds upon pieces from early childhood until the star breaks down and reunites with the inner child. Then the guide leads the star and audience in a "magic moment." The guide should be sure the participants are connected on a feeling level to the star.

A "magic moment" at this point would signal the integration of the inner child and the adult person. The inner child stand-in and the adult star might face each other. The star would thank the inner child stand-in for contributing to his or her new awareness, which has been available in no small part because the person playing the inner child has been willing to

ILLUSTRATIONS FOR MIDDLE-CHILDHOOD PIECES

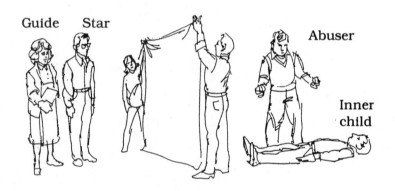

Guide   Star   Abuser

Inner
child

Guide

Star holds his own
inner child

share feelings that might have triggered memories or feelings for the star. The star can thank the inner child role-player for helping to clear up confusion and inner conflict.

At this point some teaching will take place about abuse recovery for all of the participants. It is also no longer necessary for the role-player who represents the star's inner child to function in this way, and at this point he or she can act as an audience member and the star can participate on his or her own behalf.

The teen years. This time period is meant to be filled with risk, rebellion, and searching. It is a time of tremendous physical and emotional changes. The adolescent no longer needs or wants to be under the constant attention of the parent(s) as his or her framework begins to shift from family to peers. Major struggles can arise because often the teen wants this shift to occur overnight, and the parent can permit it only slowly, if at all. Power struggles develop in which the parent may feel rejected and unappreciated and the teenager may feel stifled and misunderstood. The parent might see this as a re-visitation of a much earlier developmental stage the child went through, sort of a "terrible two's with a mouth." The adolescent is just trying to assert independence, but doesn't have all the skills necessary and is sometimes awkward, thoughtless, or careless.

According to Erik Erikson, the teenager is searching to find his own identity. It is natural to be pulling away from parents and looking towards peers for answers. Hopefully he will reach a point toward the end of this stage where he can sort through information and learn to trust himself, his own opinions and values.

Very often the innocent (inner) child has already long been lost to painful experiences, and has been put away, buried or stifled until the teen is no longer in touch with him- or herself. These shifts may have come late in adolescence, but whenever they happened, in a reconstruction it is necessary to show the star the loss of choice and the loss of self that went along with this movement.

Showing the ideas that are formed from life experience as the star moved through puberty and the normal, awkward stages of adolescence is important. Often there are extremes to look at here—sexual acting out and promiscuity, or disinterest and sublimation of sexual interest. Sexuality is often a *theme piece* in this section of the chronology. The power of a piece is often lost if given in chronological time. Theme pieces metaphorically demonstrate, through experiential role-playing, the story of repeated patterns.

For example, for a star who was a victim of incest as a child and has developed chronic low self-worth and a sense of helplessness in relationships with men, we might set up an incest situation between a female star and her brother. We might demonstrate his power over her when she was young, and her helplessness at the time. With this sculpture in view, another sculpture can be set up to show a later incident in which a young man verbally abused the star (as a young woman) and shoved her around. We might also point out at this time her repeated helplessness and chronic low self-worth. Keeping both of these sculptures in view, we could show a third in which the grown star is in relationship to her current partner, who might be abusing her verbally, physically, or emotionally. We could then help her see her need to recapture her self-worth and take action in the direction of self-protection in order to give up her state of helplessness.

SEXUALITY THEME PIECE

DAD	CHURCH	INNER CHILD	GIRLS	MOM	FRIENDS
Sex is bad	Mortal sin		Scary	Emotionally too close ("You take care of me.")	Dirty jokes

The beginnings of disease for the vast majority of alcoholics, addicts, co-dependents, people with eating disorders, overachievers, and those with other compulsions take root during adolescence. It is vital to give the star a look at early influences that may have invited this behavior.

Adolescence is a time in which many important questions arise that need to be answered: Will I start smoking? Will I choose to drink alcohol or take drugs? Will I date someone who does any of the above? When will I choose to be sexually active, and with whom? What do I believe about birth control? Abortion? How do I protect myself from dangerous sexually transmitted diseases? Will I choose to go to college? Where? What will I study? Will I be accepted by my peers? Am I okay, or is something wrong with me?

The list goes on and on. The answers to many of these questions are greatly influenced by the life experiences a person had had until that point, for these help shape the teen's very view of him- or herself.

TEEN YEARS: MESSAGES AND CONFLICTS

Conflict: Sexual abuse
Message: "You are not
           loveable."

Conflict: No guidance
Message: "You are
           stupid."

Conflict: Nobody cares
Message: "Don't feel."

Conflict: Physical abuse
Message: "I'll give you
           something to
           cry about."

Exercise 4.3: Your Teen Years

Make a list of five major decisions you made during your teen years. Write your feelings about each decision, and the personal influences that led you to decide as you did.

Many adults carry guilt, shame, or remorse about some of the decisions they made as adolescents. They don't forgive themselves for simply being ill-equipped at the time to consider all consequences before acting. The star of a reconstruction is given the opportunity to go back and face the feelings that were buried around this time, and a chance to release the feelings and move towards forgiveness, especially of him- or herself.

One possible sculpture for teen years is to set up in a circle four of the choices that the star made during this period. A person can role-play each choice, wearing a sign with the choice written on it. Other role-players can be chosen to hold signs telling some of the influences that led to the choice. The star can move from scene to scene and try to sort out the confusion, facing feelings about making life decisions he or she may not have been emotionally prepared to make.

On the other hand, some have overcome nearly impossible childhoods by finding a talent or gift to make life bearable. These gifts are evidence of the triumph of the human spirit, the miracles of some divine or higher intervention. Often these gifts are discovered and/or developed in adolescence. A reconstruction celebrates along the way whatever got the star through tough times. In the past we've had stars read their poetry or share a painting they've done; whatever the gift or talent, when presented it is appreciated by the audience.

Young adulthood.   Well into the chronology at this point in a reconstruction, the work on adolescence may have shown already the major loss of innocence and demonstrated the move into a less than satisfactory lifestyle. But this can occur in young adulthood as well. On the other hand, this may have been a time for the star to "start over" in a life outside his or her family of origin, and may illustrate the strengths, gains, or compensations made by the star. Remember that the guide will wish to validate and affirm all of the things that have gone *right* in the star's history. Scenes from young adulthood may revolve around relationships, sexuality, and marriage or other significant commitments.

Adolescents' feelings about sex and their own emerging sexuality may be influenced by multiple messages and feelings about sex which may contradict each other. The guide can help the star acknowledge this confusing time and understand how it influenced choice and behavior then, and may even be continuing to do so now. For example, a succession of unhappy or abusive relationships could each have a representative role-player, and these players could all be lined up in a row to explore as a whole. This *"gauntlet"* technique saves time. Also bear in mind that it might feel shaming to the star to list over and over painful behaviors, and a thematic piece such as a gauntlet can avoid a lot of repetition in the reconstruction.

Gauntlets can be of common people, places, themes, or events. They are used to show the repetitive dysfunctional behaviors in which the star has engaged in an attempt to medicate the pain of early childhood. For example, often a star's life has held a repetitive series of dysfunctional primary relationships. The star may be presented with a representative picture of each of the relationships that identifies the specific characteristics but the gauntlet is, more importantly, a very efficient method for revealing a common theme.

A GUANTLET FOR DYSFUNCTIONAL
PRIMARY RELATIONSHIPS

| 1ST BOYFRIEND | HUSBAND #1 | HUSBAND #2 | BOYFRIEND |
| drinking, using drugs | immature | abusive alcoholic | works & gambles |

This is often the point at which the star will realize he or she has been seeking to fill the hole of loneliness or shame. It may become clear to the star at this point that he or she has little or no concept of how to be in a mutually satisfying relationship with another loving person. This is a good opportunity to explore the issue, and a chance for the star to discover how he or she might be recapitulating unresolved childhood issues by choosing partners who are similar to one or both parents. On the other hand, there can be a great deal of relief if the star has found someone to share life with. The reconstruction may show romance or fun, good connections with another, or the fulfillment of dreams. A very good scene for this may be the re-enactment of a wedding or other commitment ceremony. It is always good in a reconstruction to celebrate a happy time.

Leaving one's family of origin is dealt with in this section. Whether happy or painful, the event is significant. The health of a family can be measured in part by its ability to allow children to become adults and separate. In terms of the star, we explore what efforts he or she made to become a fully functioning adult. Work, school, and career decisions are primary in early adulthood. Attitudes about the self can be seen in the choices made in one's early twenties.

And, again, this transitional time can also mark the onset or progression of disease. Although compulsions and addictions are understood to be rooted in one's family of origin and likely to begin during teen years, young adulthood is the time for the progression of the disease to become fairly well established.

A CELEBRATION OF A HAPPY MOMENT

Adulthood and final pieces. As the chronology winds down to the ending phase, any themes that remain unfinished or issues that have not yet been fully dealt with in the reconstruction are completed. Again, the people, places, and events that represent the star's life experiences are presented in living pictures or sculptures.

Work life may be explored in psychodramas at this time rather than in the morning session of sculptures; the star is provided an opportunity to discharge unresolved feelings towards the characters as they are presented, to finish "unfinished business," and to establish boundaries if necessary.

There is no other event as dramatic in hope or pain to family generations as the birth of children. It can be the hallmark of possibilities for love and change; it can spell the unhappy continuation of family pain. With few exceptions, everyone who becomes a parent wishes to be the best parent possible. The birth of children and the star's role as parent will have been dealt with to some degree in the current family sculpture in the morning phase of the reconstruction. Because feelings are expressed as they come up throughout the day, much of the emotion around children may have been completed by this time. One alternative at this point would be to use this section of the reconstruction as an historical re-telling. And although it can be painful and guilt-ridden, often this section serves otherwise, as a celebration, providing some relief to the intensity of the chronology.

In any case, it is important to demonstrate how the star has functioned as a representative generation within his or her family system. All of the patterns from previous parenting, the compulsive diseases, family secrets, or shame are either resolved or passed along in some form to the next generation. At this point the star can choose to celebrate the hope to be different from his or her own parents, and to provide his or her own children with healthier experiences. Often when the star became a parent, his or her inner child was still in pain and hoping for the love and nurturance that he or she is now required to provide to this young being.

The guide should affirm that the star is probably doing a better job of parenting than his or her own parents did. But it may be necessary to look at the barriers to a good relationship with one's children. If, as a parent, the star has brought unfinished business to his or her children, it is important to view this with understanding and acceptance. For example, a person raised in poverty might heap material possessions on her child. A person who was abused might fail to set limits or to discipline for fear of abusing his own children. Parents seem to react to their own unhappy childhoods either by repeating the experiences they had, or by overcompensating with opposite experiences. A good sculpture of the star's relationship to children is to show the circumstantial choices available at the time of the birth(s) and child-rearing, to line up the star, the star's inner child, the star's children, and to offer the instruction, "Children cannot parent children."

Grief pieces are used throughout the reconstruction. If strong feelings of loss are demonstrated during the family of choice sculpture, the guide will use the grief piece then. Most often, however, the grief is shown at some point during the chronology. It is up to the guide's intuition to decide the most effective use of grief work. One thing the guide should be aware of is the many contexts in which grief can arise. Grief pieces are not always about the loss of a person. Pets, belongings, time, relationships, health . . . a wide variety of losses need to be grieved. Sometimes the star feels pain around not having had any children. When disease, lifestyle decisions, or physical incapabilities (as opposed to a freely made choice) have prevented the star from having children, a grief and mourning piece can be helpful. Using one or more role-players to represent the child or children the star never had, the star can say whatever words are appropriate.

A GRIEF PIECE FOR THE LOSS OF A LOVED ONE

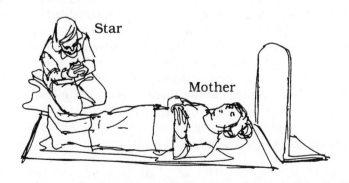

The star may have grief and guilt around the loss of a child or children to miscarriage or abortion or adoption. An effective psychodrama around the loss of a child to abortion or miscarriage can be a ceremony in which a doll (at Onsite we use a special cloth doll wrapped in a blanket) is held by the star. If appropriate, the doll can be turned over to some kind of Higher Power (e.g., in a baptism ritual). Members of the audience are often connected to feelings around such losses.

A GRIEF PIECE FOR THE LOSS OF AN UNBORN CHILD

Grief for others who have died usually consists of a role-player for a lost loved one lying on the floor with a sheet or gravestone prop. The star is asked to express his or her feelings about this person, and to verbalize the significance of the loss. A quiet time is arranged for the dead person to "come to life" for a magic moment and for the star to talk to or hold the person. If it feels appropriate, the role-player may respond with words of love or apology. This is also a good time for a connection to the inner child, who will need comfort and nurturance from the star. Soft music can be played, and the members of the audience can be invited to find another member to share the sadness they may be feeling from this piece.

Grief is a core feeling. When the star can grieve at depth the losses he or she has experienced, and empathize with his or her own inner child around these losses, a major piece of the reconstruction has been accomplished. The star will often continue this work with his or her therapist following the reconstruction. Disease pieces are also important in the late stage of the chronology. The guide will show through sculpture the progression of the disease and how the life of the star has been affected. For example, attaching the inner child to a trash can with a rope can represent all of the good things in life they have thrown away because of the disease. Covering the inner child with a sheet or black cloth represents the buried or forgotten innocence of the young self. A circle of role-players representing compulsive behaviors can surround, taunt, and bother the inner child. Pillows can be piled on top of the child, burying the innocence and feelings.

A PIECE FOR MOVING THROUGH A "STUCK SPOT"

Inner child
stand-in

Disease

Many times over the course of a reconstruction day, the guide and the star will come to "*stuck spots.*" Most often the star is stuck in some kind of denial. He or she just doesn't see a relationship as abusive, or cannot figure out how to change behavior, or how to make a decision that is crying out to be made. The participants and the guide may be very aware of certain places the star needs to be aware of feelings; meanwhile, the star is numb.

The most basic solution to stuck spots is to present enough visual pictures to allow the star to "get it" or move forward or relinquish the denial. This requires patience. Sometimes exaggerating the "stuckness" helps. Let the star walk in circles, sit in silence, or repeat some other action again and again and again and again. The use of participants can also be helpful, and gentle feedback from those who are watching can be a tolerable kind of confrontation. Rarely, the guide will need to leave the star stuck in some area, although the star should always be asked to commit to further work on this spot.

Near the end of the day, the star is presented with two pictures that represent the *generational patterns* of his or her family history. One at a time, the star is invited to look at and react to his or her mother's and then father's families of origin. After the star has worked so hard at expressing his or her feelings and, possibly, discharging a wide range of feelings towards his or her parents specifically, the reconstruction also asks the star to look carefully at the families those parents were born into. These sculptures will go back at least to the star's great-grandparents using the information gathered in the pre-interview material. The guide then provides the star an opportunity to identify the strong and weak patterns that have been passed down through the generations of his or her family, and an opportunity to symbolically return those negative generational inheritances the star chooses not to continue to carry. In this way, the gifts that have been positive are also affirmed.

RESOLUTION

The reconstruction event will begin to move toward closure when the following goals are met:

1)   Healing of the inner child and commitment of the star to the future care of the self.
2)   As much denial has been confronted as seems possible.
3)   Inner power has been awakened and established.
4)   The star is able to love and appreciate him- or herself.

Family of Choice—Where to from here?   The next step is to bring back the family of choice that was addressed earlier in the morning. The new family of choice reflects the changes the star has made. The guide will ask back only the members of the family of choice the star has asked to keep, and add to this the people from the other sculptures and vignettes that will remain a strong part of the star's life. There may be people from the work setting, from the star's mother's family, the star's father's family, and from the star's own current family.

Using the family of choice as a base and bringing in each of the other people from the sculptures should show the large support system or "safety net" around the star. Many times the star has had to give up some people from the original family of choice. This makes those who remain all the more precious. This is the final picture of the day for the star to take with him or her; it offers all the strength and self-worth that comes from these close relationships. Take a photograph of this family at the end so that the star has an actual picture to carry.

The next step is some kind of affirmation for the star. There are many different ways to do this. One is to have all of the people present stand in two long lines and clasp hands above their heads to form an archway. Let the star walk through this long archway and connect with all the people forming it while a celebratory song is played. Another means of affirming the star can involve setting up a throne in the front of the room for the star to sit on. Participants can come up and give the star a short note of affirmation that the star can keep. Or have the star stand in the center of a large circle formed by the others and have the others approach the star and offer their affirmations verbally. A parade, with some good parade music, can also be very effective. Let the star hold a baton and lead the others around the room.

In any case, it is important to select some kind of self-worth-affirming exercise that has relevance to the star, to the particular group attending that reconstruction workshop, and to use this to close on a note of celebration.

AFTERCARE PLAN

Many changes will have taken place over the day. The commitments to change become the aftercare plan. It is a good idea to have someone on staff act as a scribe for any commitments made. The scribe records all commitments to change as the day progresses.

The guide is working with the star to develop ways they can change their lives from this point on. It helps to make behavioral changes as clear and as simple as possible. it also helps to place them in short, manageable time frames. It is Sharon's belief that people do best if they have very concrete and directive plans, and she asks each of her stars to put a time frame on each decision they have made during the reconstruction process. This is called "The 3-6-9-12 Plan."

Every single time a change is committed to throughout the course of the reconstruction, the star must assign a three-month, six-month, nine-month, or twelve-month time frame within which he or she commits to changing behavior or circumstance. At the end of the day, the scribe gives the star the record of his or her commitments, along with the notes about the agreed-upon time frames. People may make small decisions such as making amends to someone or choosing to confront someone about an issue; or they may make life-changing decisions such as saying good-bye completely to a family member, choosing to get married or divorced, choosing to change careers; or there may be decisions that are between these. No matter what sort, decisions are only as good as they are executed. As people learn over time, these executions become much easier. An example of an aftercare plan looks like this:

- Within 3 months, I'm going to tell my oldest child how much I appreciate him.
- Within 6 months I am going to resign from my job.

- Within 3 months I am going to make an amend with my sister.
- Within 3 months I am going to end a relationship with a friend that is destructive for me.
- Within the next 12 months I am going to ask _____ if she will marry me.
- Within the next 12 months I am going to explore changing my career.
- Within the next 3 months I am going to let my grandmother know how much I love her.
- Within the next 6 months I am going to start looking for a different place of residence.
- Within the next 6 months I am going to purchase a pet.

POSTER AND CERTIFICATES

At the conclusion, the guide will present the star with a poster. Some time ago, Sharon had a large, beautiful poster made that is given just to the stars—it shows an outdoor, evening scene, with a special star, the moon in the sky, and it says "*Overcoming all that is past . . . celebrating all that is to come . . . shine on!*"

Certificates that have been made ahead of time are also passed out. These are simply 8" x 10" sheets of paper that are like diplomas for having completed the process. Examples of what might appear on the certificate include:

> "Congratulations for choosing to do a reconstruction."
> "Congratulations for developing a safety-net family of choice."
> "Congratulations for taking the risks you've had to take."
> "Congratulations for completing your degree process."
> "Congratulations for choosing to make a change in your marital status that is in the direction of your own self-care."
> "Congratulations for being an effective parent."
> "Congratulations for leaving an abusive situation."
> "Congratulations for ending a relationship that was not good for you."
> "Congratulations for being pro-active in seeking a relationship that is fulfilling to you."

Obviously there can be many more such certificates. It is important to have 10 or 15 printed ahead of time so that different people in the audience are able to give these to the star.

FINAL MUSIC OR READING

The very last thing to do in a reconstruction is to close with music or a reading. This is usually something that is selected during the process of the reconstruction—a song, or a particular poem or reading that had relevance to the star. Everyone stands in a big circle and we close. Very often, the serenity prayer is used here, with everyone holding hands.

> "God, grant me the serenity to accept the things I cannot change, the courage to change the things I can, and the wisdom to know the difference."

"DE-ROLING"

Participants who have played roles during the reconstruction are provided an opportunity to step away from the respective roles through the process of "de-roling." Those participants who feel that they have played difficult roles during the reconstruction are asked to stand and be recognized by other participants for their willingness to support the star in this way. Everyone is then asked to participate in a short, guided imagery designed to bring people's focus back to themselves and away from the star. After relaxing, participants are told to silently repeat to themselves three times, "My name is [fill in with their own names], I am not [fill in with the name of the role they played]." When they feel as if they have fully returned to themselves, they give themselves an affirmation for good work and "return" to the group.

CHAPTER FIVE

THE WORKSHOP SCHEDULE, SETTING, AND SMALL-GROUP PROCESS

It's hard to find happiness and peace within, yet it's impossible to find it anywhere else.
—Sharon Wegscheider-Cruse

At Onsite Training and Consulting, reconstructions are done in a "Learning to Love Yourself" workshop setting that takes place over six days (two half-days are allowed for traveling). This chapter addresses the stages of the workshop that occur prior to the reconstruction event, as well as the small-group work for all non-star participants that occurs both before and after the reconstruction day.

SCHEDULE FOR A "LEARNING TO LOVE YOURSELF" WORKSHOP

Day #1:	3:00 p.m.	Enrollment
	5:00 p.m.	Dinner
	6:00 p.m.	Introductions
Day #2:	7:00 a.m.	Optional Aerobics
	8:00 a.m.	Breakfast
	8:45 a.m.	Meditations
	9:00 a.m.	Large Groups (exercises and preparatory training for the event—includes lectures, group sharing, and teaching about sculptures)

12:00	Lunch
1:00 p.m.	One-Minute Sermons
2:00 p.m.	Small Groups (approximately 10 partici-pants and two leaders each, these small groups develop therapeutic support systems that will meet intermittently over the course of the workshop)

Day #3:   RECONSTRUCTION EVENT

Day #4:   All-day small-group therapy

Day #5:
9:00	Small-group therapy
1:00 p.m.	Parts Party
2:30 p.m.	Outing
7:00 p.m.	Autograph Party

Day #6:   Closure (Half-day)

Day #1: Introduction of Participants

It is always a mysterious, awesome thing when people come in for a reconstruction workshop. They seem to be somehow spiritually "selected." They tend to come from all over the United States as well as from other countries, yet it always seems as if the right people attend the right reconstruction. If the star happens to be a teacher, it seems as if many of the participants are also teachers, or married to teachers, or have teachers in their families. If the star is a physician, same thing. This happens despite the fact that we do not pre-select the audiences for reconstruction weeks. We accept whomever applies; it just always seems to be the right people. And although over the years we have developed some very specific reconstructions which focus on adolescents, the ministry, the helping professions, physicians, etc., there is a tremendous amount of random, non-directed selection.

> *It is always a mysterious and awesome thing when people come in for a reconstruction week.*

The first night of introductions is always fun. First, we explain to every-one there what is going to take place over the course of the week. We intro-duce the staff, and then we like to have each of the participants tell a bit about themselves. Usually they give their names, say where they're from, why they're there, and what they hope to gain from the experience. There are always some former participants and former stars at any reconstruction. They will usually tell a little bit about what it was like for them previously, and why they have chosen to come again. Sometimes there is a sense of caution or uneasiness because so many are strangers, yet there is also a feeling of excitement as people get ready to embark on this journey together. Usually in the beginning most of the participants are strangers to each other. As each person introduces him- or herself to the group and talks briefly about personal goals for the workshop, a feeling of trust develops. (Sharon always finds the introductions a special part of the workshop because she knows from experience how well these people are going to know each other in just a few short days.)

Day #2: One-Minute Sermons

On the day before the reconstruction event, all participants are asked to take one minute (it is timed) to entertain the entire group in any way they choose. The only guideline is that any stories told be of one's own experience rather than someone else's. Jokes are also out of bounds. Many people sing, dance, tell stories from their lives, share feelings, recite poetry, or display other talents. This exercise is a challenge for each participant. Extroverted people seem to think that one minute is too short, and wish they had more time to entertain; introverted people seem to think one minute is an eternity and agonize over getting up in front of an audience. But the point of the process is to provide early on in the workshop an affirming experience for everyone. (People soon learn the benefit of taking their turn sooner than later because once their minute is over, they can relax and enjoy the rest of the show!)

Exercise 5.1: One-Minute Sermon

Below is a list of possible one-minute sermons:

- a funny event in your life
- singing a song
- leading the group in a song
- teaching the group a game
- doing a dance
- telling your most embarrassing moment
- giving the group your opinion of something
- telling about a strange place you have visited
- talking about why you don't want to talk
- sharing a feeling
- briefly describing your child, grandchild, pet, job, best friend, house, where you live, etc.

Now it is your turn to think of what you would do with the one-minute opportunity. Write about it (one page of writing would take about one minute to say aloud).

CHOOSING ROLE-PLAYERS

One other purpose for the sermons in the big picture of the workshop is that while participants risk, entertain, get affirmations, and begin to trust the group, they are also "auditioning" for roles in the reconstruction.

The star will sit in the back of the room with a guide. He or she has a list of all the roles that will have to be played during his or her reconstruction. With the guide's help and the star's own intuition, participants are selected to help bring a star's story to life .It also helps that the star will already have had a chance to spend some time with these people.

There are a few guidelines for the star to keep in mind when choosing role-players. When choosing an inner child stand-in, the star is asked to choose someone who appears healthy, and not someone whom the star believes wants or needs to play the role. *The rule is to look for someone who has as much or more recovery than the star, and who has some quality or qualities the star might wish for him- or herself.* Physical resemblance is not necessary in role selection. The star often has a "gut" reaction to a person and knows that a particular person is best suited to play a particular role. The guide encourages the star not to overanalyze the choices and to let go of looking for the "perfect" role-player.

> **The star often has a "gut" reaction and knows who is best suited to play a particular role.**

As a safeguard, the guide and group leaders will pay attention to participants who may not be stable enough to play a significant role on reconstruction day. This will be considered by the guide as the star makes his or her suggestions for selections.

DEVELOPING GROUPS

Woven into the week-long workshop process is about 16 hours of small-group time. Participants are divided into groups of about 10 and given the opportunity to explore their feelings in a safe environment.

The workshop initially breaks up into small groups on the afternoon of the first day. In general, the purposes of the small group are to make a transition from large group activities, to focus on the individuals attending the workshop, to help participants bond, and to make friends and feel safe. Small group is a place to tell one's own story, and build trust in the process of the workshop itself. Small group is essential for all participants, not only to process the feelings that surface during the reconstruction event, but to work through issues they may have brought with them to the workshop.

Group facilitators also use the initial small-group meeting to assess the group members' comfort level with the process. Leaders and members will begin to get to know each other here. This is all part of the larger purpose of the initial meeting, to lay the groundwork for doing more intense work later in the week. Because the small group will provide the setting for participants' individual work on the day following the reconstruction event, it is necessary to establish trust and, hopefully, positive feelings within each group.

Small groups are often quite helpful to people who have family-of-origin problems. The group can actually provide a healthy family of choice, however temporary, by modeling the caring, acceptance, confrontation, consistency, and freedom that are characteristic of a healthy family.

The small group models a healthy family of choice.

In describing the healing characteristics of group therapy, Irving Yalom identified universality as one of the most important concepts. Universality is the recognition of common interests and needs in all human experience, and it is present in the small groups at a family reconstruction workshop. The small groups build self-worth by counteracting the idea that anyone in the group is unacceptable because of their pain or for any other reason.

The small group models concern for the individual. Low self-worth and feelings of shame keep people isolated and stuck in unhealthy patterns of behavior. A group can provide a healthy mirror that encourages acceptance of the self. The group also provides a mirror for change. The chance to see ourselves as others see us acts as a catalyst, breaking the cycle of denial and providing the freedom to make new choices.

This also applies to each individual as he or she recreates his or her own family-of-origin role in the small-group context. Feelings, demeanor, and behavior in the group setting will reflect something learned long ago in childhood because defense mechanisms, old behaviors, and mannerisms are replayed in group settings. The participant who seems to emerge as the unofficial natural leader of the group (as opposed to the actual staff leader) may have been responsible as a child or always in charge. Someone who acts out in groups probably could identify scapegoating or anger in his or her past. Someone who wants the group's approval might be able to recall feeling lonely as a child. Sometimes it even feels regressive. For example, old shyness may return. Amazingly, these dynamics and characteristics make their appearance in the group setting within a relatively short amount of time. Of course, we can't reveal or accomplish the same things in the course of one week as can a group that works together over a long period of time, but we do hope to provide an atmosphere that is a catalyst for the beginnings of change.

CHOOSING GROUP MEMBERS

On the first full day of the workshop, after the educational section has been completed and the large group has been through the introductory phase of setting ground rules, establishing the boundaries of the workshop, allowing everyone to recuperate from their trip to the site, and helping everyone feel a welcome part of the Onsite community, participants break into small groups led by a facilitator or leader and, usually, an intern.

Much of the decision as to which group a participant will be assigned is by chance. Care is taken, however, to separate people who know each other or are related. Often people from the same town are put in different groups to heighten their sense of safety and privacy and to reduce the risk familiarity can pose in such a context. The thinking behind being in a group without your friends and family members is based on the best interest of privacy and an optimum atmosphere for doing productive work. Anyone might be inhibited from talking or revealing painful information if there were any question that anonymity might not be honored. In this regard, most people feel a certain safety in a group of strangers.

Because family-of-origin issues are sometimes the central focal point of reconstructions, small-group members need to be able to talk about their own views and experiences of family. Systems theorists know that every person's perspective on his or her own family is entirely subjective. Birth order is just one circumstance that gives each person a different outlook. Often, the same family looks very different to the oldest child than it does to the youngest. For example, in the case of alcoholism, the disease may progress in the family over time, and an older sibling would have a different experience of its impact than would a child born when the disease was already in full bloom. Rather than dispute the "truth" about a family, small groups honor the perspective of each person. All of this applies to husbands and wives or other intimate partners attending a workshop as well. Any marital problems can be addressed privately in small groups without sides being taken. This also prevents the reconstruction workshop from turning into a couple's counseling session, which is a job best suited for a setting specifically designed for that purpose.

GROUP AS A SAFE PLACE

Small groups are a good place to tell the truth in a safe atmosphere. Without question, the reconstruction will address painful parts of life, including things people normally don't like to talk about: affairs, addiction, incest, sexual assault, abortion, abandonment, compulsive behavior, suicide attempts, violence, etc. But these "awful secrets" are things most of us carry. And most of us think if we tell anyone we will be rejected. Groups can effectively reduce the shame of secrets by accepting their content as more common than unique, and as painful rather than awful. The group provides a substitute family—one that is intended to be accepting and loving. Group assignments will take into account whatever considerations are necessary to create such an atmosphere for everyone involved.

WHAT DO MEMBERS WANT?

We often see three kinds of people attend a reconstruction workshop: *spectators, defendants,* and *players. Spectators* are those who will watch but remain removed from the process. They will see the work as important to others, but will try not to personalize anything for themselves. These people can be perfectly acceptable and even welcome in the workshop setting. If knowledge is the goal of the audience member, that goal will probably be attained. But it is difficult to maintain this stance in such an emotional milieu. The spectator may be hiding some painful issues that remain unresolved.

The *defendant* at a reconstruction sees the problem, but finds few solutions. This participant is stuck and unwilling to change. Such resistance is probably due to fear. Whatever its origins or reasons, it is honored. The leaders of a reconstruction are respectful of all persons and do not pressure, coerce, or shame anyone.

But most participants (probably 90% or more) in a reconstruction workshop are ready to do their own personal work. These *players* want to get their money's worth. They may come knowing what they need to work on, or they are at the workshop in order to discover what work they need to do by paying attention to the feelings and ideas that arise as they participate in the small groups or act as role-players and witnesses to the reconstruction itself.

The people who attend a reconstruction are varied, and the format of the workshop is conducive to meeting a wide range of goals. Probably the greatest majority of participants wish to do some work on family-of-origin issues. They know the process that comes out of the tradition of Virginia Satir and Sharon Wegscheider-Cruse is very intense, but they are there because they seek personal growth. The decision to feel, face, and heal with the past, present, and future puts participants in a state of readiness before groups begin. Thus they tend to "jump right in," eager to get down to business. While group therapy and experiential therapy are typically well known to about half of the participants at a given workshop, there are always a substantial number of members who have little or no group knowledge or experience. Sometimes participants are merely observing the process of reconstruction. They may have studied or read books on the subject, and want to witness first-hand the way it works. Others will be attending their first workshop of any kind that deals with families of origin. They may be very curious about their families and this will be a kind of initiating experience. Still others will have had therapy of a cognitive nature and know a great deal about their families and/or themselves. They may be seeking the healing aspect of a reconstruction, and find themselves wanting to feel their feelings and move on. They are new to experiential therapy, however, and could have fears about all the action or the intensity. The small group will serve as an introduction to them also. And for the person who has had a substantial amount of the kind of therapy that we use in reconstructions, coming to a workshop is a good way to "recharge" or to complete some work. Professionals in the field may fall into any of the categories just mentioned, and may wish to use the workshop to do personal work in addition to learning new theory and technique for work with their own clients.

Whether complete "innocents" to this form of therapy or fully experienced and prepared, people seem to get what they need out of the process.

GROUND RULES FOR SMALL GROUPS

The very first order of business for any small group is to establish the boundaries or structure of the group. It is the responsibility of the therapists to define the guidelines for the group, which should be in the interest of developing a safe environment for all group members.

Here are some general ground rules for small groups:

1. The psychological and personal safety of each person in the group is paramount.
2. Members are invited to participate, and never forced, pressured, or coerced.
3. Anyone may say "no" or "stop" at any time.
4. Any event or information discussed or disclosed in small group is confidential and must not be taken out of group. People may share with others outside the group their own experience(s), but not the experience(s) of other group members. The exception to this rule is if a person intends to harm him- or herself or others.
5. Group members are advised not to touch other members unless they ask permission to do so. Many participants have been abused and need to maintain boundaries. Some people shut down emotionally when touched.

6. Group members must attend all group sessions.
7. Feedback is encouraged. Group members are invited to tell what they are feeling, sensing, and relating to in the presence of other group members. Small-group feedback avoids giving advice or analyzing, intellectualizing, or explaining behavior or feelings.

Group leaders also may wish to have certain guidelines that pertain to the needs of their particular group. A good approach would be to use our ground rules above as structural guidelines and then, by group consensus, add any other rules that members may need.

STRUCTURE AND SUGGESTIONS FOR SMALL GROUPS

Emotional checks. A typical way to begin small group is with an emotional "check" to discover how members are feeling. Such a check simply involves each member sharing one or two sentences to describe feelings that are present. Throughout the day the leader will intermittently conduct such checks. These checks reveal something akin to an emotional patchwork quilt—some are angry while others are hopeful; some are sad while others are full of joy. The beauty of it is that all of the feelings are real, and all of them are appropriate.

Guided imageries. The beginning of small group is also a good time to do a guided imagery. This is often followed by various exercises to help members begin to feel more at ease and more connected to the group.

Many of our memories, feelings, and choices become buried over time and with experience. Particularly emotional events can be blocked in order to protect ourselves from pain that seems to persist unreleased or without reduction. An imagery can be thought of as a cycle. First, the guide helps the person to center and feel safe. One way to do this is by asking the person to pay attention to his or her breathing and to focus on any muscle tension that may be present, and to try to relax. Next, the guide invites the person to take a journey. This is followed by a detailed description of the journey which encompasses all the senses. At this point, the guide suggests whatever therapeutic work needs to be done. Examples include talking to one's inner child, meeting a parent and saying one thing he or she has always needed to say, allowing a Higher Power to send a message home, or visualizing pain subsiding or flying away. This is then followed by a slow return, in which the guide re-traces through description the steps of the journey in order to safely lead a person back to the journey's starting point. The final step is re-entry. The person is invited to return to the room at his or her own pace, fully feeling, ready to discuss, build on, or quietly absorb the experience. The following chart outlines the steps of a guided imagery.

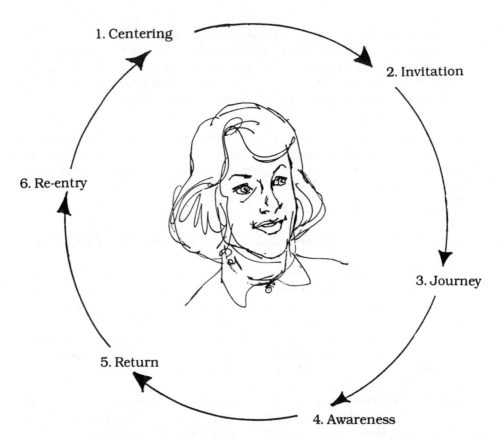

1. Centering
2. Invitation
3. Journey
4. Awareness
5. Return
6. Re-entry

Imageries can be used for various purposes such as setting a mood, stirring up feelings, helping a person reconnect with past events, or calming a person or group after deep, intense work. (It can also set the stage for a theme piece that may be used with the whole group—for more on theme pieces see Chapter Four.)

There are many types of imageries. Here are some ideas and brief explanations.

1. *Inner child.* Connection with an inner child in imagery helps a person to understand and feel the connection with an often-denied part of the self. It can also provide a focus point so that the person can remember this child and his or her needs when he or she (the adult) gets blocked or scared.

2. *Safe place.* The person is asked to remember a safe place he or she had as a child. It might have been under the bed or in the woods or up in a tree fort or at a grandparent's house or deep inside the self. In this imagery, the person is asked to visualize and feel him- or herself in that place. Further instruction/guidance might involve imagining a potentially harmful force in the picture, and feeling safe regardless of that

force because in the safe place, nothing and no one can harm the person. This imagery can be used in times of stress to regain serenity simply by revisiting the safe place for a few moments.

3.   *Childhood home.* Imagery can help a person to revisit the events and feelings around the home in which he or she grew up. The guide can invite a person to visit the town, the street, and the house or residence of childhood. The person can visit each room or one room in particular.

4.   *Nature.* An imagery might simply be a walk through nature to affirm oneself and appreciate the outside world. Some possible scenes might be a beach, mountains, a tropical rain forest, a meadow, a park, etc. It is possible to see friendly animals along the way who offer helpful or loving words.

5.   *Healing.* Imagery can be a wonderful healing tool. When Kathy's daughter Deanna was seven years old, and they were two and-a-half hours away from home at 8:00 p.m., she was injured by a huge dinner bell, which caused a cut on the side of her nose just beside her eye. The cut bled and it hurt. Though it wasn't deep enough for stitches, Deanna was scared. Kathy used an imagery technique of Milton Erickson's to help with the pain. Deanna envisioned a little bird on her shoulder. Kathy told her that when she was ready, the bird would fly away and the bleeding would stop. It did. And when Kathy's children were even younger, she used "switches." She taught them that they had tiny wires connecting all parts of their bodies. The control center had rows of light bulbs; each one had a switch, and a wire that led to a different body part. When there was pain, a light bulb would come on. They soon learned that they could close their eyes, locate the proper light bulb, and turn off the switch.

6.   *Higher Power.* There are many ways for a person to connect with his or her Higher Power. Imagery gives a person the opportunity to be creative and safe. A soft warm light of any color can shine down and encourage a person to be enveloped. The image can start with a black screen. The guide can encourage a color to be seen, and then ask for the color to take a shape, and a size. The person can be asked to experience the feelings that come up in the presence of what he or she has created. The creation can also be changed at will.

The guide in any of these imageries can be the person him- or herself once the technique becomes familiar. Music can be extremely helpful in setting the stage or mood for what is happening. And remember, these are just a few examples—there are many different types of imageries.

When the imagery is completed, there are different ways to expand the experience. The person can draw the experience and share the drawing verbally, or write a journal entry about the experience. In group, he or she can sculpt the scene and intensify the feelings and the message. In or out of group, a list of changes to be made as a result of the experience can be developed.

The following is a sample "script" for the guide's role in a guided imagery. It is intended to illustrate the imagery cycle, and show one possible way in which the tool can be used. The steps are numbered for your convenience.

Guide: (1)   Today I am going to invite you to locate a warm spot in your body. Let your breathing help you to find it. Breathe slowly, and as you inhale and exhale, pay careful attention to where the warm spot is. When you locate it, focus on that warm spot. You may want to close your eyes now if you haven't already.

Warmth is a nurturing feeling. It has a glow to it. Often, warmth expands. It is hard to keep it contained in one place. Notice where it appears, and how fast it spreads.

Your body will continue to take care of your warmth and your safety and your ability to let go as you need to.

(2)   In the meantime, I'd like to invite you on a journey. I'd like you to imagine yourself on a path. The path leads through your favorite place in nature. It could be a park or a mountainside or a field of flowers or a body of water—wherever you choose is a safe place. No one will harm you there.

(3)   As you walk, notice somewhere along the path a small child—your inner child. Go to that child. Kneel down and look at him [her]. He [She] knows what you need, and what you feel.

Reach out and embrace your child. As you do, pull the child close. He [She] will become part of you as the child that has always been. You will be aware of your child inside. As you continue the journey, this will be allowed to be so.

(4)   Stand and continue to walk along the path. As you look ahead you may notice that the path takes a sharp turn. Go to the turn and take it. As you turn, the path changes. It becomes colors and shapes. You have turned down the path of feelings. Walk along and watch the colors and shapes change as the feelings change.

Keeping walking until you find a feeling in which you need to spend some time. Allow yourself to sit in those feelings, to feel them. Look at the colors, the shapes. Notice their detail. Are there smells and tastes as well? Stay there for a minute and take it all in.

[Pause here for a minute or two before continuing.]

(5)   Now it's time to stand and start back toward the turn in the path. Bring your feelings with you as you head back. As you take the turn and the path changes back to the place in nature that you chose, be aware of that place. Feel the safety. Allow yourself to continue to walk back to where your journey began, back to the room.

(6)   Be aware again of the warmth, and of your breathing. [Take another pause before finishing.]

Gently allow yourself to return to this room, bringing your feelings with you. Take your time. Allow yourself to open your eyes as you are ready to return.

SAMPLE INTRODUCTORY GROUP EXERCISES

All of the sample exercises that follow are suggestions for small-group work. Instructions within each description are intended for the official group leader(s).

What does your name mean?   This provides a safe subject to share, and may carry meaning to family-of-origin issues. Group members all share the origin of their names—who they were named for, the name's meaning in general, and the personal meaning of their names for themselves.

Go-arounds.   This gives each person equal time, builds trust, creates safety, and increases group knowledge. A go-around is any sharing of information by each group member. Examples of things to share include a feeling, a happy childhood memory, a wish, a safe place, or an "angel" in their lives. ("Angels" were defined and discussed in detail in the section on Family-of-Choice Sculptures in Chapter Four. It is sufficient here to understand angels as those people who have brought special gifts or messages into our lives.)

Finding an introductory prop.   This exercise helps share feelings, build trust, learn about issues, and become familiar with props. Each member chooses a prop that seems meaningful (or symbolic) to him or her, and then shares with the group.

Walk-around.   This is intended to relax and build trust, to take a break from intellectualizing, and to promote nonverbal communication. Soft music can play while members of the group walk around the room in random fashion. At first there should be no touching or talking. Then change the style of music being played to something more lively, and then back to soft. Add eye contact.

Ball toss.   This promotes bonding and allows a member to identify strengths and weaknesses. The group leader tosses a ball to one group member. The member shares a fear and a hope he or she has for the week, and then shares a positive character trait he or she has to offer before passing the ball to another member. This continues until all members have caught the ball, shared, and the group leader has the ball again.

12-Step sharing.   This promotes bonding and provides information. Ask each group member to share his or her involvement with or lack of connection to 12-Step programs.

Blockade drawing.   This reveals participants' current issues, exposes some defenses, and offers hope. Each group member is given three pieces of paper, to be numbered 1, 2, and 3 in the corner. On sheet #1, members draw (using the non-dominant hand to avoid perfectionist tendencies) a response to the question, "Where are you right now in your recovery?" Then members take sheet #3 and draw a response to the question, "Where would you like to be?" Finally, on sheet #2, members draw a response to the question, "What's in the way?" The sheets are lined up in numerical order. Each member can share the drawings verbally and hang them on the wall. These may simply be used as a sharing exercises, or for material to sculpt with later on.

SAMPLE PRELIMINARY GOAL-SETTING EXERCISES

Hands-and-feet mural.   This promotes bonding, assesses some needs, and encourages participants to work together and share. The group will need one large piece of newsprint and markers. Members trace their hands and feet, and draw their eyes and ears anywhere on the paper. They are encouraged to ask for help when necessary. The whole group works at the same time. They share markers and space. When this is done, they are asked to go back and write inside each tracing/drawing: in the feet they are asked to write somewhere they need to go in recovery, in their hands they are asked to write something they need to have in recovery, in the eyes they are asked to write something they need to see, and in the ears, something they need to listen to.

Drawing pain.   This helps in becoming aware of feelings and issues and acts as an exercise in risking disclosure. Each person divides a 12" x 18" piece of paper in half. On one half, members draw their pain, and on the other half, they draw their anger. Again, encourage people to use their opposite hands in drawing exercises. Color, symbols, lines, shapes, stick figures, etc. are all acceptable to represent the abstract ideas.

Drawing the inner child.   This is a good exercise to do along with a guided inner-child imagery, and facilitates the sharing of feelings and family-of-origin material as well as helping people risk disclosure and build trust. On a large piece of paper, members draw a childhood picture of themselves. As in the previous exercise, any drawing or representation is acceptable.

"Taking a photograph."   This allows group members to attempt sculpture work, to disclose issues, and to build trust and share information. Group members create "portraits" of their issues by putting together a still picture using role-players, objects, and props in the room. For example, someone might say her issues are a powerful mother, too much work, and the death of her father. She would put a mother role-player on a chair to represent power, a father role-player lying on the floor to represent his death, and many pieces of paper or pillows to represent the overwhelming work. Let the participants use their own imaginations to come up with their own scenes or pictures, which, though not comprehensive in scope, may serve as metaphors for their lives—lonely, frantic, overwhelming, etc. Let the group give feedback.

EARLY EXPERIENTIAL ACTIVITIES

Four corners of feelings.   This exercise encourages members to express their feelings, and to risk and build trust. Divide the room into four areas. Label each area with a feeling (e.g., happy, sad, scared, angry, etc.) Have each person stand in each of the four areas, and tell about that feeling in his or her life: how it has been experienced, what its origins are, and what it costs to hold onto the feeling. Decide where the majority of the group's time is spent and which issues (feelings) might be worked on during the workshop.

Show the inner child.   This is another exercise to reveal the inner child. It uses sculpture, encourages the expression of feelings, and promotes sharing about families of origin. Have each person choose a role-player for his or her inner child. Place that role-player in a body position (with props, if helpful) to represent feelings.

Anger discharge.   This helps to practice the expression of feelings, to build trust and relax, and to have less fear of anger and other feelings. Build a pile of pillows in the middle of the room. Put on dramatic music, drums, or classical music. Pass around an encounter bat or another pillow, and take turns allowing each person to learn how to discharge feelings in a group. Instruct people to "put it on the pillows," or to name their anger. Some people will be uncomfortable with the physical nature of this exercise, and will only want to verbalize their feelings.

ANGER-DISCHARGE WORK IN A SMALL-GROUP SETTING

THEME PIECES

Theme pieces help access feelings, bond group members, and make it easier for individuals to participate if they are shy or reluctant.

The disease. This exercise introduces experiential techniques and avoids blame of specific persons. Have group members build a pile of pillows in the middle of the floor. Add props to make a heap or garbage pile. Let each person write on a 3" x 5" card something he or she has lost because of the disease of alcoholism, drugs, food disorders, co-dependency, or other compulsive behavior (examples include, but are in no way limited to time, money, childhood, relationships, education, children, marriage, self-worth, jobs, opportunities, parents, happiness, love, attention, nurturing, and spirituality). Put the cards on the pile. Let the group share feelings and discharge them onto the pile if they wish.

Exercise 5.2: Losses to the Disease

Write your losses to the disease.

Empty chair. This allows members an opportunity to work on some unfinished business, and to access emotions and discharge them. Place an empty chair in the middle of the room. Invite group members to take turns closing their eyes, taking a few slow breaths to relax, and then imagining someone sitting in the chair—someone they know they need to talk to, or wish they could talk to, in order to finish some business; someone they have some feelings about. Then they can open their eyes and keep imagining that person in the chair, and sharing the identity of that person with the group, maybe even describing them physically a little bit. You may wish to use role-players, and have them take the chair and "become" the person (the participant whose turn it is may tell the role-player what the person might say). Whether using a role-player or not, when it is their turn, participants may sit directly opposite to the chair to talk and discharge feelings.

The family triangle.   This exercise teaches expression of feelings and addresses family-of-origin issues. Build a sculpture of the mother, father, and child, and use this as a teaching sculpture by letting each person in the group use role-players to reset the triangle as they remember the relationship triangle formed by themselves and their parents. Check for feelings, and suggest discharge if needed.

Secret circle.   This helps members share and build trust, express feelings, and understand the burden of unfinished business. Have the group stand in a circle, with each person holding a pillow on his or her back. Have everyone imagine that this is the weight of something unfinished—it may be guilt or anger or fear; it could be an event never spoken about. Let anyone name the burden. Group leaders can pull or press a little on the pillow to add a little weight and stress. This will be just enough to irritate the person, who will then be able to get in touch with the feelings he or she has around carrying the burden of some unfinished business.

CHAPTER SIX

THE REST OF THE WORKSHOP: MORE SMALL-GROUP WORK, THE PARTS PARTY, AND CLOSING ACTIVITIES

I am not responsible for my feelings
—only what I do with them.

> —Dr. Coephus Martin
> as quoted in Days of Healing,
> Days of Joy (Larsen and Hegarty,
> New York: Harper/Hazelden, 1987)

Focused on one star, the reconstruction event serves as a catalyst for all workshop participants. Small group process was discussed in detail in Chapter Five. The small group process that will take place on the two days following the reconstruction event will allow non-star group members to take the feelings that surfaced for them during the reconstruction event, personalize them, and so do some of their own work in a safe and nurturing environment. This work may range from highly individualized and specific pieces to generalized pieces that most participants can relate to, and theme pieces.

The small-group leaders will make the decision as to what type of work will be done. This will depend on several factors. As mentioned earlier, some groups have many new members who are not accustomed to group process or to experiential therapy. The facilitators in groups such as this may decide to rely more heavily on teaching and theme pieces than on very specific individual work. Some groups may have several people who had specific issues surface on reconstruction day, or who came to the workshop with certain goals. The facilitators in groups such as this may decide to allow each group member to select the issue that he or she needs to address and do a sculpture around it.

Most groups will be a combination of these two types, and the facilitators need to be very sensitive to the level and needs of each participant.

It is important to note that small groups will finish the experiential part of their work on the morning of the last full day of the program. Participants need to be made aware that they will be together again for a final closure, but on this morning a shift is made. It is often helpful to allow each group member to say thank you to his or her small group, and to share one thing he or she is taking, and one thing he or she is leaving. A special song is often a nice way to close.

THE PARTS PARTY: AN OVERVIEW

At the conclusion of the intensive work phase of the "Learning to Love Yourself" workshops, we return to the large group and have a "Parts Party." Parts parties are included at this point in the workshop experience to leave each participant with a sense of renewed self-worth and hope for the future. The Party provides an opportunity to examine the positive and negative characteristics we all possess, bring them to life experientially, and make decisions about them. Participants learn to acknowledge strengths and negotiate weaknesses in an atmosphere of validation and fun. It is intended to bring the large group together again after small-group work, to teach a basic exercise in the integration of self and the acceptance of all parts of the self, to raise self-worth, to have fun and laugh, and to begin the transition from the workshop back to life.

Virginia Satir conceived the idea of a Parts Party and it is one of her experiential tools. Like reconstruction itself, this technique uses role-play, imagery, psychodrama, Gestalt, improvisation, humor, and decision-making and problem-solving skills.

> **The Parts Party is both an exercise in self-worth and a vehicle to facilitate change.**

The Parts Party is one of those tools or techniques that can be used in a variety of settings and ways. It is adaptable and can change with each new therapist who uses it. Virginia Satir taught this technique to her students and proteges, and Sharon Wegscheider-Cruse expanded it to use in her reconstruction workshops.

The premise of the Parts Party is that there is some value in examining our strengths and weaknesses. In the theories of personality from Freud to Berne, the personality has been conceptualized into different parts. Freud looked at the super-ego, the ego, and the id. Jung depicted the self and shadow, archetypes, and the masculine and feminine. Eric Berne described ego states of parent, adult, and child. Recent research has looked into dissociation as an ability to develop and compartmentalize aspects of experience. In the most extreme cases, an individual may actually develop what we call "multiple personalities" to carry certain information and emotions.

Twelve-Step recovery requires an examination and awareness of character defects. It also requires the naming of strengths and weaknesses.

Here is a listing of the 12 steps as taken from *The Big Book of Alcoholics Anonymous*:†

1. We admitted we were powerless over alcohol—that our lives had become unmanageable,
2. Came to believe that a power greater than ourselves could restore us to sanity,
3. Made a decision to turn our will and our lives over to the care of God as we understood Him,
4. Made a searching and fearless moral inventory of ourselves,
5. Admitted to God, ourselves, and to another human being the exact nature of our wrongs,
6. Were entirely ready to have God remove all these defects of character,
7. Humbly asked Him to remove our shortcomings,
8. Made a list of all pesons we had harmed, and became willing to make amends to them all,
9. Made direct amends to such people wherever possible, except when to do so would injure them or others,
10. Continued to take personal inventory and when we were wrong promptly admitted it,
11. Sought through prayer and meditation to improve our conscious contact with God as we understood Him, praying only for knowledge of His will for us and the power to carry that out,
12. Having had a spiritual awakening as a result of these steps, we tried to carry this message to alcoholics, and to practice these principles in all our affairs.

---

† The 12 Steps are reprinted with permission of Alcoholics Anonymous World Services, Inc. Permission to reprint does not mean that A.A. has reviwed or approved the contents of this volume, nor that A.A. agrees with the views expressed herein. A.A. is a program of recovery from alcoholism - use of the 12 Steps in connection with programs and activities which are patterned after A.A. but which address other problems does not imply otherwise.

These steps can be adapted (with permission) to fit all addictions and compulsions.

We are often not fully aware of how to live with the parts of ourselves that we don't like, and even less aware of how to diminish or improve them. The Parts Party addresses awareness of parts of ourselves and how they might interact. It presents the inner dialogue or "committee" that meets in the head, the inner conflicts of who we each are. All the facets of our personalities do not live in harmony. We do not accept ourselves and, in fact, often loathe certain parts of ourselves. We do not see the value of being indecisive or judgmental or depressed. The Parts Party is designed to show the balance or imbalance of positive and negative characteristics. Almost everything has a purpose, even the most pesky or loathsome character traits. A Parts Party honors the need for all the facets of the self. We must learn to see the payoff for our behaviors in order to make changes. So the Parts party serves as a validation of the self, but it also illustrates some methodology for change.

Step 1: Identification.   The experience begins by thinking of four positive and four not-so-positive characteristics about oneself. (More than four can be used, but for the purposes of a group exercise that is structured to last no more than ninety minutes, it is simpler to confine the activity in this way.) This step is one of *awareness*. What are our most prevalent characteristics? What is our internal structure?

For example, in thinking about the parts of self that are positive, one might come up with a list that includes *smart, honest, persistent,* and *spiritual.* In thinking about the parts of self that are negative, the list might include *insecure, sarcastic, judgmental,* and *controlling.*

Step 2: Personification.   Next, by personifying the list that has been made, we can conceptualize further what our complexities are. The audience is asked to think of a person, real or fictional, present or past, who is strongly identified with each of the characteristics we have listed for ourselves. These people can be movie stars, political figures, athletes, historical figures, cartoon characters, fictional characters (both heroes and villains), etc. The requirement for selection is only that the person be generally known to most people. For example, someone might choose Hillary Clinton or Albert Einstein as a representative *smart* person. Ideally, for purposes of balance, people should choose half male figures and half female figures, regardless of their own gender.

Examples:

Characteristic	**Character**
Smart	Albert Einstein
Honest	George Washington
Spiritual	Mother Teresa
Judgmental	Radio Talk Show Host
Controlling	Adolf Hitler

Then, as a warm-up to what follows, the audience is asked to play charades. First, they break into groups of about 5-7 people. Each person in the group takes a turn acting out one of the famous people he or she has thought of, revealing to the group only the characteristic that the person represents until the group guesses the well-known person or character.

Step 3: Interaction.   The next step is to select one person and bring his or her characters, all eight, to life in the large group setting in order to see the interaction and conflict. In watching this, everyone learns. One person is selected by the guide to bring his or her list to the front and choose role-players from the large group for each characteristic. The role-players are given about 5-10 minutes to come up with costumes for the characters they have been chosen to play. They also need to come up with a snappy entrance (this can be up to a few lines) for their characters.

When role-players are ready, the *experiential party* can begin. The guide or an audience member role-playing a maid or butler announces each character and allows him or her to make an entrance, say a few lines, and engage the audience.

Step 4: Conflict.   The guide instructs the players that they should talk and interact with each other at a dinner party or meeting. This is a party for the focus person who was chosen to share his or her characters. For the role-players, the key is to remember the essence of the character in terms of the characteristic he or she was chosen to represent, and to play that up in any interaction. As the role-players interact, a conversation or "committee meeting" among different characteristics or aspects of the self takes place. When the guide instructs the players to "freeze" or "stop," they halt the action so that the focus person can talk and make decisions.

Given these directions, the party begins. Parts talk, argue, and otherwise interact. Music may be played to add party atmosphere. The focus person watches and gets a feel for the parts until he or she finds a place to begin working and tells the guide that he or she wants to speak with a certain character. This is when the guide brings the action to a stop.

An important task for the role-players is to show the host how they influence (or even control) the host's other parts. Again, the key to this whole exercise is the *interaction of the parts.*

Step 5: Change and Decision Making.   The focus person talks to each part, articulating the advantages and disadvantages of having this characteristic. The guide may coach by beginning a sentence, "The price I pay for having you is _____." And "The payoff I get from having you is _____." At this point, the guide will ask the focus person how he or she wants to deal with this part. The focus person may choose to:

1. Accept the part. The person may be grateful for and proud of many parts, such as perseverance, humor, intelligence, courage, kindness, and spunkiness. We can honor these parts.
2. Ask a part to leave. This can be appropriate for a part that has served its purpose and is no longer useful. An obese person who has learned how the obesity has functioned to protect him from intimacy and other forms of relationship may now realize that the obesity no longer serves him and he can bid it farewell.
3. Modify a part. This is when we need to change a part in some way, perhaps to temper weaker parts. Intelligence can step into reason with avoidance by helping a person make decisions as to when avoidance is necessary vs. when it is unhealthy. A person may want to get rid of depression, but still has a healthy need to feel sad and to experience sadness, so we'll get rid of the state of depression while retaining the capacity to be sad.
4. Use role models. In a group exercise, call upon audience members to share how they may have acquired or discarded certain characteristics of their own.

No matter what the person's decision concerning a part, it is important that the star identify and thank each part for what it has given him or her, and for how it has helped in the past.

Step 6: Integration. To conclude a Parts Party, it is important to celebrate the parts of a person. A good way to do this is with a ritual. Place the host in the center. Let him or her place the parts around him- or herself in various proximities that are meaningful. (The important parts that offer the host safety and well-being are placed close by, etc.)

One woman placed her sensitivity and intelligence next to her to guide her, her spirituality above her, and her kindness grounding her (by her feet). Her fears stood next to her spirituality for reality-testing.

Close the party with a ritual: *"Close your eyes. Feel around you all of your parts—those you honor and those that have been painful. Inwardly thank all of them for helping you to survive, for challenging you to change, and for encouraging you to grow."*

VARIATIONS

Listed below are several different activities that can be used with the positive and negative parts lists. There are many ways to use a Parts Party. Here are some techniques by which we can begin to modify our internal structures.

1. *Pencil-and-paper exercise.* After listing positive and negative parts, write a dialogue showing the conflicting messages of the parts. Ask for

strength from some parts to modify or lessen certain other characteristics as appropriate.

2. *Sociogram.* Draw a circle and line picture of parts. Instead of dialogue, make a visual interpretation of the parts and their interaction.

3. *Gestalt.* Allow a single individual to act out all the parts that would appear at his or her own Parts Party.

4. *Guided imagery.* After getting into a relaxed state, an individual and guide can walk through the Parts Party using the imagination.

5. *Charades.* As a group activity, it can be fun to act out without dialogue the interaction of personality features either in nonverbal still sculpture or in mime. Props can be used in either case.

6. *A therapy group.* In a well-bonded group of 5-10 people, have the host choose one group member to play each characteristic of a chosen focus person.

SCHEMATA FOR A PARTS PARTY

Butler

Announcing the arrival of Mother Teresa

Star

(Smart)
Albert
Einstein

(Honest)
George
Washington

(Controlling)
Adolf Hitler

(Judgmental)
Radio Talk Host

Exercise 6.1: Your Own Parts Party

The reader is invited to make a list of his or her own character traits.

Positive	**Negative**
1.	1.
2.	2.
3.	3.
4.	4.

Do the dialogue exercise with each part; write it out.

Then think of a famous character to personify each part.

Characteristic	**Character**
1.	1.
2.	2.
3.	3.
4.	4.
5.	5.
6.	6.
7.	7.
8.	8.

Now draw a picture of yourself with all of these parts around you. Have each part saying one thing. How does it feel?

Try a guided imagery exercise in which you imagine yourself being the star of a Parts Party, interacting and modifying all your parts.

THE OUTING

Following the Parts Party, all the workshop participants leave the grounds of the reconstruction site for an outing. This is a mandatory activity.

The outing allows people to begin to re-orient themselves to the outside world. It is also a wonderful opportunity for the participants to release some of the week's tension in a relaxed and peaceful atmosphere.

After three days of intense emotional and physical work, the opportunity for some fun, contact with nature, new visual stimulation, taking photographs, etc., is most welcome. On the way back, participants on the bus can often be heard talking about what they are going home to, or about how

ready they are to be with friends and family again. For many, this is the first time they'll have talked this way in several days. The process of re-entry has thus begun.

AFFIRMATIONS

After the outing, the participants are brought together in their small groups one last time for affirmations and closing. At this time, each group member can hear how he or she has been perceived by peers.

At our site, this exercise is presently done in the small-group rooms. In the past it has also been done in the large meeting room, with small-group members sitting in circles all around the room.

The affirmation circle is a testament to the bonding and sharing that has occurred over the past several days. This exercise consists of each small group seated in a circle, with one group member at a time sitting in the center of the circle with his or her eyes closed. Soft music is played in the background while, one at a time, each of the group members approaches the person seated in the center. An affirmation is whispered to the person by each fellow member, and a self-stick label on which the same affirmation is written is placed on the person's shirt or blouse. People usually wear these "affirmations" the rest of the day. We refer to these labels as "dressing for dinner." Participants often do wear them to dinner that evening.

The person in the middle is asked to just take it all in, to realize that he or she is receiving so much now because of what he or she has given all week. The exercise continues until all group members have been in the center of the circle to receive affirmations.

Other closing activities include the ceremonial small-group closing chosen by the group leader, and an informal large-group time with participants signing posters and sharing affirmations.

Has it become increasingly apparent how much emphasis is placed on closing and on saying good-bye as part of the process of the reconstruction workshop? We do this because all too often in our lives we have learned to avoid or ignore endings. Abandonment and grief issues often surface, and because they are so painful, we repress them.

This workshop begins to teach people to view good-byes in a different way, as lessons in celebrating positive endings and in appreciating ourselves.

Exercise 6.2: Affirmations for Yourself

List ten positive affirmations about yourself. Put these on an index card, and put them in a photo album. Keep them in a special place where you can refer to them often, and add to them on a regular basis with a long-term goal of filling the entire album.

FINAL CLOSURE TO THE RECONSTRUCTION PROCESS

People will feel as though they have been going through this process for many, many days—much longer than the actual time spent. Participants will find that they have gotten closer to people than they have in other settings. Some people feel closer to the people they've met through the reconstruction process than they do to those with whom they live and work each day, or to those with whom they grew up. This is attributable at least in part to the level of trust, the level of sharing, and the unconditional acceptance that are all present at a reconstruction workshop.

> *It is important that people recognize that this experience is only one of many they may have on the path to change and growth.*

The reconstruction workshop is a place where people will have learned some new tools and some new ways of relating and communicating that they did not have before. But it is important that the workshop not be viewed as the only place where these feelings and behaviors can exist, simply the first place they have been able to try them out.

So part of the formal closing on the last day seeks to encourage participants to take everything they have learned and felt and to integrate it all. They need to allow there to be an organic change inside themselves so that they do not depend on the workshop experience for their self-worth, but, rather, use the workshop experience to help them enter other experiences in which even more self-worth can be gained.

> *The ending of a reconstruction workshop is actually the promise of a new beginning for participants.*

The last morning of the workshop consists of a formal, large-group closing. This is a way for people to thank each other, and to express gratitude for the growing they have done together. Then, in a very formalized way, accompanied by sharing sessions and music, people prepare to leave this warm, safe place.

The final step on the day of closure is to let each person share with the large group a little bit about themselves as their way to say good-bye. (Most people choose to share one thing they got out of the week.)

A wonderful song that is often played at the end of the workshop is "I Set Myself Free," which is probably the best final statement for the process.

At this point, everyone scurries to give final hugs and gather their things for boarding the bus to the airport or packing up their cars for the drive home.

PART III

JOURNEYS: PERSONAL EXPERIENCES OF FAMILY RECONSTRUCTION

Beyond a wholesome discipline, be gentle with yourself. You are a child of the universe, no less than the trees or the stars; you have a right to be here.

—Desiderata

CHAPTER SEVEN

A WITNESS' STORY

Many people are hesitant to join in such a private, self-revealing process as family reconstruction. One such person was Patrick Cotter, who signed up to attend a reconstruction workshop as a participant and watch a star go through the process. Patrick found it a profound experience, and wrote about it for *Changes* magazine. His article is included here by permission, with only slight editorial changes.

RECONSTRUCTING BROKEN LIVES
By Patrick Cotter

A preschool-aged girl cried with abandon in the cafeteria as I waited in line. Tears streamed down her face and her little body heaved with sobs at having been left with the older man next to her, who I presumed to be her grandfather. A woman next to me opined that she'd give the girl "something to cry about—a good smack on the bottom."

I replied that I wouldn't because my memories of having been hit as a child were too unpleasant. She changed her tack. "I never had any kids." I said to myself: "Thank God for that." My silence proved uncomfortable and she tacked again. "My sister says I saved myself a lot of trouble by not having children." Again I kept my thoughts to myself: "Think of the trouble that saved the kids." In the meantime, the older man was trying to console the girl by holding a half-eaten hamburger to her lips and handing her a can of soda. It was a picture-perfect lesson in feeling-stuffing.

This scenario played out at a cafeteria in a visitor pavilion at Mt. Rushmore National Monument in the Black Hills of South Dakota. The faces of the four Presidents carved out of granite there have become a symbol of our many freedoms. Ironically, the children in this land of liberty are still not generally accorded one very precious freedom. It's the one freedom without which there is no true independence—the freedom to have and express one's feelings.

The incident was doubly ironic for me. I was in the Black Hills participating in a Family Reconstruction Workshop at Onsite Training & Consulting in nearby Rapid City. In the five-day residential workshop some 40 people came together to come to grips with painful, long-suppressed feelings through experiential therapy. What follows is how it felt to go back to re-experience and release the pain of childhood feelings.

It's a very scary proposition. But before one can allow these feelings to surface, fear must give way to trust. My fear was that I would be shamed as I had been as a child for having my feelings in the first place. I was afraid I'd end up mired in misery again after yet another effort to "get better."

My trust was that Onsite would be a safe place to experience and let go of the pain and sorrow of the dangerous, forbidden, discarded, and shameful parts of myself that had been mapped but never claimed in almost three years of group and one-on-one therapy. After 40 years of being secretly scared and sad most of the time, I know well the bitter fruits of fear. The workshop proved to be a lesson in the immense rewards of trust.

As usual, fear took the early lead. And, as usual, I was not alone. In the opening session we introduced ourselves to the group, one by one. Most admitted they were afraid and hurting. Fear and pain make me notice and judge things: The words the workshop leaders and participants use, the clothes they wear, the way they look at me, how it feels to be with them. With every heartbeat a voice murmured: *Am I safe here?* The setting didn't exactly inspire confidence. The workshop was held in a very ordinary motel on the outskirts of Rapid City.

Fear also makes me suspicious and cynical. The personalized coffee mugs we were given at the first night's dinner bore the slogan, "Celebrate the Miracles." As a recovering Catholic, the word "miracles" summons holy-card images of saints burning at the stake, martyrs riddled with arrows— grotesque proof of the "glory" that awaits those who suffer unto death. On the wall was another slogan, "Trust the Process." My reflexive response was to ask: *Why should I?*

Even with such protective armor, as I looked around and listened to the recovery stories of our "group," I began to relax my guard. These people were just like me. They had had enough suffering, were willing to take a risk to do something about it. Few people travel hundreds—or in some cases— thousands of miles to spend money and devote five days risking their innermost feelings with perfect strangers unless they are strongly motivated to find a healthy way out of their pain. Score Day One: Fear 4, Trust 1.

The next day was a guided tour of the frontiers of thinking on the causes, complications, and treatment of co-dependency. The guide was Joe Cruse, M.D., Onsite's Clinical Director. His easy manner, medical background, and track record—he was the founding medical director of the Betty Ford Clinic—made it easy to trust that this guy knows his stuff. Any guy who peppers his presentation with the phrase, "el toro poopoo" probably isn't throwing too much of the same your way.

Space does not allow a detailed explanation of Onsite's view of co-dependency, but it's clearly laid out in the book, *Understanding Co-Dependency*, written by Onsite's President Sharon Wegscheider-Cruse and Joe, her husband. It is important to note that they see co-dependency as a disease, the complications of which can disable a person physically, socially, and spiritually. They also believe it is a disease for which there is effective treatment.

A key to Onsite's approach to treatment is using past events in a person's life as a scalpel to lance and drain the "emotional abscess" caused by suppressed feelings. The abscess causes the constant pain that one medicates with alcohol, drugs, food, work, sex, religion.

Woven into Joe's presentation were brief breaks in which the large group broke into groups of three and began shedding masks and building trust through self-disclosure exercises. It's hard not to feel closer to someone when they've told you something secret about themselves.

Other ground rules reinforced what they call a "program community." Attendance at meals was compulsory. Leaving the grounds was cause for dismissal. Watching t.v. and making outside phone calls was discouraged, but not forbidden. The idea was to focus on the here-and-now, not on home.

The restrictions had the desired effect. Onsite felt like summer camp. People started hanging out, chatting on the long benches outside the big room where we ate and met as a big group, going for walks, swimming, and playing volleyball or baseball.

Later that day there was an exercise called One-Minute Sermons in which participants and leaders spent a minute in front of the group doing whatever came to mind. Some of the talents displayed were worthy of "America's Funniest People": a tongue contortionist, dislocating body parts, putting a fist in the mouth, silly singing and dancing. In no time at all the group was roaring with laughter. My suspicious self could see they were trying to get us comfortable with each other. My trusting self had to admit it was working. Score Day Two: Fear 3, Trust 1.

The next day was only the second full day, but it already felt like I'd been there several days. This was Reconstruction Day. One person, chosen long before the workshop starts, starred in this 10-hour event. Considerable advance preparation is involved. The significant people and events of her life were re-created, and then re-structured, in work, deed, and symbol. Other group members, selected by the star, play the parts of the people, and even pets, in the star's life.

Before the reconstruction got under way under Sharon's direction, she explained how re-experiencing the feelings that lead to co-dependency— and letting them go— can free one in ways that cognitive therapy can't.

Okay, I said to myself, I want to believe that's true. But I was afraid I wouldn't feel anything. I didn't have to wait long for the feelings to come.

Sharon and the star first reconstructed her family of choice—the people she chose to have in her life, including her inner child. They looked at how close they stood—literally and figuratively—to her, how they both hurt and support her, what she would change about those relationships and what she had to do or say to make those changes.

The honesty and sadness, the joy and anger, the hope and loss were moving. I was glad to be crying along with the star as I watched her begin to reconstruct her life in a way that would give life to her. Many of the people in the room were moved to tears as she moved a friend farther away, confronted, then embraced another, and said good-bye to a third whom she loved but whose denial made it painful to have as a friend.

The first session was only Act One. The second session involved her primary family—her husband and children. Now the feelings cut closer to the bone. Feelings of loss and helplessness, feelings of tenderness and heartrending sorrow. The weeping grew more unrestrained, the sobs deeper, the anger more direct, the peace more serene, the laughter lighter and more infectious. I felt like we were pulling for her. Like we were with her in body as well as in spirit.

By the end of the second session that day, I felt like I was at a championship boxing match. The star, the champ, was taking on all the pretenders to her authentic self. This was definitely not "Queen for a Day." Sharon seemed more than a director. She was a guide, a coach, an ally—and a geiger counter for emotional truth.

After lunch came the main event, the bout with her family of origin and later, her life with her husband. Mother, Father, and Siblings were depicted by role-players who acted out scenes from her life. Here the psychodramas grew more elaborate. The roles more defined. The tragedy that befell the family more compelling and heartbreaking. It felt as though it were really happening again before my eyes.

We watched how a young, innocent child was bent and warped, beaten and bruised by a disease against which she had no protection. We saw how she had to abandon her inner child, her true self, to survive the madness that surrounded her—and how she had turned to multiple medicators to numb herself from the relentless pain of having abandoned herself. First nicotine. Then alcohol. Then achievement. And all along, caretaking.

We watched as the disease claimed her whole family. My heart pumped wildly as she raged, smashing the bataka bat—a plastic stick sheathed with foam—into the pillow again and again and again. I took heart as she reclaimed the self she had surrendered so long ago. My heart heaved with hers as she summoned the courage to accept the pain of losing her family, and to accept that she was powerless to save them. We wept with her as she said good-bye. Now the tears fell freely.

Sharon seemed to use and respond to the feelings in the room the way a seasoned skipper uses the power of the wind and waves to keep a sailboat on course to safe harbor. She lifted the weight of the star's (and our) losses by providing "magic moments." One of the most moving was when the star had a tender interlude with her father, the father she had always wished she had. Sharon played a song, "My Dad Can Beat Up Your Dad, But He Wouldn't," which brought down the house—in tears. Many sobbed with abandon. It felt like this was a moment we all wished we'd had.

It was but one of the many resolutions that were achieved as the day progressed. The destruction we had witnessed became reconstruction as the star came to terms with every aspect of her past and present life. She made choices to refashion her life to nourish and protect her inner child. And Sharon extracted promises to meet certain commitments within specific time frames. The star abandoned all her medicators, and gave the pain that had traveled down through her family for generations back to its rightful owners. She had freed herself.

Winning freedom is not easy, but the star never shied form the work she had taken on for all of us to see. The reconstruction had taken from 9:00 a.m. to 8:00 p.m., with breaks for meals. Imagine replaying the most shameful parts of your life for almost 10 hours before 40 strangers. The payoff is that this time you get to reconstruct life as you would have it. Score Day Three: Fear 1, Trust 2.

The next day it was our turn—the 40 of us who watched and helped the star. We split in groups of 12 to 14 and met in stripped down motel rooms with only cushions and a bataka bat. Each group had a therapist leader and a therapist intern. Both leaders and interns had their own private practices elsewhere. They came to Onsite by invitation. But how were they going to create the trust we needed to grapple with our own feelings in public in the two days that remained?

My fear was stronger than ever now that it was our turn. I was afraid I would shut down. And I did when the first member of our small group let loose. The wails and screams brought me right back to being four years old. This was weird, scary. But then the next one wasn't so bad. I was asked to play a role in her psychodrama. The therapists were right on top of the action, keeping the ball rolling, helping the person through with the right word or touch. I felt safer. Tears came. Then I played another role in another's work. The bataka flew. Raging screams filled room. Tears flowed. Now I felt brave enough to try.

I began speaking of my sadness and anger. Two emotions that were absolutely unacceptable for me to display in public. Within a half a minute I was swept away by a torrent of wordless wails. It was as if the desperate, aching sobs were flowing through me from somewhere else, from some other time, some other country. I could not stop them welling up from deep within. They washed me overboard.

My guess is that the storm raged for three minutes, maybe four. Gradually the sobbing subsided. I was weak and spent. Two members of the group helped me to my feet and I began to breathe deeply. My rage rose and boiled over. I screamed my anger and my hurt with abandon as my supports held me back like I was a mad dog. My body shook, as though it could not contain the power coursing through it. My voice erupted like a volcano, spewing words hot with rage. When the eruption abated, I was trembling all over. My fingers tingled. My legs shook uncontrollably. There was blood on my hands where the fingernails had dug into the skin. But it felt wonderful to be free of such intense pain and sorrow.

The group gained momentum. Member after member found their courage and confronted their demons. They re-experienced the shame of physical, sexual, and emotional abuse, and expunged their grief with tears and rage. The therapists were always there with a word or touch to help us identify, own, and express our feelings. This was done by invitation, not confrontation. As each person took the risk and did his or her "work," the sense of trust grew deeper. We would be there for each other. It was safe to be unsafe. It felt like victory.

By the end of the day 8 of the 12 had "done their work." It was apparently the same in other small groups. The feeling in the air was palpably different at the motel. Now there was laughter as unrestrained as the tears. There was a looseness and uninhibited air. The way kids behave when they're free to be themselves. Score Day Three: Fear 1, Trust 3.

On the fourth, and last full day of the workshop, the small groups met in the morning. Two more of our group did their work. But there seemed to be no shame attached to those who declined to do their work center stage in the group. Their "private" work was respected.

In the afternoon, we reconvened as a large group for a "Parts Party." Group members chose eight traits about themselves, four they liked and four they didn't. Then we chose characters, real or imagined, living or dead, we felt embodied those traits. There was one character per trait, but overall four male and four female characters.

Sharon asked me to be the one whose characters had a party. I chose eight members of the group to play the different parts. While those eight prepared costumes and a party, the rest of us waited outside. When we returned, the fun began. Remember, we've been wrestling with heavy emotions for three days and we're feeling pretty free. We're giddy and acting like kids at camp who've been cooped up because of rain.

The party was a nice taste of what one can do with oneself as the pain and sorrow of the past slip away. It was also well-earned playtime after a lot of work. Score Day Four: Fear 1 (it was a bit scary being the center of attention in the big group), Trust 4.

The workshop ended the next day after breakfast. We came together as a big group for the last time and received a certificate of participation (and 42 continuing education credits). Each participant said a few words to the group. Most were grateful and thrilled at what they had experienced. I admitted I had been cynical about the miracles, but that I now believed because I had experienced a small one of my own.

We then broke into small groups and sang a farewell song, the only line of which I remember is this: "All I ask is that you remember me loving you." After the intensity of feeling and level of trust reached over the previous three days, those words carried real weight. There wasn't a dry eye in the house by the time the song finished. At least I didn't see one. And then we all turned out from the circle, symbolizing that this circle had served its purpose and was now broken. And then we went home, each having taken a big step to begin reconstructing our broken lives. Final Score: Fear ½, Trust 5.

CHAPTER EIGHT

KATHY'S STORY

INTRODUCTION

When I first began my journey of recovery I had very little memory of my childhood. My feelings were frozen and my needs were not yet known, even to me. Things have changed a lot since then. I remember much more. I am a feeling being. I feel pain and anger and loss, and more. These feelings have freed me to experience more love and joy than I ever dreamed possible.

The next pages tell the story of my life according to me. It is wonderful to know this much about my life, and to feel this much about my life.

MOM'S FAMILY

My mother was the first daughter of a family of eight children. She had one older half-brother, one older brother, and one twin brother. She also had one sister and three younger brothers. Their family was very poor. My grandfather was a binge drinker and refused to work steadily. He was explosive and abusive to my grandmother and to the children. Their roles were often to protect their mother physically and to take the abuse themselves, especially the older ones. My grandfather also had affairs and he would disappear for days at a time. My grandmother did what she could to meet the physical needs of the children, but she was unemotional and overwhelmed.

My mother's role was that of caretaker to her younger siblings. She tells stories of trying to make sure her younger brother would have shoes to wear to school and a warm jacket. The older boys would torture the two girls. They would tie them up and tease them with snakes. (My mother is still petrified by snakes, and can't even watch them on television.) Her youngest brother was killed in an elevator shaft when he was 16.

Many of the children, including my mother, developed alcohol problems. Relationship and sex addiction also ran high among her male siblings.

At family functions I remember a lot of drinking and usually a fight as it got later, with one family member or another jumping on the table. The family as I remember it always had a pretense of being close, and always secretly had internal wars.

DAD'S FAMILY

My father was the younger of two children. The story goes that he only weighed about two pounds at birth, and they kept him in a shoe box in back of the stove where it was warm in order to keep him alive. He had an older sister who took most of the abuse in the family. My father was the favored and smothered child.

I loved my grandfather. He was an easygoing man. He sang and smiled and had very little power. I understand, however, that he had an ongoing affair for many years. He also drank. When I was about seven or eight years old, he was diagnosed with diabetes and lost both his legs. He became quieter—still good-natured, but with a broken spirit. He quit drinking then, sort of.

My grandmother was a compulsive overeater as well as an alcoholic. By the time I knew her she was cute and old and funny. Apparently she had been mean and abusive to her husband and daughter. It is said that she used to hit my grandfather with a frying pan. She also had problems with her "nerves" and there were times when she would become overwhelmed and drop my father and aunt off at the orphanage for a little while. My grandmother was lazy, and never did more than she had to. My aunt was the caretaker and my father the fair-haired boy. I was told that when he went into the service, my grandmother covered her furniture and blocked the windows until he came home. As she grew older, and this includes almost all of my memories of her, my grandmother sat in a chair and insisted on everyone waiting on her. No one resisted. She would ask my sister or me to get her "milk," citing that we were younger than she, and we would scurry out to the kitchen to get her beer. We thought it was funny.

Grandma also had the best lap in the world. It was soft and squishy and she always let us curl up in it. Thank goodness it was big enough for two! I loved my grandmother.

My aunt was also a compulsive overeater with "nerve" problems. She would become quite frightened or anxious at various points in her life, and she would go to bed and stay there for months. At the age of 59, during one of these bedridden periods, she died. My aunt had used pills for her nerves. My father used alcohol for his.

My father's nickname was Junior, and that's all I ever heard his family call him.

MOM

My mother is a mix of so many things. She was definitely the organizer of our family. We had little money, but our clothes were always clean and ironed. I never felt poor. There was always just enough to get by. We also always kept moving up just a little.

My mother worked in jewelry factories most of her life. She set stones and was proud of how fast she was at her work. Often she would work from September to June, and then quit or find a way to get laid off for the summer to be home with us.

I don't remember hugs from my mother. We had ritualistic pecks on the cheek at the appropriate times, but never that feeling I had on my grandmother's lap. Mom was also very negative. The emphasis was always more on what couldn't be rather than on what could be. She was a screamer—loud, domineering, and controlling. There was a lot of criticism of me and of others. She believed that if she praised us too much or told us we were pretty, our heads would swell. She said again and again that she would trust me until I screwed up once, so by my teen years, I was trying very hard not to screw up. I took very few risks, I did not believe in myself, and I withdrew.

It was also in my early teens that Mom started drinking and my world caved in. I was scared and embarrassed, and I wanted to hide. There were many crises related to my mother's drinking as time went on: broken bones, calls from her job, stories from her friends, and embarrassments when friends would see her drunk. Eventually, my Mom stopped drinking on her own. She insisted—and still insists—that doing it on her own represents a major strength. I'm grateful she no longer drinks or smokes (she quit that on her own, too). Her drinking, smoking, rage, and insistence that she did not need help all took their toll, however, and she has paid dearly.

My contact with my mother had been very limited for years. She had no idea who I was. Then, last fall, a miracle happened and our relationship changed. Unfortunately, my mother had to suffer a stroke for this to occur. But now she is vulnerable, she accepts help when she needs it, and she is beginning to know her youngest child a little.

DAD

I loved my Dad. I felt sorry for him. Mom picked on him, and that's why he had to drink.

I believed that for years.

My Dad was quiet. He cried. He used to touch my Mom's hair and call her pet names. He would sing in the kitchen and make up his own words to the songs. Actually, he was like another child.

He took no responsibility for anything but going to work. He would do what my mother told him to do, and seemed to have no power of his own. I would never ask my Dad for help with anything or for his opinion. He was just "there."

He would always drink daily. He had his quart of Narragansett Beer beside him in his special chair, and he would drink until he fell asleep. My five-year-old nephew found my father dead in that chair at the age of 49. I now know that my Dad was always depressed. My last memories of him are in a lawn chair in our garage with his head in his hands. It was his 49th birthday, and he was crying. He said he had nothing to live for. He had lost his job. My sister and I were married and on our own. He and mother fought constantly (nothing new).

He died about two weeks later. The death certificate says he died of a heart attack. I wonder, though, if it wasn't heartbreak, or alcoholism, or suicide from the heartbreak and through the alcoholism.

ME

I vaguely remember myself as a very young child; I don't remember with my head, though, but rather with my heart. I had a strong spirit, a great sense of humor, and I was vulnerable and loveable. I was also scared and unsure where I belonged in my family.

I am the younger of two children. My sister is four years older than me. She was born with congenital heart problems and had surgery at the age of seven. Much of the focus in our family was around illness. She was sick and I was well. I learned to be good, and not to seek attention. I felt unimportant, unnecessary, on the outside looking in.

My earliest memory is of staying at a relative's house while my sister was having her heart surgery. I was four years old at the time. The image in my mind is of me standing on a stool at the telephone, calling Mom and Dad to come and get me. I was scared and alone (I now know I felt abandoned). Would my sister die? I had heard adults saying she had a 50-50 chance. Would my family forget me? Didn't they know I was afraid of my uncle? Didn't they care?

My parents did come to get me, but those feelings of fear, loneliness, unimportance, and abandonment stayed with me for years.

I had a lot of trouble in the first grade. I wrote all my letters backwards. I was left-handed and had a hard time making the letters at all. They were big, my name was long, and my handwriting was messy.

Often, I would get "sick" at school (I said I had backaches) and insist on going home. They would get my sister out of class and make her walk me home. She didn't appreciate it, and let me know about it. But I was afraid of my teacher. I was also accused of cheating in front of the whole class. I felt scared and stupid and, once again, alone.

In second grade, they discovered I needed glasses—relief (I could see) and embarrassment (I looked different). Now I didn't belong at home and I didn't belong at school.

I don't remember Dad's drinking at this time, although I know he did. Mom yelled a lot. There was a lot of rage towards Dad most of the time. Dad took it, but occasionally he would fight back. I don't remember it getting physical, but I do remember my fear. Stomach aches and constipation were part of my daily existence as I tried to cope with the tension and terror.

We did have a big, extended family, and I loved that. My Grandma and Grandpa on my father's side were always around. Grandma used to babysit a lot for us when we were little. She'd make batches of French fries for all our friends while we were outside playing. (Thanks, Grandma.)

My Dad's sister and my Mom's brother were married—Aunt Jane and Uncle Ron. They had no children. They kind of adopted us, especially me. They paid attention to me, and thought I was cute and funny and special. They encouraged my free spirit. (I used to laugh at my Aunt's dirty jokes whereas my sister was too prim and proper to enjoy them.) I loved them both. They had ulterior motives, but I didn't know this then. I just needed to be noticed.

My family celebrated everything. Whenever there was a birthday, we would all get together for ice cream and cake and beer. (To this day, I cherish the ice cream and cake part of the tradition.) At about the age of nine, I started gaining weight. My grandfather who had diabetes had had his legs amputated, and I always believed these two things were related. My father withdrew and probably started drinking more. Fights in the house escalated.

Going to school each morning was a major event. My mother always woke up cranky, and she used to lose things—the comb, her purse, her shoes. Each morning she would scream at my sister and me until we left for school. We always left crying and shaken. To my knowledge, my mother rarely drank during this period, but the effects of her rage and criticism were devastating enough.

Dad was quiet. He didn't yell very often, and he didn't intervene. He didn't interact very much at all. He was the good guy, but he failed to come to our rescue.

I vacillate between "I" and "we." It is hard to separate myself from my sister during this period. We were all each other had. Any sense of security I had was because of her. We fought some, but basically we pulled together to survive.

By junior high, I was no longer overweight, but unfortunately, I hadn't gotten over the feeling of being overweight. I always thought I was fat. I still struggled with food, and had to be careful. My mother and sister, on the other hand, were always very thin. I had been told from a young age that I looked like my grandmother and was built like my father. In my eyes, my grandmother was fat, toothless, and old. I didn't understand what they meant about looking like my father except that he was 6'2" and wasn't like my sister and my mother. I had a very distorted body image and I felt ugly. Despite these feelings, I blossomed. School got better. I discovered I could do well and decided to excel (in contrast to my sister, who chose not to focus on her education), although inside I still felt stupid and inadequate and I was waiting for someone to "find me out."

Things began to deteriorate grossly during my adolescence. My father's drinking began to show its effects. His depression and isolation worsened. He lost his job. He began drinking whiskey as well as beer, and he started fighting back, loudly. It was scary. At one point I was dressing as many did in the late 60s—jeans, a white shirt, and love beads. My father called me a slut and yelled until I was angry and in tears. There were a few such scenes. No one felt safe to me anymore. My new school was too big and it overwhelmed me. My grandparents had died. Aunt Rita had touched me inappropriately once when I cuddled up next to her, and I never got that close again. Uncle Cliff had withdrawn, my sister had married. The most crushing factor, though, was that my mother had begun to drink.

My spirit broke. I had a small group of friends with whom I could be myself, but outside of that circle I was shy, ashamed, and withdrawn. I dated primarily guys who didn't go to my school. My one high school love that I felt good about was someone in one of my classes—Charlie. I knew what I wanted and went for it. I dated Charlie for two years. My parents hated him and made life miserable for me. During this period—and this was the only time it happened, when they were screaming about my relationship, I would scream back, hysterically. Just scream, desperately, again and again. Finally they would be quiet, scared I was going crazy. I know now that I was fighting for my own reality. It was incredibly scary.

While still dating Charlie, I met my husband. It was on a blind date. My very best friend, Sandy, and my husband's best friend, Alan, were dating. They saw our pain and fixed us up.

On our first date, I experienced a gentleness and deep connection that I had never felt before. This person was safe. I felt as though I had been lost in a desert and finally found something to drink. My spirit had been parched and dry. In Ray, I saw hope for life and freedom.

We dated long-distance for three years. Ray was in medical school in Philadelphia and I was in college in Rhode Island. We cherished each other, and really learned to appreciate each letter, each phone call, each visit.

Things at home, meanwhile, were worse. I went home every weekend during college, afraid that if I didn't my parents would kill each other or themselves. I now know also that I had no idea how to relate to college life, so it was safer to withdraw.

Ray and I married six days after he graduated from medical school. We thought everything in our lives would be wonderful from that day forward. He was starting his internship and I was teaching.

Ray's father died one month later. We were crushed. I really loved him and he thought I was wonderful. He was fun, and he cared about us. I later learned he had not been very effective as a parent, though—similar to my father in many ways, but at least more outgoing.

Ray and I clung to each other. He felt he had to take care of his mother. She depended on him to take her husband's place. For a long time, he tried to fill the gap. I felt abandoned and grew angry.

My own father died five months later. Another blow. Another responsibility. Our honeymoon was short-lived. We continued to cling to each other, but there was so much pain buried on both sides. My mother's drinking was more out of control than ever.

Almost a year-and-a-half later, our oldest daughter Jodie was born. Another oasis. I loved motherhood. Jodie was beautiful, precious, sweet, and she loved me unconditionally. What a blessing.

Twenty-one months later, we had Deanna. There was a special sparkle in her eyes from birth, and she, too, was (and is) beautiful and wonderful and special.

I was happy. My family loved me and I loved them. My relationship with my husband was based partly on pain and need, but it was based also on love. I didn't realize it, but I had decided somewhere along the way that if I could control everything in my life, I would be safe—there wouldn't be any surprises or disappointments, and I wouldn't get hurt. Through the pain and emotional abuse I had suffered, I had become rigid and controlling and angry as well as lost, and it showed.

I got pregnant again. This time we had a son, Brett. He was born ten weeks early, had lung problems, and died five days after he was born.

My theory hadn't worked. I blamed my body and the doctors. I fell into depression, and my eating got out of control. I didn't get into recovery for several years, but to me, this was my bottom. Somehow, my spirituality was born. I loved my son. I remember seeing him in the hospital, touching him, feeling the despair about what might happen, trying desperately to hold on to some hope. Ray and I had no idea how to handle this one. It wasn't supposed to happen. Our relationship improved and it suffered. We pulled together and we pulled apart.

Much of this time is still a blur. Today my son is my special angel, and I love him still. Ray and I wanted another child very much. Almost two years and a miscarriage later, our youngest daughter, Kerri, was born. The pregnancy was scary (I needed surgery to hold her), and the delivery was scary because I worried about something going wrong again. But the result was miraculous—that beautiful baby was a gift from God that I cherish.

I delighted in my children. I was a good mother, but I was rough around the edges. I was a screamer like my own mother, more than I like to admit. I was depressed and didn't realize it. I was a compulsive overeater and didn't realize it.

But life went on. I went back to school to become a counselor. Maybe I could fix my family. Both Ray's mother and mine interfered in our relationship; my sister was having problems in her marriage, so I went to the rescue. I was overwhelmed, exhausted, and trying to hold it all together. In school I had started to learn that I couldn't fix anyone, but I could help myself. I went to a conference in 1985 where I heard Sharon Wegscheider-Cruse speak for the first time, and the message changed my life.

I found out that my pain affected my children. I found out that love is not about taking care of everyone in sight. I found out that my sense of control was an illusion. The biggest discovery was finding out that I had deep pain inside, and that I had to let it out in order to live. I cried through the entire lecture, which was pretty unusual for me. A special angel was there that day, though. I had never seen her before and I haven't seen her since. She held my hand and told me I could get help and that I deserved it—I was important enough. My spirit leapt for joy. I could break the chain.

I went to a reconstruction workshop with Sharon and I cried for five days. When I came home, I could actually begin to feel the love I knew I had. I made amends to my children, to my husband, and to others.

I went to another reconstruction workshop. This time I got angry. I went home and set boundaries with everyone I knew.

Then I took a risk and asked to be a star at a reconstruction. My Higher Power led Sharon to hear my tiny voice. In June of 1987, I was the star of my own reconstruction. I allowed my life to be unfolded before a large group of people. I publicly decided not to stay lost. I faced the foundation of pain and need on which my relationship with my husband had been built. And this time, I went home, and my life has been unfolding ever since.

My husband had his own reconstruction in May of 1992, and he feels as free as I do. The love we've always had has grown, and is now cherished and nurtured. There is so much less pain, that we have more room for joy. We are both constantly changing and growing and this is exciting. I love you, Ray— thank you.

My children are now teenagers, and they are so much wiser than I was. I have given them the best gift a mother can possibly give her children—my own recovery. With that, I've given them a life based on honesty and love. I know in my heart that their spirits have flourished under this. I can see the effects of recovery in each of them, and I'm so proud. They are not perfect, and I have not been perfect, but who cares? Jodie, Deanna, and Kerri, I invite you to fly—I love you all. You are special!

CHAPTER NINE

TED'S STORY

*As he stepped from behind the partition, I burst into un-
controllable tears of relief and gratitude.*

I was so moved that I woke from the dream still crying. Although I did not
know the full significance of my dream, somehow I knew that I had witnessed something very important.

My healing process began some twenty years prior to my reconstruction
in 1990. I was raised in a physically and emotionally abusive environment
that had the full weight of generations of shameful secrets and was ravaged
by the complications and emotional pain of a generational chronic illness,
the bleeding disorder known as hemophilia, which I carry.

When I was a young adolescent, my parents became deeply involved in a
fundamentalist "fire and brimstone" religion which served to reinforce the
family mores of control through instilling feelings of guilt, shame, and
personal unworthiness. Personal difficulty or unhappiness were interpreted as personal failures due to an "incorrect" relationship with God. As a
young man, and through my early adulthood, I tried to "get right" with God,
"be right" with God, "stay right" with God, and "do the right thing."

At the age of 26, I was experiencing great difficulties in my marriage,
suffering the physical symptoms of a pre-ulcer condition, and receiving
from my spiritual leader the "You'll know why God has given you this
burden when you die" advice. I made the most difficult decision I have ever
had to make when I left my church, my wife, and my two young children and
all of our friends. I threw into turmoil my relationships with my parents, my
brother, and my sister, all of whom were deeply and powerfully enmeshed in
the religious system I was abandoning.

What moved me to act with such uncharacteristic courage was the
degree of pain I was in, and a little voice inside myself, long ignored, telling
me that if I didn't get out I was going to be dead. Whether this death was

going to be physical or spiritual didn't matter—either possibility was something I wasn't willing to risk.

I spent the next 20 years angry at religion and those who had practiced it "on" me. I became an agnostic, seeking meaning through voracious reading, attending workshops and training, and through my work as a high school counselor. I became more and more intrigued by what I was learning about the history, philosophy, and spiritual beliefs of the Native American people. My interest was piqued enough to actually spend parts of two years on Native reservations in Arizona.

Living on the reservation in the midst of unbelievable poverty, I found a peace and serenity that I had never known. About the time I felt that I had found a place to be, that now familiar little voice inside said, "Now you know what it feels like. It's time for you to find it in your own culture and among your own people." This seemed an impossible task, since I knew of no one anywhere in my culture who possessed the qualities of acceptance, peace, and serenity in the degree I had found them with Native Americans.

My quest led me to become professionally involved in the alcoholism treatment field. The public school system I was associated with was one of the first to respond institutionally in an appropriate manner to the effects on students of alcoholism and other drug addiction; compulsive behaviors; chronic stress; and rigid family or religious systems. In the course of my professional training while I was serving as the supervisor for this student assistance program, I became aware of the work of Dr. Joseph Cruse, and Sharon Wegscheider-Cruse, and of Onsite Training and Consulting, the organization they had created to address the family issues raised by family dysfunction.

I eventually attended one of Onsite's five-day "Learning to Love Yourself" family reconstruction workshops. While witnessing the star's psychodrama, the little voice inside me (which I had begun to trust more and more all the time) said that I, too, deserved a chance to experience what I was witnessing. After arguing with myself about the wisdom of following that urging voice, I applied and was accepted as a star in the family reconstruction process. Two years of very intense personal therapy as well as extensive research into my family history lay ahead of me as I prepared for my own reconstruction day.

July 16, 1990, was the date of my reconstruction. I now look back on it in many ways as my "emotional birthday." I arrived at the site from Michigan, having brought with me some important artifiacts I had collected during the previous couple of years which held special meaning for me and served as physical reminders of all the hard work that had gone into my preparation for this event: an arrowhead my second wife and I found on our property, a miniature statue of a wolf, a special stone, and more. I had wanted to add a feather to this collection, but spent the first two days of the program without finding one, or even seeing or hearing a bird, which was quite unusual for the mountains of South Dakota. The feather was to make its appearance at a later date.

The night before my reconstruction, I had a vivid dream about the day ahead. In the dream, I imagined the various scenes that would be a part of my psychodrama. The dream culminated in a scene in which the guide said to me, "I know you've had difficulty connecting with a Higher Power or God— would you like to meet Him?" I was stunned by the question, since I believed that in order to save my life 20 years earlier, I had chosen to abandon God. I managed to say yes, though, and the guide motioned to someone, and as he stepped from behind the partition, a man dressed in a deerskin fringed shirt with his arms wide open and a smile on his face seemed to fill the room. I recognized him immediately as a Native American medicine man or *shaman.*

As I realized the implications of his presence, I burst into tears of joy, relief, gratitude, and an awe so profound that it woke me from my sleep. As I lay awake, still crying, I knew for the first time that I had not abandoned God and God had not abandoned me, but that God had been made manifest to me over the last two decades in a form that I could see and accept. I suddenly understood my interest in learning and experiencing Native American culture—their history, their value system, and their spirituality.

The next morning my reconstruction began. The major theme that emerged during the day was one of tying up loose ends and of letting go. I completed unfinished business with my hometown therapist, my friends, my deceased grandmother, my children and ex-wife, medical and religious communities, and my childhood environment of abuse, terror, and neglect.

The weather during my reconstruction seemed to match the mood of my life chronologically, especially as I confronted the terror, abuse, and fear of my childhood environment. At times it was raining with high winds whistling around the building; it was "dark and stormy." At one key moment while I was doing anger work about my religious abuse, a bolt of lightening hit the ground very close to the building, with an accompanying thunderclap that literally shook the room.

About a year-and-a-half earlier, during a time when doctors had said that for some reason my immune system had decided that my skin did not belong to me, and that my body was trying to reject my own skin, I had had a dream about observing an operation in a hospital. A wolf was being operated on—he was on his back in a semi-reclined position. As I watched, the doctors seemed to pull a zipper down the wolf's front and lift a small baby from inside its body. I asked the doctors what was happening and one said, "Sometimes when children are born, it's not safe for them to be people, so they are put into an animal's body until it is safe. It is now safe for this little boy to be in the world."

I had awakened near the end of this profound dream and I knew that its meaning was significant, but I was quite unaware of the exact meaning. I included this information in my written materials in preparation for the reconstruction.

The climax of my reconstruction brought full meaning to this dream. During this scene, I was asked to sit in a chair and close my eyes. The lights were dimmed and the curtains pulled. It felt as if a cloak was put across my shoulders. Soft music was playing. The guide read a very moving poem entitled "I Give You Back" from Joy Harjo's collection *She Had Some Horses.* After the reading, the guide said, "I give you the name of Little Wolf, in honor of your dream, and to symbolize this sacred moment, I give you this—" and as I turned to look, I was given a white feather. Suddenly I knew why I had not been able to find a feather earlier in the week. At that moment, I was filled with a feeling of instant healing, like an immediate cauterization of my psychic wounds.

The audience was also profoundly moved by this experience, because although I was unaware of it, the weather outside had changed during this ceremony. The storms had passed, the winds had calmed, and through a torn section of the curtain, a beam of sunlight had illuminated the chair in which I was seated. Later, a Native American woman approached me to ask, "You were healed during that ceremony, weren't you?" I answered that yes, it had felt like some kind of healing had occurred, though I couldn't put it into words, and she said, "I knew that, because I was healed too."

Three years have passed since my reconstruction, and every aspect of my life has changed. The most immediate effect of my experience was my increased ability to see, hear, and feel more clearly the world I lived in and interacted with.

This increased sensitivity was both painful and pleasurable. The new awareness and subsequent decisions I've made have resulted in many changes. The quality of my relationships with my partner, my children, my family of origin, my Higher Power, and most of all myself, has improved beyond my greatest imaginings. I have chosen a different profession and I have re-located to a more spiritual place. I have experienced an increased ability to let go of the people and things I cannot control. I and others have noticed my own increased willingness to do some of the "hard" things such as confronting, setting boundaries, and arguing that are frequently involved in maintaining the quality of my important relationships.

I used to dream and hope for a time (perhaps I could only imagine it occurring on my deathbed) of healing with my children, of closeness with my partner, of peace with my Higher Power, and of peace with myself. The effect of the reconstruction process and my recovery program has been that I have received and continued to receive these things while I still have life. The reconstruction process has been a life-changing, life-giving event for me.

CHAPTER TEN

ANN'S STORY

For me, the reconstruction process was a spiritual pathway, the ultimate exercise in trust in a Higher Power. I knew I was being led to places I needed and wanted to be, yet I had no sense that I knew the direction. There is a German word—I have forgotten it—but translated, it means "homesickness for a place you've never been." I couldn't believe there was a word that stated so clearly the feeling I carried inside myself most of my life. That word sums up where I was before reconstruction, which turned out to be about finding the way back to a place I dreamed of. I feel I have come home.

My process really began thanks to my husband. His alcoholism and my caretaking of him nearly killed us both. When I look back at those 18 years of alcoholic marriage, I don't know how either of us survived. Luck, stubbornness, and the terrible fear of being or doing something differently kept us together. But when he hit his final crisis and bottomed out, he found sobriety and recovery in A.A.; I didn't know what to do next.

I was skeptical, angry, and resistent, but I tried AlAnon. About four months into our shaky new life, we were invited to a talk about the disease of alcoholism and how it affects the family. The presenter was a therapist named Mary Lee Zawadski. She showed a film in which she was reconstructed by Sharon Wegscheider-Cruse called *Another Chance*. It was 1982, and the film was brand new. We were stunned and moved by what we saw. The film was to change our lives. When someone tells the story of your own life in a movie, the story you have carried as a secret for years, the impact is profound. This was the first time either of us faced the emotional pain of our early lives. We both went into a 28-day treatment program for chemical and co-dependency. We began communicating, changing our behavior, and making the amends for past mistakes that were necessary to save our marriage. Neither of us had much faith in God after those drinking years, but we learned to pray for our relationship and live a spiritual marriage. We continued to be active in 12-Step groups.

About three years later, my husband and I hit a new level of pain as we faced the issue of our nicotine addiction. Clean and sober—even emotional sobriety—looked a little ridiculous while puffing on cigarettes. But not smoking seemed to unleash frightening feelings.

Although we both worked hard to embrace A.A. and AlAnon, we seemed stuck in old grief, anger, and hurt. I couldn't shake the depression and low self-worth that had been my friend since childhood.

Bill's sponsor told us about a place called Onsite, in Rapid City, South Dakota, where Sharon Wegscheider-Cruse (there was that name again!) helped people deal with the emotional pain of recovering families. Again, Bill led the way. I went to my first reconstruction in July of 1985 with my "heels in the asphalt," so to speak.

I was stunned again! The beautiful unfolding of a person's life—the star told it all! She raged, cried, laughed, and celebrated. The audience had the same emotions. I have always loved the theater. This was an incredible play of reality and humanity.

At the same time I was totally miserable. I had a headache, a stomach ache, and couldn't sleep. I was terrified to tell the group who I was or to show my feeling. I felt naked and alone. Looking back, it doesn't seem that I got much out of the workshop, but the seed was planted there. I knew I needed what this place had to offer. I commmitted to begin to change and feel, whatever it took. I stopped smoking for good, and got help to start feeling.

I came back to Onsite over the next five years until it was comfortable. I learned about my painful issues and how to express feelings. Onsite became my siritual home as I fell in love with the sacred Black Hills of the Lakota Indians. I trained to do the experiential therapy and began to work at Onsite. I got to know Sharon and her husband Joe as employers, as mentors, and as friends.

Then one day Sharon gave me one of her gentle and loving but firm nudges. "I think you can train to do reconstructions, but only if you are willing to be reconstructed yourself." Another stop-in-my-tracks moment. I had never considered myself worthy of being a star (my unresolved shame and low self-worth again). I couldn't imagine my life being interesting enough to create a day of work. Everyone would be bored to death. My family wasn't even very dysfunctional! My fear and denial were working overtime. Because deep down inside, I knew Sharon was right. As a person who had always overachieved and tried to look good and be good, I couldn't see a way to refuse. So I delved into my reconstruction investigation. I started with my reasons and issues—especially those ongoing feelings of shame and depression and low self-worth after so many years of therapy.

I researched by parents' families. My mother had some historical documents and my Dad had an aunt who had studied their genealogy. They sent me what they had and told me the stories they knew. I believe they were happy one of their children was interested in family history. They copied old family photographs and birth certificates.

MOTHER'S FAMILY

My maternal great-grandfathers were cowboys and pioneers. They were rugged men who settled in the West and ran in the Oklahoma land rush. One a German and the other an Englishman, they settled in the south-westernmost county of Oklahoma and built sod houses to live in. One of my great-grandfathers was a very respected, successful businessman and banker. He was one of the first legislators in the state of Oklahoma and a friend of the Apache Indians. His oldest son, my granddaddy, had big shoes to fill. The Depression hit as he became an adult, and he never lived up to his father. The bank failed and the family fortunes were lost. I remember him as an extremely quiet man who was hard of hearing. He lived within himself and had no visible emotions. But he was a man of great faith in his quiet way—he knew how to meditate and be still with God. He read the Bible all the way through every year, and walked to church every Sunday and on Wednesday evenings. He was the kind of granddaddy who bounced you on his knee. He put a wooden Santa ornament in the front yard at Christmas. He lived to be 97 years old, and was a safe and loving role model for me.

My other maternal great-grandfather was an alcoholic and a womanizer. He was a source of embarrassment and shame to a small community in Southwest Oklahoma. His wife was an oldest daughter who had raised some of her own sisters and brothers. She must have been tired, married to an alcoholic, because she passed her own parental responsibilities onto her first-born daughter, my grandmother.

My maternal grandmother was strong-willed. Until almost the end of her life, she took care of and ran the lives of her two younger brothers and four younger sisters. She ran the local welfare office and held a position that would be considered a forerunner of a social worker. Her religion was stern and righteous, perhaps to compensate for the embarrassment of a father who was a drunk and had affairs with women her own age.

She loved me as her oldest granddaughter. My happiest childhood memories were of summers spent shucking corn and picking flowers from her garden. Maybe she knew we were a lot alike. She went to college by paying her own way—pretty special for a frontier woman at the turn of the century. She became my role model in life as a strong, intelligent woman whose job was to care for others and who carried the unfinished shame of her alcoholic family.

Her oldest daughter was my mother. My mother did not have the out-going self-confidence of her own mother. She was shy and insecure—more like her father. She didn't seem to inherit the responsibilities of the oldest female child, but she learned well how to be a caretaker. She learned to hide the shame and carry on unfinished family business.

My mother doesn't talk about her childhood pain. But it seems she was frightened of a lot of things, had little confidence in herself, and tried always to avoid conflict or anger. Some of her aunts and uncles were what I would call "ashamed alcoholics," that is, they were quiet and secret drinkers. Many were overweight or obese. I saw in my mother's family a preoccupation with weight and food.

FATHER'S FAMILY

My father's family were farmers in Kansas. In fact, a family story goes that my great-grandfather left a good farm in Indiana to buy "the worst piece of farmland in Kansas." His sense of failure turned him to drink and he died when my paternal grandfather was eight years old.

The youngest of nine children with nine of her own left to care for, my paternal great-grandmother was an unhappy and bitter woman left in poverty. She told her daughters to never marry, and four of them stayed "old maids." Pictures and my childhood memories of them showed a continuation of bitterness and repressed anger. They relied heavily on my grandfather in their old age. He didn't much like women for that.

My grandfather did a variety of things for a living, none of which were more than moderately successful. He lived a modest and uneventful life, and carried on a sense of failure and repressed anger about it. He did have one special quality that he passed on in his family, and that was his sense of humor. It was fun, and he liked to make puns. Sometimes the teasing was kind of angry, though. They never drank or had liquor in their houses, but my grandfather did have some very scary mannerisms that bothered me as a child. When I sat on his lap he would caress my arms and legs in a way that felt very bad. He washed his hands with lava soap, and to this day the smell of lava soap nauseates me.

My mother wouldn't stop him, but she would watch in great alarm, and we never spent the night there. I don't fully understand the extent of his sexual inappropriateness. But his behavior, in addition to other sexual behavior in my family, made me very frightened. I knew instinctively that sex wasn't talked about no matter what. I believed it was shameful and bad—too bad to talk about. Even if Mom knew, she wouldn't say anything.

My paternal grandmother came from a family in which there are many secrets. It is known that her parents were first cousins and had no contact with their families. Looking at old photos, the women in her family were very obese.

My grandmother never wanted to marry, hated the idea of sex, and didn't want children. The family story is that she was persuaded with a lot of effort on my grandfather's part to do all three. Much to her chagrin, she became pregnant, and accidentally lost the baby in a fall. She felt God was punishing her for her bad attitude. She then had my Dad and his sister. She seemed to view children as a duty rather than as a joy.

As a child, I didn't think she liked me at all. I don't remember her much liking my Dad or being a loving grandmother. She seemed angry, bitter, and unhappy. She never had toys or allowed her grandchildren to play. She was very obese and arthritic.

My Dad is a very smart man. He has enjoyed the benefits of reading and learning all of his life. I think he would have been a good teacher. He has also done a variety of things to make a living. This was especially true during the first 11 years of my life when we moved a lot with his job changes. It doesn't feel to me that he feels any more successful though, than his father or grandfather. He seemed to carry that unresolved anger that his family all possessed. He wasn't violent or abusive, but he simmered with frustration and could use words to be very hurtful.

MY PARENTS

My parents met during the second world war. They were both in college, and married when my father began his Officer's Training toward the end of the war. They seem to be genuinely in love with each other. They brought to their newly created family the values of honest hard work, decency, loyalty, and faith in God. They gave their three daughters, of whom I am the oldest, all the love and care they were capable of giving. Times were often hard for them—money and success were difficult to come by. Their relationship danced around his anger and her fears, but their love and simple virtues were never in doubt.

As I wrote and gathered materials for my reconstruction day, themes began to emerge. I realized I had a heritage of many gifts from strong, hardy people, but I also saw the alcoholism, eating disorders, sexual acting out, shame, caretaking (especially among eldest daughters), and the inability to express feelings or resolve family pain. None of these issues were talked about openly. We were a looking-good, feeling-bad family.

I believe that my perceptions as a child of all these unspoken pieces of family baggage translated to an idea that there was something wrong with me. I loved these people and they loved me. What was wrong with this picture?

PREPARATIONS

Many feelings surfaced for me as I wrote my life story and identified issues. I had to keep in touch with my therapist and keep myself emotionally stable while waiting to process what I was learning and beginning to feel.

One of the most beautiful and painful parts of the process was the gathering of my photograph albums. There were boxes and albums of photographs and slides, old scrapbooks, and memorabilia stuck in cubby-holes. These were the mementos of 46 years. Choosing those that personified or epitomized my life, I put them in chronological order. As I looked, really looked, at the eyes and facial expressions of that baby, then toddler, child, and adolescent, I could see the history of the emotional pain that I carried.

An important decision made in the preparation of my reconstruction was whether my husband would attend. He had a good, solid recovery of his own. We had worked hard to clean up the conflicts of 25 years of marriage. As he watched me working to prepare for the reconstruction, he realized that he had some more anger and hurt from my behavior during the drinking years. Off he went to get some individual counseling. He was a great support.

My son and daughter, who are now grown and live in their own homes, talked a lot about remembering me as I was when they were growing up. I told them about their grandparents' families as I learned myself. They had some of their own secrets that they shared. They are on their own individual paths now, but the process brought us closer together. They didn't attend my reconstructon, but they gave me their support.

I also wanted to invite some of my close friends and support system. As I prepared, I realized I had feelings to work through and boundaries to set with them, also.

The preparation period was rich and productive in terms of my emotional awareness. If nothing else happened, I believe my efforts and discoveries in just that part of the process alone would have changed my life significantly.

THE BIG DAY

It's hard to describe in words the reconstruction day itself. It felt like an altered state, mostly a surrender to the process in which I felt my feelings for a lifetime. I saw my childhood as a painful time with too little understanding of what was happening to me at the time. Instead of beating myself up and being full of self-loathing, I began to have empathy and forgiveness for the child that was me.

I saw the heavy load of caretaking and shame my mother carried and passed on to me. She used religion to feel better, and wanted me to have that, too. But I only heard the talk about sin and fear of hell as a message that I was a bad girl.

My father brought his family sense of failure and repressed anger. He drove us hard to be smart, to be educated, and to succeed. He never felt the success for himself. To a little girl who wanted to please, only perfection was good enough.

The sexual repression on both sides of my family prevented me from telling my parents about being sexually abused as a child. Because it couldn't be talked about, it must have meant that I was shameful and dirty. I carried the fear and blamed myself. As I raged at my perpetrators and claimed my power, the shame slipped away.

There were many moments of anger, and I fought for that frightened and shamed little girl. There were many losses. I grieved the angels who had passed through my life—my granddaddy and grandmother, a special therapist, and my first sponsor. All were gone now.

Twenty years before, my husband and I lost a child to a sudden, traumatic illness. We re-lived the trauma together that day and I laid it to rest. It was a moment of great closeness in our relationship.

I could look at the cost of my disease of caretaking and celebrate recovery.

I rejoiced in the pageantry of my life. I had survived! I felt I had triumphed. The final scene of my reconstruction was a re-enactment of being crowned princess of a high school dance. This time I was able to feel the joy and pride of this honor, and dance a special dance with my sweetheart and the love of my life, my husband.

AFTERCARE

The months, and now years, after the reconstruction have been an affirmation of the process. Many pieces of business that had hung on from the past felt finished at last. Truck-fulls of shame were gone, along with the vague depression and low self-worth.

I learned to trust my "inner voice" when things felt unsafe or against my best interest. I gave up some work relationships and friendships that somehow just didn't seem to work anymore. As *The Big Book of Alcoholics Anonymous* promised, I was beginning to "know how to handle those situations which used to baffle us."

There are still struggles. The desire to be a hero and overachieve lessened, but work habits die hard and it looked like change would come slowly in that area. I now know how to ask for help. Sometimes I have to go back and correct mistakes I have made in judgement. I learn on a daily basis to rely on my faith in a Higher Power, and to stop trying to run the universe.

My feelings of fear and resentment towards my family of origin diminished and then left me. I have learned to return to my family as an adult rather than as a needy child.

There are many definitions of "angels." One of them is *messengers*. Sharon Cruse has been one of mine. She saw something in me I could not find for myself. She gave me that gentle, firm nudge toward growth and happiness. She urged me to take risks and realize dreams.

I told someone unfamiliar with therapy or personal growth work that I was undergoing a reconstruction. "Oh, what kind of surgery are you having?" I started to explain that is wasn't surgery when I realized that in many ways, it was. So much was removed, the heart was restored, and the healing began.

CHAPTER ELEVEN

BEYOND VIRGINIA SATIR: SHARON'S PATH TO A NEW MODEL

The story began for me in the early 1970s when I was a young therapist, eager to learn everything I could about what made families tick. I had grown up in a family that had been most loving, and yet painful.

Over the years of my college work, already on my way to becoming a therapist, I really wanted to specialize in working with alcoholism and drug abuse. The culture had just emerged from the 60s, and I had grown up in a family where alcoholism was an issue—addictions were my primary interest. I wondered how families were involved in the illness of alcoholism. At that time, there wasn't anyone in the field of alcoholism who was conducting any studies or reporting treatment that focused on the family aspects of the disease, but I came across a one-page article written by Virginia Satir. On that single sheet she addressed many of the thoughts and questions that had been going through my mind. I knew I had to find her, meet her, that there was much that she could teach me. I tried for at least two years to track her down. I wasn't, at the time, aware of any additional writings by her. Later I learned that it was just about that time that *People-Making* was in press. But I didn't have the faintest idea about tracking her down through a publisher.

I was then teaching night classes at a local campus of the University of Minnesota. One night as I was driving home a strange thing happened. My car stalled in a suburban neighborhood. It was very late, and many of the houses were dark, but there was one house with lights on. I left my car, walked over, and rang the bell to ask if I might use their phone to call road service. The couple who lived there welcomed me in. While I was on the phone making arrangements for getting some help with my car, the couple started talking about a trip they were taking the next week to Saskatoon, Canada, to spend a week-long workshop with Virginia Satir.

I was amazed! Immediately, I asked them for information about the seminar and they told me I wouldn't be able to go because it was being sponsored by the social service program of Canada, and it was for Canadians only. They were being invited as special quests of a Canadian couple, but the program wasn't open to the public. Well, I had gotten this close—I wasn't going to give up so easily.

I asked them for the address where the workshop was going to take place, and they gave it to me from the hotel's brochure. When I got home with my restored car later that night, I thought, "I've got to find a way to go."

Now, there were several complicating factors I hadn't even thought about. First of all, I was a single parent raising three young children with very, very limited funds. Also, I was 33 years old and had never flown in an airplane before. Yet there was something inside me that knew that taking this trip was of the utmost, urgent importance. What's so interesting about it as I look back now is that in my 20-year career, I have probably flown well in excess of a million miles. But back then, it seemed a problem. Also, the money, which brings me to another part of the story.

A couple of years earlier, I had been chosen to be part of an experimental prison program that was going on in Minnesota. A few therapists were selected to spend three weeks living in the same quarters with a group of prisoners. The purpose was to see what kind of intervention could be made into the alcoholsm and drug abuse that was going on for the prisoners, both prior to being incarcerated and once in prison. There were approximately 40 prisoners and four or five therapists housed in a college in Southern Minnesota for the duration of the program.

One of the other therapists was an older man who was part of a halfway house system in Minneapolis. He had many, many years of sobriety under his own belt. He didn't have a lot of formal education, but he certainly knew about addiction, as well as recovery, and he was an important element in this pilot program. Lovingly referred to by everyone as "The Colonel," this man was old enough to be my grandfather. He was a single man, and had been alone for many years. On occasion, I would invite some of the staff out to my house for dinner, supper, or a Sunday afternoon picnic. During the course of the time we were involved in this project, the Colonel became very fond of all three of my children, and long after the project ended, we continued to see him every two or three weeks. He would stop by, bringing Chinese food, or something for the kids—he served as a sort of grandparent figure for them.

One night, he and I were sitting in the living room, discussing our careers, and addiction, and what addiction did to families, and I mentioned to him very briefly that I had finally found the person from whom I wanted to learn. I told him I was hoping at some point to be able to track down this

Virginia Satir, and I told him of my recent phone calls with the Canadian Social Service to see if they would let me into the workshop. They had told me in no uncertain terms, several times, that this was not a workshop that was open to people from the United States. It was a Canadian-sponsored workshop, being paid for by the Canadian government, there was no way to enroll, etc. etc. I kept calling and talking to different people, and I kept getting shuffled around the agency, and at that point had still not been able to make any inroads. But finally, they were getting frustrated with me, and somebody said, "Listen, if you can get here and you're willing to pay for your own materials (which was a $15.00 charge and included the brand new book, *People-Making*), go ahead and come—we'll get you in somehow." I felt like Santa Claus, the Easter Bunny, and the Tooth Fairy had all come at once and brought me a huge gift. All I had to do was figure out how to pay for it. A good friend of mine offered to take care of the kids, so that issue was resolved.

Later that night, I was sitting on the couch doing some school work with an afghan across my lap. When I rose to go to bed, something fell out of the afghan. I reached down to pick it up—an envelope. Inside was $450.00 (the airfare to Canada at that time was $438.00.) and a short note: "Go and learn what you can and pass it on. With love for all that you and your children have brought into my life—The Colonel." He didn't have much money, but he had more than I did at the time, and I recognized him as an angel in my life who had given me a blessing. I was one very excited, very grateful lady. I could take all that I had learned about addiction, alcoholism, drug abuse, and prescription pills, and, hopefully, learn all that I could from Virginia Satir about family systems, and try to find some way to bridge the two fields.

I went to Canada, and met Virginia, a very wonderful, powerful person. She was sitting in a booth right across from me the first morning I had breakfast at the hotel. I approached her and began, "I don't want to interrupt you, but—" Immediately she cut me off and said, "You have already interrupted me; let's make it useful."

She left me with my mouth open, and I just briefly said, "I've been interested in your work for years." She gave me that dismissive smile that people in the public eye often have. I was fascinated. I attended the entire workshop and learned a great deal that I brought home. I had almost three full notebooks, and I immediately began working with the new information at a small center I had started in Robbinsdale, Minnesota called "Family Factory."

The journey into the reconstruction model was life-changing. Virginia had certainly impressed me with her ability to assess a family's situation. She could go right to the core of the family pain, and at the same time identify and build on the family's strength. My start with Virginia Satir, together with my addictions training, opened the door to a flood of new opportunity and possibility. Every time I worked with families from that point on, I saw miracles happening that certainly hadn't been happening when I had simply been working in the addictons field alone.

That week in Saskatoon, Virginia at some point asked me if I came from a happy family or a painful family. I said, "Well, both."

She said, "No. Did you come from a happy family where your emotional needs were met, your self-worth needs were met, and there was much nurturing going on, or did you come from a painful family where nobody's needs got met and there was much crisis and trauma?'

I said, "Both."

"I don't think you understand," she said."

"No," I found myself saying, "I don't think you understand. I came from two families—I came from a family where, when things were sober, it was the most nurturing family possible. Our home was filled with music and people and laughter and flowers, and I learned what love was all about. But when my family was drinking or using prescription medicine, I came from a home of negativity and criticism and violence and emptiness and insecurity."

"Very interesting," she said.

"Virginia," I went on, "all of the work that you do, and what I'm learning from you is very, very wonderful. However, some of it won't work in a family where addiction is primary."

"Very interesting," she said again.

Some time later, almost two or three years, I was invited to a Christmas party at the home of good friends in Minnesota. These people were also good friends of Virginia's although I didn't know this at the time. When I got to the party that night, there were only six guests, including me and Virginia! That night, we had much more chance to interact than we had had in Canada. It seemed like a miraculous coincidence to me. Later that night she took me aside and said, "Sharon, you are more like me than I sometimes feel myself. There is something very connected between the two of us. I think you need to travel with me, and learn from me. Will you do that?" She was looking at me with her deep, deep eyes, and I said yes, but I didn't know how, or when or where. Yet before the evening was over, she said, "I'd like you to be on an airplane with me three days from now—we're going to Mexico for 30 days and I want you to be part of that learning experience."

I remember saying I would be there, and over the next three days, my life once more unfolded financially and in terms of child care. In three days I was on that plane to Mexico to begin the first of my studies with Virginia Satir. There were many, many trips over the next few years, many opportunities to learn from Virginia professionally, and to share and talk personally. In both arenas, she did much to nurture me during those years. I am happy to be able to say that she told me later that I had greatly enriched her life as well. She became much more interested in the subject of addiction, and later on was able to share with me some of her own personal family issues around the subject. I was also able to bring her to treatment centers and to introduce her to people in the field. She incorported a much bigger picture of family systems when she realized that addiction played a very primary role when it was present.

Our friendship and professional careers together have been one of the special gifts of my life. One of my dreams has been to take what I have learned from Virginia and to be able to pass it on to others, as Virginia was able to do for me. She later said to me, "Many people say that imitation is a great compliment. But what really feeds my soul is when someone takes what I have given, adds some skills as well as another piece of the Spirit to it, and transforms it into something that is much more than it was when it was just with me. . . . If you have a choice, don't become simply a technician, though there are many around who do good work. Become a spirited artist—go into the depths of your soul, add to what already exists, and make it something new. Then, as you pass it on, encourage people to do the same."

Interestingly enough, Virginia started out working with all family systems, and all kinds of problems. In my own need to address addictions, I transformed much of her work in order to address the addicted family. This newer form has been important as addictions work has entered the mainstream in a much more profound way by virtue of its incorporation of family systems work. But now we may be returning to the place where we apply our model to all kinds of families. For example, my current interest is in working with families in which someone is chronically or severely ill. I think the model has a lot of applicability there.

In any case, it's a model that is ever changing, and much bigger than it was when I learned about it over 20 years ago. It's my further belief that as time goes on, the model will continue to change with the new insights and awareness that each artist will bring to it.

I will always be grateful to Virginia Satir for the gifts of courage, clarity, compassion, and confidence. It's been my hope over all these years, and with this book, to embrace those gifts and pass them on to others.

NUGGETS AND PEARLS: MORE DETAILS, MORE EXERCISES, AND MORE WISDOM

Years of working with people have yielded many, many ideas and techniques that have been proven to work effectively. We have chosen to include here some of the exercises and ideas that have been important and useful to those who have embarked on the journey of recovery and/or those helping others on the journey. Many of these are a regular part of every reconstruction we perform, were mentioned throughout this book, and, so, have already been described in some detail. For those exercises, this section serves as a kind of "cross-reference," and may be helpful in breaking down further the steps involved. Others are mentioned for the first time here. Some instructions are clearly worded for therapists and potential reconstruction guides; others are directed to the general reader. Ideally, all of these exercises are done in a reconstruction setting, which necessarily implies a group of participants. But for many of the exercises, we have included a modifed "Reader's Exercise" to help the individual reader do some of this work immediately. In other instances, the exercise itself is appropriate for an individual.

1. Excess Baggage

This sculpture exercise is designed to help gain an understanding of the emotional burdens that accumulate over time and affect our current lives. Role-players are required, and necessary props include bags or pillowcases partially filled with dirt or rocks.

Stand a person in the middle of the room. Add the different kinds of baggage he or she has in life currently, including expectations, guilt, unresolved feelings and pressures from past relationships (e.g., with a parent), etc. by using labeled role-players, or bags filled with dirt or rocks. Remember to label the baggage, whether represented by people or weighted bags. Bear in mind that the current pressures will typically echo an original unresolved kind of pressure or feeling that is rooted in some historic experience.

For example, Tom is a man who has many frustrations in his life. Choose role-players to represent the people who add pressure to Tom's life, and let them come into the center of the room and hold on to Tom. One player represents the expectations a father has had of a son; someone else represents a former marriage, with all of the expectations of a partner; children also have many needs, and if there are three children, then have three role-players come up to represent those children. An employer who really wants Tom to do a particular kind of work will also need to be represented. Keep adding as many players as necessary to fully represent all the people in Tom's life adding pressure, label each of them, and let them all hang on to Tom's clothing in some way. Add bags of rocks or pillowcases of dirt to represent the non-personal pressures, such as work, family, money, unresolved issues or feelings from his past, etc. Label the bags or cases and tie, pin, or otherwise attach them to Tom. With all of the weight, and all of the people hanging on to Tom's clothing, let Tom try to walk. Let him feel whether he can move with any ease or mobility, and then have him describe the experience of trying to move in this way. With eight to ten people pulling on him, and with the strain of carrying the weight of other pressures, Tom is going to feel constricted, to say the least. He may even feel out of breath or panicky.

Many feelings may emerge in Tom. Give him enough time to really verbalize each aspect of his feelings in this moment. Hopefully this experience will make it more possible for him to explore these feelings than it would be if he were just sitting and discussing the reality of these pressures in his life.

Reader's Exercise: Draw a picture of what this sculpture would look like if you were the central figure.

2. Draining Relationships

This sculpture exercise teaches about draining relationships. Role-players will be necessary, as will several two-foot lengths of ordinary garden hose.

Very often people who caretake or give away much of themselves feel tired, depressed, or "drained." And they are drained—of their resources, their energy, their creativity, and their spirit.

As in the exercise above, choose a star to stand in the center. For example, Janet is a person who allows many people to make demands on her, and she feels it necessary to please all of them. Each of these people is represented with a role-player, who comes up to Janet with a piece of hose, and makes remarks such as these:

> "Janet, I really need you to be at the Church on Sunday morning to teach the Sunday School class. There's no one we can count on more than you."

> "Janet, if I need to give a company dinner Saturday night, then, as my wife, you need to do that for me."

> "Mom, you told me I could have a slumber party Friday night."

> "Janet, your father and I were expecting you to come home for Christmas this year. We haven't seen the kids in over a year and they're our only grandchildren!"

> "Janet, you work for me, and if I'm going to pay you a regular salary, then sometimes you're going to have to stay late and come early until the project at hand is finished, and that includes this Friday night."

Each player comes up, makes his or her demand, and hands Janet a piece of hose. As she starts to have to hold more hoses, Janet may start to feel out of breath, panicky, or angry. Whatever she feels, help her access that feeling and work with the vividness of it all as she holds the hoses.

Reader's Exercise: Make a list of people, places, and things, that drain your energy. You may want to go a step further and, after evaluating your list, write a commitment to make some changes in this aspect of your life.

3. Magic Time

The goal of this exercise is to allow the use of fantasy to help access feelings. The only prop needed will be a beautiful wand of whatever type you wish.

There are moments in the reconstruction process that will call for a magic time. This is when we can make anything "happen" in accordance to what feels right for the moment. Magic time is not about what is real, but about what we wish were real. It is often a great contrast to reality, and can therefore be profoundly sad. Nonetheless, it is a way of letting the star do things that aren't in the exact framework of what's happening, but might still be necessary.

For example, sometimes a star is so filled with anger at an abandoning parent that he or she can work and work and work on that anger, yet the rage remains. It seems the star just isn't getting where he or she need to go. This would be the time for the guide to pull out the magic wand and say, "It's time for a magic moment." The guide may go on to say to the star something along these lines: "I know you are just filled with anger and rage. I know this is the reality of the situation. But I also feel as though maybe inside you are also sad for what you never had. Now, granted, your father left you, and granted, your father is probably the biggest source of all that anger and rage, and he deserves it. But you also deserve to be held, and cuddled, and to grieve for your losses."

Have a role-player from the audience agree to take the part of the father. Have this person take the star in his arms and tell him or her all of the things he or she never got to hear from the real father. Let the star feel the comfort of this person's presence. Magic time can allow years and years of grief to surface, be expressed, and begin to heal.

Magic time in no way invalidates the anger, or the reality of the father's absence, but it allows room for grief. Another example of a good time for magic time is when a star is working through the grief of an abortion. The guide can pull out the wand and let the star go back and breathe life into that child, and let herself tell the baby all the things she has second-guessed or had shame about. The guide or someone from the audience can help the whole group develop an appropriate ceremony, whether religious or otherwise, for honoring that child who wasn't born, and this can help the mother return this child to God or to a Higher Power in a very healed way. This may not have happened at the time of the actual abortion, but through magic time, it can happen now. The healing can happen for both the star and the audience.

There are many uses for the magic wand, and it may appear two or three times in a given reconstruction. The purpose is to allow the impossible to be true for a moment in order to let feelings around a reality heal. Afterwards, we can return to the reality, but from a stronger place.

Reader's exercise: Draw a picture of a scene you wish had happened in your life.

4. The Relationship Gauntlet

Many times in a reconstruction, a pattern of behavior in relationships becomes apparent. Rather than slowing down the process in order to develop each instance into a full sculpture or psychodrama of its own, we can line up all of the thematically linked relationships to deal with at once.

For example, if you are working with someone who has had multiple relationships with members of the opposite sex that have a similar theme (this may include live-in relationships and marriages and dating), this might be a good occasion for using a relationship gauntlet.

Let's say that Marylou grew up in a family in which the father was absent, and as a small child, her whole identification as a female was manifest around trying to get some time and attention from this man who was not really available. It's quite likely that Marylou is going to develop a pattern in her adult life of seeking and pursuing men who are in one way or another unavailable.

In the gauntlet, line up all ten (or whatever number is actually representative) male relationships, and include the original relationship with her father.

Another appropriate time to do a gauntlet piece would be with someone who felt very one-down: in his relationship with his employer, with his neighbor, with his college professor, with his older sister, etc. Working back, it becomes clear he felt one-down with one of his parents.

Line up the whole gauntlet of people, represented by role-players, who have left this star feeling one-down. He can deal with each of them in this gauntlet as well as returning to the source to deal with the emotion in that original context. This can make it quite clear to the star how he needs to change his behavior in the future.

Relationship gauntlets are intended to tie together many similar relationships or many relationships that share a similar theme. When the source becomes apparent, then the star can "return" and do some healing work with the player representing the figure (usually, but not always, a parent) in his or her life with whom this theme originated. Not only does this provide the star with some tools for dealing with this theme in current and future relationships, but it can be healing enough to prevent any more such gauntlets in real life.

Reader's Exercise: List similar patterns of relationship in your own life.

5. Humor

This exercise is intended to illustrate the healing power of humor.

Any process that ignores the power of humor and laughter in healing and building self-worth is incomplete. The ability to use our emotional senses includes using our sense of humor. The child within each of us, who is often buried beneath a great deal of emotional pain, deserves to be released and to be able to celebrate with laughter and play. Yet often that child is filled with shame that destroys self-worth.

Humor, which is spiritual, and so can restore a person's sense of self-worth, is often the best antidote to shame. As Norman Cousins once stated, "Medicine is becoming spiritual and spirituality is becoming more important and more pervasive and is free. It costs nothing and its rewards are so great."

Virginia Satir often talked about the "cosmic joke," defining this as the moment or moments when we are able to laugh at ourselves. She believed that all good jokes could be very healing, especially the cosmic sort, when we see the ridiculous or the humorous aspect in some experience we might have taken seriously. Sharon tells a story:

> I was so serious in my early days of being a therapist. Every-
> thing was executed and taken with a great deal of profes-

sionalism and absolute correctness. I was invited to come to the state of Louisiana and speak to a group of nurses about how important it was that nursing students begin to articulate and use anatomically correct words with people about their bodies, and correct, explicit sexual words in describing what was going on in male-female relationships. My role in doing this workshop was to share with the nursing students a comfort level in using such words. So I packed up my materials and took off on an airplane to Baton Rouge with three films I had purchased after undergoing a graduate course in sexuality. On the airplane, I had my three films in a bag, and I slipped them under my seat. As the airplane ascended for flying altitude, all of my films slid out of my bag and all the way to the back of the cabin. There I was, sitting in all my prim properness, on my way to give one of my first out-of-state presentations, when the flight attendant said over the loudspeaker, "Will the owner of the following three films please claim them: *Sensuous Orange, Love Toads* and *Fun in the Afternoon*." Now, this was back in the days when there weren't as many women traveling on business trips as there are today, and as I sat there, I could feel the eyes of many of the men on the plane staring at me while my cheeks flushed. I stood up in total seriousness, and very professionally walked to the rear of the cabin as the stewardess repeated, "Would the owner of the three films, *Sensuous Orange, Love Toads,* and *Fun in the Afternoon* please claim them." Well, I had a good laugh at myself that day, and I think this is a good example of learning to laugh at oneself in a serious, potentially embarrassing, if not shaming, situation.

One of the best ways to employ humor is through the use of props and sculptures. Many times this short-cuts a situation and provides a very real picture that reveals a painful truth with humor. One example involves working with someone who has been seriously abused by Bible-thumping religion. We might make a cross and a church and set up a scene or dress people up in certain costumes that bring a laugh. Now, we are in no way ridiculing religion or spirituality, but the exaggeration of something very proper and very value-laden can sometimes help us to see a situation more clearly.

Often we work with workaholics, or with the children of workaholics. It's one thing to say your father was a workaholic. It's quite another to be very graphic and put the father in a sculpture holding a briefcase, probably six or seven reference books under his arms, a telephone in one hand, another telephone in a pocket, with someone tugging on him and applying some more external pressure around his job. There is a humorous tone to this image, but there is also compassion with the reality it represents.

What about someone who is a chaos addict? We have put together a sculpture with someone standing in the middle with ski poles, a tennis racket, a telephone, a brief case, and two people talking to him at once and it all begins to get very clear. The sculpture may have gotten a laugh, but that laughter quickly dissolved into real, deep feelings, and even ended up in tears.

The point is that humor can be a really non-painful, even pleasurable means for getting at some difficult truths, without sacrificing the complexity of feelings that truth may generate. It is also worth noting that there is probably no better place to use humor in a family reconstruction than in a Parts Party.

Reader's Exercise: Tell a story about yourself that uses humor to relay something painful or reveals the humor inherent in a painful situation.

6. Music

The reconstruction process involves considerable risk-taking on the part of the star. Music can facilitate the star's access to feelings by setting or enhancing a mood. There are situations, especially during the chronology, in which one particular piece of music can be established and used several times throughout the rest of the reconstruction to indicate or reveal a theme.

The star can also provide his or her own favorite or meaningful music to the guide to supplement the music the guide has on hand.

Reader's Exercise: List the five most significant pieces of music in your life.

7. Safe Places

Role-players are again useful in this method for introducing or reinforcing the concept of "safe places."

The guide invites the star to consider "places" in his or her past or present that have felt safe. Be broad-minded in this exercise—a "safe place" can be a person, a place, or a spiritual relationship (e.g., with a Higher Power). Having identified past and present safe places, the star is better able to identify potentially safe people and places for his or her future.

Reader's Exercise: Draw a representation of your concept of a safe place.

8. Bookmarking

This method allows a safe way to "tag" feelings that arise in a reconstruction for further work at a later time in the process. You can use a real bookmark.

"Bookmarking" is a technique used throughout the reconstruction process, beginning on the day of the star's pre-event interview. Whereas when doing specific counseling work, it is important never to postpone a feeling (because whatever feeling surfaces should be felt, addressed, and worked through or further explored), there are times when it isn't appropriate to do that sort of work. On the day of the event, the technique is used primarily in dealing with the audience and their feelings because this is the *star's* day. When an audience member becomes aware of a powerful feeling emerging, he or she is asked to take note of the feeling, to note the incident(s) or information that appears to have triggered the feeling, and to hold onto this awareness until an appropriate time and place for expression of the feeling (most likely in small-group process work over the next days).

Reader's Exercise: List some feelings you need to contain for now, but which you will work on later.

9. Saying Goodby to Medicators: Binge Foods as an Example

The goals of this sculpture exercise can be modified to address issues of saying goodbye to any substance that has been used as a medicator. Our example focuses on overeaters who want to identify binge foods, face feelings around compulsive eating, and encourage a change in food plan.

This sculpture is particularly helpful to clients who are compulsive eaters and are trying to develop a food plan that still includes foods which have consistently been problematic in the past. It helps clients who minimize the pain and loss of control they feel around their compulsive eating.

It's important to note that many people who do not have an eating disorder may nonetheless be using particular foods to comfort themselves, stuff anger, or avoid feeling pain. This piece is often a trigger for these people to face the reality of their own relationships with food.

Have the person identify binge foods (e.g., pizza, ice cream, rice cakes, whatever). Choose a role-player to be the inner child stand-in. Choose players to represent each binge food, and have the person tell each food how he or she feels about it. Have the foods start calling the person to come closer with increasing volume (e.g., "*I know you want me...You can't resist me...Come and get me...I've always been in control of you, how dare you think of giving me up...What will you do when you need me?...You can't give me up...*").

The person will usually have some feelings at this point—maybe tears or anger about the lack of control. Encourage him or her to reclaim power by using a bataka bat toward the binge foods, or by screaming, or by pushing on pillows. If the star gets to the point where he or she is ready to say goodbye and to remove these binge foods from his or her life, let him or her say goodbye to each food, one at a time, feeling each loss. Thanks can be given for what the foods have provided at the same time that hurt and anger is acknowledged, and then goodbyes are said. The star can take the drawing or name tag from the role-player, rip it up, and throw it away. He or she can then tell the inner child what the process felt like, and articulate exactly what commitments and changes he or she is ready to make. The guide should have someone record this in writing for the client to have as part of his or her aftercare plan. Then the star is encouraged to connect with the inner child in whatever way feels comfortable, and the whole group is encouraged to give the star a standing ovation for his or her courage. Finally, group members process the piece through feedback and sharing around their own relationships to food. Grief process work may be appropriate (this can be done by moving through the stages described by Kubler-Ross, i.e., shock, denial, anger, bargaining, depression, and acceptance.)

Reader's Exercise: This exercise can work well with any compulsive behavior—write a letter saying goodbye to something you've used as a medicator.

10. Antagonist - Angel

This exercise allows the person to recognize positive and negative influences in his or her life, and to begin the process of unlocking feelings and letting go of grief and anger so that he or she can move from focusing on pain to an awareness of positive people who have made a difference. All that is needed for this exercise is four pieces of paper and a pencil or pen.

Everyone goes through a variety of life experiences, some of which are painful. Often, the people we rely on to be there for us are not, which can be due to many factors, e.g., emotional unavailability, addictions, violence, etc. There are also people in our lives who have harmed us, whether physically, emotionally, sexually, or spiritually.

Reader's Exercise: Take a few moments to reflect on your life. Recall some of those who have caused you harm. make a list of up to ten of these people. Refer to this list when you start to believe that "it wasn't that bad." Then take another piece of paper and write a letter to one of these people. Include how this person harmed you, what you had expected or wanted from the relationship originally, how you felt when you were hurt instead, and what your present feelings are about this person.

Now, in the midst of our pain, there have also been people who have been there for us to provide encouraging words, a safe place, acceptance, and/or love. Take a few moments to reflect once again on your life, and to recall some of the people who were there when you needed them. Sometimes some of the same people will appear on both your lists—this is okay. Make a list of up to ten of your "angels." Refer to this list when you start to feel as though your entire life was terrible, and that no one was ever there for you. Then take another piece of paper and write a thank you letter to one of the people on this list. Include the circumstances around which this person gave you something you needed, how you felt about that, and what this person currently means to you.

At a later date, a letter can be written to each person on each of these lists. Whereas letters to angels can always be sent, it may be much more volatile to send the letters you write to your antagonists about the harm they have caused you. The best advice we can give is to work with a professional therapist and decide together, not too rapidly, whether any of these letters should be sent. Letters to angels can be sent or read to a safe person (who may or may not be the person the letter is addressed to), and then kept in what we call a "gratitude file." (We often teach people in therapy to keep a gratitude file—every time someone does something that makes you happy, note it and stick it in the file. On a low day, go to your gratitude file and feel good about yourself.)

This exercise allows us to recognize that there is a balance of negative and positive experiences and people in our lives, and allows us to experience awarness and acceptance around feelings of pain, anger, and gratitude.

11. Body Image

This exercise can help promote the honesty, acceptance, and peace-making that are part of loving ourselves and our bodies. For this exercise, we need two pieces of paper, and markers, pen, or pencil.

Put some soft music on in the background. Find a comfortable position and relax. Allow yourself to reflect on your body. Begin with your toes and feet, and think about their shape, their size, things you have said about them, things others have said about them, and how you feel about them. Slowly move up your body in the same way. Be honest with yourself. Allow yourself to feel all of your feelings. When you have finished the self-appraisal, take a piece of paper and, with your opposite hand (to discourage perfectionism), draw youself naked. Feel as you draw. When you are done, look at the drawing. Remember that this is the body that has been with you since birth. It has grown and changed. Perhaps it has been abused. It has also served you, however. If it is imperfect, it is not alone. We all tend to concentrate more on what we need to change than on our good qualities. Point out some of the finer characteristics of your body, and label them on the picture.

Write a love letter to your body. In this letter, try to let go of what you think your body "should" be, and let yourself write to the wonderful body that is.

12. Resistance

This exercise can help you see and begin to tear down the walls that keep change from occurring.

To describe a refusal or inability to see something for what it really is, Virginia Satir tended to use the conventional term, "resistance." In the field of addictions, the favored term for this kind of behavior or thought process is "denial." Most people don't arrive at the truth by having people shove it down their throats. Truth is most often recognized when one feels safe enough and strong enough and clear enough to be able to see and accept things as they are.

For example, Jean had been living in a marriage of emotional and financial abuse, though so far there had been no physical abuse. Each time that Jean tried to make changes in her marriage to Bob, either by leaving it altogether or by setting some boundaries, she has found herself slipping back. Most of the time she was afraid that she is being unreasonable and unfair while Bob continued to abuse her emotionally and verbally. In talking with Jean, her therapist has many times tried to get her to see the situation for what it is, but Jean couldn't do that.

In the process of Jean's reconstruction, a sculpture was set up to show how Bob's behavior and verbal abuse were very destructive to her. The sculpture set up Bob's family, showing how they had abused him and how he was simply passing this along to Jean.

Jean resisted this truth. So it became important to change the sculpture in order to bring clarity and focus to Jean's feelings. We operated from the premise that Jean would not be resisting this knowledge if she were not protecting her emotions in some way. This then became the focus. The guide asked Jean what she was afraid would happen with her and Bob. Jean talked about being lonely and fearing that Bob would leave if she confronted him. In talking with her about her loneliness and fears, feelings about her own inadequacies and what it might be like for her if she were alone came forward. Soon the entire focus was off of what was happening between Jean and Bob and was fixed, rather, on what was going on inside of Jean in terms of her feelings of inadequacy and fear and guilt and so forth. This was harder for Jean to deny or resist because it was her own truth, and because she felt safe. The emphasis was now on her well-being, so Jean felt cared for. Before long she was pouring out all of the feelings she had kept inside because she did not feel safe and because she felt alone.

After she had expressed these feelings, and was able to connect and feel the strength and power of the reconstruction group, it became less scary for her to look at the reality of the situation with Bob. The more Jean was in touch with her own feelings, the more she was able to see that these feelings had been badly damaged in her relationship to Bob. Her resistance had been protecting her—once she felt the feelings, however, it was less scary to begin to look at the truth. She had to make certain decisions regarding the termination of her relationship with Bob, but this was not as scary as she had thought.

The sculpture could then be re-set and she could look at it, face it, and decide what she was going to do.

It is important to remember that resistance and denial serve as methods of self-protection for a person who is frightened or hurting, and that when we meet the needs of that frightened, hurting person, the walls of resistance or denial tend to fall away more easily.

Reader's Exercise: Try to identify a current problem that may be presenting in your life as a "stuck spot" where you're not making much progress. Beneath every stuck spot are powerful feelings. Try to identify the feelings you have around this issue (not just the feelings you have about being stuck). So first you're naming the wall, or stuck spot, then the feelings. Now try to identify the consequences of your resistance around getting "unstuck," and then imagine what the payoff would be.

13. Initiation into Manhood

This exercise for men teaches about the experience of being a part of the company of men.

The therapist invites a member of the group to come forward and share with the male star what he has learned about what "being a man" means. Other men are then invited, one at a time, to join, sharing as the first man did, until all of the men are gathered around the star. At this time an appropriate piece of music, a poem, or a reading is used to close the exercise.

14. The Dinner Table

This exercise helps re-enact rigid roles and family dialogues. Props include a table and chairs and role-players are necessary.

Role-players are chosen to represent a nuclear family—mother, father, and four children. All the players are instructed to sit at the table and pretend they are at a family dinner in which they are to keep eating and talking. No other instructions are given.

After a period of time that varies from group to group (usually at least five minutes but seldom longer than ten minutes), a discussion is held with the participants regarding what they experienced, and then with the audience and, finally, the guide, sharing what was observed.

Often what emerges are the rigid roles that those playing the family develop, even in so short a period of time. The children's roles almost always parallel those of hero, scapegoat, mascot, and/or lost child.

Reader's Exercise: Draw a typical family dinner in your childhood. Look for the roles in your family, and note whether the roles were rigid. Explore who's sitting next to whom, and how close together or far apart people are. What can you learn from looking at your drawing?

15. Forgiveness

This exercise helps to practice the art of forgiveness, which is both a decision and a process. It often takes years to forgive completely. But forgiveness is an act of self-worth that often benefits the person forgiving more than anyone else.

Realizing that the biggest piece of work in a family reconstruction is the honest expression of the perceptions and truth of feelings, forgiveness is the next logical step to freedom. Write a letter to yourself from someone who has hurt you, listing in as great detail as possible all of the wrongs for which this person is responsible. Include an apology and a request for your forgiveness. When you finish writing the letter, read it aloud to yourself, and then tear it up. This can help release you from the fantasy that you will ever receive a letter such as this from this person, and gives you back the time and energy you might spend hoping.

16. Feelings

The goal here is to practice articulating feelings.

Using the common feelings of anger, sadness, happiness, fear, hurt, shame, etc., finish the following statements:

If my anger could speak, it would say . . .
If my sadness could speak, it would say . . .
If my happiness could speak, it would say . . .
If my fear could speak, it would say . . .
If my hurt could speak, it would say . . .
If my shame could speak, it would say . . .

17. Poetry Machine

The goal here is to use poetic expression for feelings and memories.

Close your eyes and bring back memories from your childhood of a sound, a smell, a style of movement (e.g., running, jumping, swinging, crouching, dodging, hitting), a safe place, a scary place, a musical instrument, an animal, and a flower.

After completing this list, expand each one into a phrase or sentence using present-tense verbs. For example:

Sound = Tractor
Sentence: "I know my Grandpa's almost home when I hear the tractor downshift."

Smell = Alcohol
Sentence: "I know my mother is drunk when I smell the too-sweet alcohol on her breath."

Movement = Running
Sentence: "The wild spearmint breaks as I run up the hill."

Safe Place = Abandoned Stairwell
Sentence: "The abandoned stairwell is my safe harbor."

Scary Place = Basement
Sentence: "I can feel my fear swell as we go into the basement where I know my father is going to hit me."

18. Spirituality: Four Concepts of God

This exercise involves a teaching sculpture intended to promote awareness that people do have choice in their relationship with God. Role-players will be necessary.

Quite often a star has had considerable difficulty in establishing an appropriate spiritual relationship with a Higher Power. Because a child's first impressions of a Higher Power come through their primary caregivers, and because those caregivers may have demonstrated a considerable degree of pathology, such difficulty in embracing a healthy sense of a Higher Power should come as no surprise.

Select four individuals to stand and face the larger group. Have the first person put his or her body in the shape that would best express a punishing attitude. Have the next put his or her body in the shape that would best express an unapproachable attitude. Have the next position him- or herself to best express the attitude of being conditional. Finally, have the fourth person position him- or herself to best express the attitude of being unconditional. The guide then asks the larger group, "How many would want a relationship with a punishing God, a God that would kiss you and then punch you, a God who made you feel as though you never knew when the other shoe was going to drop?" Next the guide asks, "How many would want a relationship with an unapproachable God, one who is not present for you?" Third, the guide asks, "How many would want a relationship with a conditional God, one who requires needless sacrifice and whom you can never satisfy?" And, finally, the guide asks, "How many would want a relationship with a God that means that there is nothing you can do to make God love you more or less; God simply loves you?"

These are the four concepts of relationship with God. One may choose whichever appeals most, and that choice will almost always be compatible with one's own religion.

19. Anger

The goal of this exercise is to practice the healthy discharge of emotions.

During the day of the reconstruction event, the discharge of unresolved, repressed anger by the star is quite common. Many choices exist for how to manage these anger-reduction opportunities. Below are listed a few of the most commonly used options the guide provides for the star: touching hands firmly ("patty cake" style) and pushing; clenching fists; pushing against a wall, floor, or pillow; pulling on a rope or sheet; twisting a towel into knots; tearing a newspaper into strips; tearing a telephone book; rolling a towel into a tight long tube and then using it like a bat; kicking pillows; throwing a trantrum on a bed of pillows; exaggerating a song, poem, word, phrase, or vowel sound; growling like an animal; pointing and yelling; whispering, hissing, dancing, or other non-verbal sounds or movements; repeating a significant phrase; running or stomping in place; clenching then releasing hand grips; drawing on paper; using a bataka bat.

20. Pets

This exercise is used to acknowledge the presence of unconditional love often found with pets and to illustrate the importance of these close emotional connections. It can also be used to initiate the experience of grief around the loss of a pet, and/or to celebrate a pet angel. Props needed are paper and markers.

The importance of a special pet or pets in a person's life is often underestimated. A lonely child will often cling to an animal for the love he or she needs, and a very strong bond forms. Yet often the loss of a pet is minimized.

In the first part of this exercise, have group members draw (with their opposite hand to discourage perfectionism) a pet they had as children or wish(ed) they had had. Invite them to write adjectives on the picture to describe their feelings about this pet, and to name it. Have people share their pictures with the group, introducing their pets and telling stories about them, whether real or imaginary. Ask each member to describe how he or she feels while sharing and when finished. Encourage emotions.

In the second part of the exercise, choose a group member who has had a pet that died or ran away. Allow him or her to choose another person from the group to role-play the pet. Give the person who has lost the pet an opportunity to thank it, to hold the pet one more time, to grieve the loss, and to say good-bye.

The third part of the exercise is excellent for "piggy-backing," that is, for letting others feel the feelings that surface while one person is the center of the work. Invite group members who wish to do so to come up to the "pet," make it their own, and say and feel what they need to say and feel. The person playing the pet may change attributes in order to fulfill the needs of whomever wants to address a pet in that moment.

Finally, all the picture tags of the pets can be placed somewhere special on the wall in a ceremony to symbolically give the pets over to a Higher Power for safe keeping. These pets become angels.

Reader's Exercise: Draw your pet.

21. What Does the Cake Really Mean?

The goal of this exercise is to help the star and the group as a whole understand the narcissism of a parent who would do this, and to discharge feelings around abusive smothering. Props needed include plastic food.

Sometimes parents, adults, and societies force ideas or beliefs upon children. The message is that whatever is being forced upon the child is good for the child, when in reality the benefits are to the parent or adult. A good example of this involves forcing a child to eat rich foods because they were prepared by the parent or because the parent needs a celebratory mood.

Set up a sculpture of the inner-child on its knees, and the parent standing over him or her with a tray of plastic food saying, "Eat this ... I fixed it for you ... I went to a lot of trouble ... It will make me happy if you eat this ..."

As the role-play of the parent continues, it may look more and more like physical abuse. Allow the star to discharge feelings around having something forced on him or her.

22. Information Exercise

The goal of this exercise is to appreciate the way that understanding information without facilitating change can lead to depression.

Often a person in pain believes that if he or she reads the right books, attends the right lectures, or hears the right information, then the pain will go away. Alcoholics have tried to believe that if they can just find out why they drink in the first place, everything will be okay, and then they will be able to drink safely. Thousands upon thousands have discovered that this doesn't work. Information is only as useful as what is done with it, but people often get stuck in the "action" phase of recovery. This can be not only frustrating, but dangerous.

Information is essential to growth. It is important to learn about co-dependency, dysfunctional families, addiction, self-worth, etc. Information about the cycle of co-dependency can show what happens to children of families with addictions and/or compulsions. The information is useful, as is feeling and re-feeling one's feelings, however these are not enough and can, in fact, be dangerous if not combined with action and changes in behavior. The alcoholic needs to give up alcohol no matter how he understands the situation. The adult who is being physically abused needs to get out of the abusive situation no matter how many books he or she has read or how well he or she understands the pattern. Having the information and not taking action can lead to a deep sense of hopelessness and despair. It seems an impossible situation, and it is. Nothing changes if nothing changes.

It's important with adult children from painful families to have in therapy both verbal and experiential means of expressing and experiencing feelings. But it's especially important for young children who do not yet have the verbal skills to express all of their feelings that they have non-verbal or less direct means of doing so (e.g., art; make believe with dolls, stuffed animals, or other figures; music, etc.). Otherwise their feelings can overwhelm them, leading to depression.

Four components to change and healing are awareness, feeling, healing, and behavior change. The order in which they occur can vary, but each component is necessary for real growth.

23. Facts vs. Hunches & Guesses: Equal Payoff for Unequal Work

The goal here is to learn to use intuitive guesses as healing tools.

In many arenas, facts need to be kept in perspective. For example, interviewing several members of the same family may produce conflicting "facts." But each individual's truth is important. The interpreter of the information needs to use his or her own "gut" response to process the data. Not only is it impossible to fully digest every last detail of a person's life, but it is not necessary to the process. It is equally important to realize that in order to break the chains of the past, it is necessary to have awareness and understanding, but it is not essential to search for more and more details.

The reconstruction guide takes the multitude of facts provided by the star about him- or herself and begins a process of formulating a picture of this person's life. The guide gathers the facts, studies and sorts them, gets to know them on a feeling level (i.e., pays attention to the feelings that come up inside him- or herself as this process is undertaken), and then sets them aside. A strongly developed intuition will aid the guide in selecting key patterns, relationships, and events that need to be explored. (It may be worth noting that this is not very different from what many therapists do in more conventional talk therapies. They are only presented with the facts that a person brings into the sessions; these facts are, in most cases, not investigated or verified, or even considered as important as the feelings the person presents *around* the sharing of the actual information. Therapists pay attention not only to the actual content of what the person says, but also to the feelings the person presents, and to the feelings that come up inside themselves as the person shares or sits with them. From all of this comes a sense of the person's pain, his or her needs, and a strategy for treatment.)

The star is told at the interview that some of the facts as they are presented in the reconstruction itself may not mesh exactly with the facts of the star's own life, but that it is to the star's benefit not to focus on the deviations in sequence or detail. Rather, if the star concentrates on feelings, relationships, and patterns, the work that needs to be done will get done. On the other hand, if the focus shifts to exact detail, the flow will be lost and the reconstruction can become an intellectualized discussion of the star's life instead of an experiential exploration.

This is true in many areas of recovery. For example, many people from painful childhoods start a search in early recovery to understand their pasts. A search is begun for answers to their pain. Some of the questions most often asked are, *What happened? When? How? Why? Who is to blame?* They begin exploring and reading to find the answers. There are books and lectures and new techniques. The hope is to find the answer to the pain. While all of these routes can be helpful, there is not, fortunately or unfortunately, a set of facts out in the world that will relieve the pain. The pain must be felt, perhaps even as if re-lived, then let go, and new decisions must be made about how we choose to live our lives. As noted in the exercise on information, external materials are supportive, but they are not curative.

Reader's Exercise: One exercise that may help to clarify these areas of recovery and delineate the benefits is to list three painful, important facts that you have learned about yourself, three books or other readings that have been helpful in understanding these facts, and three ways you have dealt with or plan to deal with the feelings around these fact.

Another place where facts can get in the way is at support groups and 12-Step meetings. Often there seems to be a need to hear a story exactly like our own in order to feel as though we belong. If we allow ourselves to listen not to the surface facts but to the deeper feelings and patterns, then we begin to realize there are more stories similar to ours than we may have thought. At meetings we are asked to identify, not to compare. This means we need to set facts aside and trust our feelings and intuition. If we pay attention to our bodies, we can learn so much. If your body tightens and your mind says it wants to leave because whatever is being said is too different from your own story, then ask yourself what that tension might really be about. Are there feelings being expressed that are difficult for you? How can something very different from you make you this uncomfortable? Is it possible you identify with these feelings, even if the facts are all different from your own?

Reader's Exercise: Attend four support group meetings. Identify and note in writing one area of discomfort at each meeting. During or after the meeting, allow the feelings to surface, and note these. Relate these feelings to an event from your past and write about it. Then choose one of the sets of feelings, take a piece of paper and some markers, and draw the feelings (with your opposite hand to discourage perfectionism). Allow the drawing to express your pain, rage, etc. Say the words that go with the feelings, and then create a ceremony of some sort to let the feelings go (e.g., rip up the drawing, throw it way, burn it, etc.).

Banner Nuggets & Pearls

Over the years that Virginia Satir and Sharon Wegscheider-Cruse have worked with people in family reconstructions and in other workshops and therapies of many kinds, certain phrases of wisdom have been remembered and collected. They often seem like simple slogans, but these simple words can carry important, helpful truths. These slogans make good banners to be hung in the room in which reconstructions are going to take place, or in the small-group rooms. They can be a means of subtle confrontation and challenge while offering support and hope at the same time. Here we offer a sampler of some of the best:

Everything grows with love.

Calling all little children to come out and play.

Choices—what are yours?

People are like flowers, beautiful and special. Thanks for letting me stroll through your garden.

I've outgrown the need to suffer.

Celebrate the miracle that is you.

In a healthy family, the parents are there to meet the needs of the children. In an unhealthy family, the children are there to meet the needs of the parents.

Humor can be used to avoid or to heal.

Laughter is a feeling too—honor it and use it, even if it comes from the audience.

There is a handicap and an opportunity in every event.

Clients do better when they see the truth represented visually than when they just hear it verbally.

You will grow and find intimacy when you share your pain as well as your joy with others.

When you have access to feelings you can begin to understand them.

Happy families are made up of people who give of themselves to make the family happy.

Saints are neither sweet nor victimized, rather they act with great courage.

Honesty results in intimacy.

Neither big people nor little people have the right to hurt others.

Personal power and confidence come from within—they come spiritually, emotionally, mentally, physically, and socially.

Recovery is when a person's inner life matches his or her outer behavior.

Sexuality is an important part of one's identity, and is to be cherished by ourselves and by others.

Recovery comes with effort, risks, and choices.

The truth of who we are is the sum of our experiences.

Never postpone a star's feeling during the reconstruction process.

Presenting information to the star without providing choices or options is abusive, frustrating, and will bring on depression.

You cannot heal what you cannot feel, and you cannot feel what you medicate.

ABOUT THE AUTHORS

Sharon Wegscheider-Cruse is president of Onsite Training and Consulting, formerly based in Rapid City, SD, and currently at Sierra-Tucson in Tucson, AZ. She has developed residential programs for both co-dependency and family reconstruction, as well as a couples' treatment program. A family therapist with more than 25 years of experience working with people of all ages, Sharon is the Founding Board Chairperson of the National Association for Children of Alcoholics, and the author of 13 books, including the best sellers *The Family Trap, Another Chance: Hope and Health for the Alcoholic Family, Choicemaking,* and *Learning to Love Yourself.*

Kathy Higby is a therapist in private practice in Las Vegas, NV, specializing in eating disorders and family recovery. She has received training in experiential therapy and the family reconstruction process from Sharon Wegscheider-Cruse, and is on staff at Onsite Training and Consulting.

Ted Klontz is Executive Director of Onsite Training and Consulting at Sierra-Tucson in Tucson, AZ. He is a founding member of the American Society of Experiential Therapists, a therapist, teacher, trainer, and consultant. He has received specialized training in experiential therapy and the family reconstruction process from Sharon Wegscheider-Cruse.

Ann Rainey is a psychotherapist and substance abuse counselor in private practice in Joplin, MO. She has also worked in private and community treatment centers, and has done research and presented workshops on experiential techniques in family-of-origin therapy, trauma and abuse, parenting, and relationship therapy. On staff at Onsite Training and Consulting, she has received specialized training in experiential therapy and the family reconstruction process from Sharon Wegscheider-Cruse.

Other Books by Sharon Wegscheider-Cruse

Another Chance: Hope and Health for the Alcoholic Family
Experiential Therapy for Co-Dependency: A Manual
Learning to Know Yourself Workbook
Grandparenting

The above titles are available from:
Science & Behavior Books
2225 Grand Road #3
Los Altos, CA 94024
(415) 965-0954
FAX: (415) 965-8998

★ ★ ★

Choicemaking
Learning to Love Yourself
Coupleship
The Miracle of Recovery
Understanding Co-Dependency
Life After Divorce

The above titles are available from:
Health Communications, Inc.
3201 S.W. 15th Street
Deerfield Beach, FL 33442
1-800-851-9100

★ ★ ★

The Family Trap
Intimacy and Sexuality

The above titles are available from:
Onsite Training and Consulting at Sierra-Tucson
16500 N. Lago del Oro Parkway
Tucson, AZ 95737
1-800-341-7432